The Construction of Racial Identity
in Children of Mixed Parentage

of related interest

The Dynamics of Adoption
Social and Personal Perspectives
Edited by Amal Treacher and Ilan Katz
ISBN 978 1 85302 782 6

Permanent Family Placement for Children of Minority Ethnic Origin
June Thoburn, Liz Norford and Stephen Parvez Rashid
ISBN 978 1 85302 875 5

The Adoption Experience
Families Who Give Children a Second Chance
Ann Morris
Adoption UK
Published in association with The Daily Telegraph
ISBN 978 1 85302 783 3

First Steps in Parenting the Child Who Hurts
Tiddlers and Toddlers
Second Edition
Caroline Archer
Adoption UK
ISBN 978 1 85302 801 4

Next Steps in Parenting the Child Who Hurts
Tykes and Teens
Caroline Archer
ISBN 978 1 85302 802 1

Child Adoption
A Guidebook for Adoptive Parents and Their Advisors
R.A.C. Hoksbergen
ISBN 978 1 85302 415 3

The Child's World
The Comprehensive Guide to Assessing Children in Need
Second Edition
Edited by Jan Horwath
ISBN 978 1 84310 568 8

The Construction of Racial Identity in Children of Mixed Parentage

Mixed Metaphors

Ilan Katz

Jessica Kingsley Publishers
London and Philadelphia

First published in the United Kingdom in 1996
by Jessica Kingsley Publishers
116 Pentonville Road
London N1 9JB, UK
and
400 Market Street, Suite 400
Philadelphia, PA 19106, USA

www.jkp.com

Copyright © Ilan Katz 1996
Printed digitally since 2010

Library of Congress Cataloging in Publication Data
A CIP catalogue record for this book is available from the Library of Congress

British Library Cataloguing in Publication Data
A CIP catalogue record for this book is available from the British Library

ISBN 978 1 85302 376 7

Contents

CHAPTER ONE

Introduction

Work on this book began in the mid 1980s when race and racism were perhaps the most important and certainly the most contentious issues within the social work profession. For many white professionals this debate, together with the earlier 'radical' critique of social work was one of the first real challenges to their basic notions of the aims of social work and the 'good society' it was aimed at promoting. These critiques showed that other positions were equally valid, and that a complacent belief in the liberal status quo of the profession could lead to inequality and oppression. The anti-racist critique demonstrated that not only individual practitioners but also the structures of the profession were discriminatory. Perhaps the biggest challenge to the liberal orthodoxy was the growing opposition to trans-racial adoption and the concomitant focus on natural inter-racial families.

Issues of race and culture were a central aspect of my own personal and political identity as a white Jewish South African. The way the debate was framed in Britain, however, differed from South Africa, particularly in its focus on personal relationships and racists rather than on political and economic struggle.

The purpose of the first part of the study was to study mothers and infants, to see how race affected their relationship and specifically the identity development of the child. White mothers were chosen because they are the group who were seen to be most problematic according to the current anti-racist theory. Black mothers, having experienced racism, were seen to be more appropriate parents, at least in terms of the racial identity of their children. Anti-racist theory posits a direct link between racism and racial identity and asserts that because they will be subject to racism the children will have to develop a black identity. The question was how positive would this identity be, and how would the mother affect its development? Mothers were chosen because of the emphasis all theories placed on their centrality to children's development.

The notion of 'identity' used in this first part of the study was the conventional 'structural-developmental' view, which conceives of identity as a hierarchy of psychological structures developing and becoming more complex over time.

The aim was to seek commonalities and to begin to develop a 'theory' of early identity development in children of mixed parentage. This stage confirmed the central role of race in the first years of the children's lives, but also showed the diversity in the ways the families dealt with race. They showed that culture, gender and class, which were not seen by anti-racist theory as fundamental aspects of black identity, were at least as important as race in the life-choices of the mothers and the identity development of the children. However, current conceptions of identity and race made it difficult to conceptualise these factors in a theory of racial identity development.

By the mid 1990s new concepts of anti-racism and identity had become available, though not in the social work literature. Writers such as Paul Gilroy, Philip Cohen and Stuart Hall had re-examined current concepts of 'race' in the light of post-modernist theory. They developed notions of race which were wider than simply responses to racism, itself seen as multi-faceted rather than a single phenomenon. Identity was seen as the process by which individuals and families made sense of and negotiated their own situation, rather than as the acquisition of characteristics and traits. Class, culture and gender were therefore seen as integral components of identity rather than being added on to a core positive or negative racial identity. Identity was seen as based on 'difference' rather than 'race'. The concepts white and black were seen as constructions, developed in particular historical and social circumstances, rather than as essential types.

The fieldwork confirmed the enormous diversity in the way inter-racial families make sense of issues of race and culture and how these issues change according to family circumstances. The children's identity development was seen to be similarly diverse, discontinuous and dependent on many subtle influences, not just mother's behaviour. The father's role was seen as being of equal importance and even in those families where fathers lived apart. Interactions between the parents were also integral to the process.

In the last chapter I return to contemporary versions of the original anti-racist theories and show how inadequate they are in dealing with these complex notions of identity. I develop the notion of 'narrative identity' which seems to provide a much sounder basis for conceptualising 'racial' identity than the cumulative model provided by psychoanalysis and social work anti-racism.

CHAPTER TWO

The Inter-Racial Debate

Introduction

The debate about the role of racial differences and their impact on children's services has been raging in the United States for several decades, but only became a focus of concern in the United Kingdom during the 1980s. Central to the debate are the experiences of members of inter-racial families where the wider political issues are reflected in intimate personal relationships, where young children's development is dominated by powerful family forces.

This book aims to

- explore the origins of identity development in mixed-race infants
- consider how the infants' early relationships affect this development
- study some of the effects of parents' background and attitudes on the development of racial identity in children
- consider how identity is constructed within inter-racial families
- consider how this relates to the wider social circumstances of the family
- develop a notion of identity which accounts for these processes.

In order to place the current study into context, some of the relevant literature relating to race relations, trans-racial adoption, the development of racial identity, the position of mixed-race people in society and theories of identity development will be discussed. Previous studies on the development of racial awareness and identity will also be considered and their methodology will be analysed. Explanations of the methodologies used in the study will be offered. Finally a new conception of how the identity of mixed-race children can be understood will be presented.

The term 'mixed-race' is used despite the fact that it is not value-free and many people feel that these children should be described as black (Small, 1986; Hayes, 1990). Much of this book is devoted to differentiating between the situations of children both of whose parents are black and children from inter-racial families.

It would therefore be very confusing to use the term black to describe both. In addition, all anti-racist theorists use the terms black, white and 'race' so it seems to me that the term 'mixed-race' is legitimate. 'Children of mixed parentage', which I also use, is very cumbersome in certain circumstances. 'Mixed-ethnicity' and 'mixed-origin', which have been used by some theorists, are no more satisfactory than 'mixed-race', because of their assumption that 'ethnicity' is somehow more real than 'race'. These terms also have the disadvantage of not being used by the families themselves or by professionals.

Trans-Racial Adoption

The concerns surrounding race and racism are highlighted in the area of child care policy and practice, especially fostering and adoption. They have changed over the years with the changing political and social climate (Cheetham *et al.* 1981; Gill and Jackson, 1983; Rhodes, 1993).

Before the 1960s, there was very little awareness of racial issues in the personal social services. The generally accepted philosophy was that everybody should be treated equally and that services should be 'colour blind' (Nanton, 1989). By the mid 1960s, however, a large number of black children remained in institutional care while their white counterparts could be placed in substitute families. As a result of this, the British Adoption Project (BAP) was instituted to find homes for black children. The vast majority of the adoptive families were white.

Placing black children with white families was considered to be a progressive step. Social workers felt that this would improve understanding on both sides and would demonstrate to the wider community that different races can live together (Gill and Jackson, 1983). Subsequent follow-up studies on these children have shown that the adoptions were remarkably successful:

> In terms of what could be regarded as four crucial measures of outcome (relationships within the family, peer group, level of self-esteem and behaviour disorders) the research suggests that only a small number of these adoptions can be considered problematic. (Gill and Jackson, 1983, p.131)

Johnson, Shireman and Watson (1987) speaking of American research, say:

> Among preschool children, transracially adopted children have been reported to develop a concept of blackness and of themselves that is more positive than that of black children adopted by black parents. (p.46)

Nevertheless, criticisms of trans-racial adoptions began to surface, often voiced by the growing number of black professionals. Small (1986), for example, challenged many of Gill and Jackson's conclusions. The criticisms fall into two interrelated categories:

Political Criticisms

Political criticisms are concerned with the historically exploitative relationship between the black and white communities. In this view, children are yet another resource with which the white community enriches itself at the expense of the black community. The black community is thereby deprived of the very essence of its future – its own offspring. These critics point out that trans-racial adoption is a one-way flow of black children into white homes. They are particularly scathing of the 'colour blind' policies of the 1960s and 1970s (Penny and Best, 1990).

Psychological Criticisms

It is asserted that growing up in white families instils in black children a profound sense of separateness, depriving them of the intimate bonds essential to psychological well-being. They are likely to become isolated and withdrawn. This isolation extends to the extra-familial milieu which inevitably reflects white social attitudes. Moreover, because they have been brought up in a white environment, the children are isolated from the black community which would normally be a source of support for them, thus increasing their sense of isolation.

Black children in white families will grow up with confused racial identities. Chestang, (1972) talking of the American experience says:

> A child reared in a white family will lose contact with the black experience... Having been socialised largely to the white experience, such a child is likely to experience an identity crisis throughout his life; thus he will be truly fragmented. (p.103)

In Britain, Samuels (1979) stated that:

> The transracially adopted child is bound to undergo severe psychological and emotional problems of identity. Racially black and culturally white, what is his cultural inheritance? (p.238)

Not only are the children confused, they also suffer from low self-esteem because their white families are unable to help them deal with the problems of racism in society.

> All black children in Britain are constantly at risk of having their self-esteem eroded by the image of themselves as black in a society where white culture and white values predominate. For the black child brought up in a white family, this risk is increased because there are no black role models immediately available, and no black family members on hand to deal with negative experiences the child may undergo. (Mullender and Miller, 1985, p.34)

These arguments are supported by a body of anecdotal evidence which shows that children often try to cover up their black skin, for example, by scrubbing the skin to get off the 'dirt' and putting on talcum powder (Mullender and Miller, 1985; Penny and Best, 1990; Maximé, 1993).

Policy Changes

As a result of these criticisms local authorities began to change their practices and by the mid 1980s same-race placements were adopted in most local authorities (Rhodes, 1992).

The political arguments against trans-racial adoption are not amenable to research. Research on the psychological consequences, both in the USA (Johnson *et al.* 1987) and in Britain (Gill and Jackson, 1983; Tizard and Phoenix, 1989, Bagley, 1993a) has found that black children in white families are no worse off in terms of self-esteem, although they tend to be rather distanced from the black community. Nevertheless, the arguments against trans-racial adoption are persuasive and are propounded by the majority of professionals (Hayes, 1990; Rhodes, 1992). The research itself has been accused of being imbued with ethnocentric assumptions (Small, 1991). In fact both sides have used research to bolster their arguments (Rhodes, 1992).

Inter-Racial Families

The debate has been formulated mainly in terms of white *adoptive* families. However, many of these arguments apply to inter-racial families, particularly where the mother is white. Attacks on miscegenation have been made for several centuries and often the children's confused identity has been a major element of the reasoning (Henriques, 1974; Benson, 1981). These arguments have historically emanated from the 'right', usually from whites fearing that their 'superior' race will be tainted by 'inferior' stock.

Inter-racial families have been part of the dynamics of race relations in Britain for many years and were preceded by a long history of colonialism where British men had relationships with black women outside this country (Henriques, 1974). Benson (1981) claims that:

> Inter-racial unions are above all else the exceptions that prove the rule of ethnic differentiation, the outcome of deviations from a statistical and cultural norm...
> To study the everyday lives of inter-racial families then, is to study the nature of British race relations as it impinges on the lives of individuals. (p.1)

The families can be seen as examples of racial harmony, a threat to the British tradition, or as a theft by the dominant culture of minority members (Banks, 1992c). They are 'natural' in the sense that, unlike adoptive families, they occur spontaneously and without the sanction of professionals.

Because race is such an important component of both social relationships and personal identity, racial identity and attitudes are likely to permeate these families in subtle ways. Milner (1983) points out that although 'race' is an abstract term denoting a group of people, racial attitudes and identity begin at the same place and time as weaning, toilet training, and so forth.

Racial Attitudes

Psychological Theories of Prejudice

Racial attitudes have been studied for several decades, both in terms of how they develop and the effect they have on individuals and groups. In the 1930s and 1940s the thrust of most of the research was directed at trying to explain the nature of racial prejudice, discrimination and ethnocentricity. Most of the theories developed at this time used psychodynamic concepts to explain racial discrimination in terms of the psychopathological states of the discriminator (Milner, 1983). The two most prominent of these theories were The Frustration–Aggression Theory developed by Dollard et al. (1939) and The Authoritarian Personality, developed by Adorno et al. (1950).

Dollard et al. postulated that when frustration builds up it is expressed by the individual as aggression. When, for some reason, the aggression is not directed at its true object the cause of the frustration, it is 'displaced' elsewhere. Thus the frustrations of relationships, jobs, and so forth, become displaced towards an easily identified and less powerful group, such as Jews and black people.

Although scapegoating commonly occurs in human relationships the theory does not explain why racial prejudice is so endemic in society. As Milner (1983) points out, in relation to large social groups:

> There is the issue of masses of people experiencing similar frustrations at the same time, while the scapegoat theory can help to account for individual prejudice,…it requires the assistance of a variety of social and cognitive factors, such as ideology and conformity to social norms if it is to explain how these individual reactions are translated into collective, coherent actions. (p.27)

This theory perhaps explains the behaviour of *oppressed* groups which are likely to be more frustrated than the oppressors (Rex, 1986). After World War II social scientists sought to explain the phenomena of Nazism and racism and to answer the question of how racism develops in individuals. The most influential work was undertaken by Adorno et al.

Adorno and his colleagues (1950) tried to apply Freudian theories of personality and psychopathology to social phenomena. They hypothesised that:

> …The political, economic and social convictions of an individual often form a broad and coherent pattern, as if bound together by a 'mentality' or 'spirit' and that this pattern is an expression of deep-lying trends in his personality. The major concern was with the potentially fascistic individual. (p.1)

Authoritarian personalities were not only likely to be anti-semitic and ethnocentric, they were also likely to be resistant to change; conform strictly to social norms;

and to idealise authority figures such as parents and charismatic leaders. Adorno concluded that there is:

> A close correspondence in the type of approach and outlook a subject is likely to have in a wide variety of areas, ranging from the most intimate features of family and sex adjustment through relationships to other people in general, to religion and to social and political philosophy. (p.971)

He postulated that hierarchical, exploitative, authoritarian patterns of parent–child relationships lead to power-oriented, exploitatively dependent attitudes towards sex partners and God and ultimately to a political philosophy and social outlook with no room for anything but strong and disdainful rejection of whatever is relegated to the bottom.

Adorno goes much further than Dollard in explaining the roots of racist attitudes by seeing those attitudes in the context of a coherent personality. Moreover, he demonstrates that racist attitudes are neither inherent nor an inevitable consequence of frustration, but are largely the result of a complex process of social relationships within the family. It is therefore possible for racism to be diminished or even eradicated by a change in child-rearing practices.

Allport (1979), however, offers a cautionary note:

> The basic fact is firmly established – prejudice is more than an incident in many lives; it is often lockstitched into the very fabric of personality...to change it, the whole pattern of life would have to be altered. (p.142)

Allport

The discussion so far pertains to the dominant or majority group and the racial attitudes within it. But what are the psychological consequences of being a *victim* of prejudice? Allport (1979) suggests that there are particular traits characteristic of the victim of racial prejudice. These traits develop because of the need to use *ego-defences* or ways of defending the psyche against the trauma of abuse and low expectation. Ego-defences are of two types.

- ° **Extropunitive** – victims blame an outer cause for the handicap

- ° **Intropunitive** – victims either blame themselves for the situation or at least take responsibility for adjusting to it.

These traits do not occur in every victim but are widespread and offer a cause for further discrimination because they confirm the oppressors' preconceptions. Not all the traits are negative; suffering can lead to moral and spiritual upliftment. Ritchie (1973) confirms that victims of ethnocentrism are not always psychologically adversely affected and he chides contemporary social science for being over-concerned with pathology and with the sources of prejudice in white society rather than the victim as a person.

Little has been written about the development of black identity in terms of the early parent–child relationship (McAdoo, 1988). Nevertheless it seems logical to assume that early childhood experiences will influence the development of identity and attitudes as much in black people as in white.

Social Theories of Prejudice

Comprehensive as they are, psychological theories have severe limitations in explaining racial attitudes. By defining the racist as a deviant Adorno precludes an explanation of large-scale racism as manifested in societies like Nazi Germany or Apartheid South Africa. In fact, psychological factors can *never* fully account for racist behaviour – the growth and decline of Nazism in Germany was surely not caused by a change of child-rearing practices. Wider social and political forces must be taken into account in any adequate explanation.

In another classic study Sherif (1966) demonstrated the social dimension of prejudice. Using 'normal' American boys as his subjects, he divided them into teams and created a competitive environment between them. Soon the teams behaved towards each other in a manner very reminiscent of racist behaviour. Sherif showed that group processes can be very powerful determinants of inter-group attitudes and behaviour. The psycho-social theories indicate that the potential for racist behaviour exists in any social situation in which groups are differentiated from each other.

In Britain and the USA, black people are regularly and systematically discriminated against even in situations where no overt racism is evident. These situations are defined by Rex (1986) as instances of 'institutional racism'. Institutional racism has several meanings, but I will concentrate here on so-called 'unconscious racism'. Rex contrasts this with the 'psychological racism' of by Adorno and Dollard. He claims:

> Much more important is the racism inherent in the belief system of a society... Even in a society committed to universalism and equality of opportunity, such common-sense knowledge is marked by the use of stereotypes of minority individuals which are derogatory to them or which place them in questionable settings. (p.110)

Institutional racism permeates the very structures of which Western society is constituted.

Cultural Racism

There is a further way in which racism permeates society – it is evident in the language and culture with which we grow up. At its simplest this is demonstrated by the association in the English language between the words black and 'dark' with evil, mystery and fear. In contrast white is defined as pure, spotless, innocent or happy.

These associations do not necessarily mean that racism is caused by the use of the words in the language – black is used in many languages and cultures as a derogatory term (Gergen, 1967). Also, discrimination does not necessarily depend on linguistic negatives, and groups are discriminated against whose names have no pejorative connotation in the language (Harbin and Williams, 1966). Nevertheless, language is a vital channel of communication for children and the ubiquity of the negative connotations of the word black is likely to have some effect on both black and white children.

To give a full picture of the nature of racial prejudice and the effect it has on children, we must take into account three dimensions:

- **the psychological dimension** – including the individual personalities of those involved and their antecedent experiences, especially relationships with their parents

- **the social dimension** – the structure of groups, institutions, and the social context in which they are interacting

- **the cultural dimension** – the elements of language, symbolism and belief that make up the fabric of the cultures of those involved.

If early childhood experiences are central to the development of racial attitudes and identity, and if all white people display some measure of ethnocentric or racist behaviour and attitudes, it is easy to understand the anxiety of those who disapprove of trans-racial adoption and inter-racial families on the grounds that the children are likely to be given negative self-images by white parents. No matter how egalitarian or even anti-racist the parents' *opinions* are, they still carry the cultural baggage which comes with being white in Western society. This means that parents are likely to convey often unconscious attitudes and beliefs in very subtle ways as part of the everyday interactions which make up family life.

The psychological dimension may appear first in the parents' own histories, their reasons for coming together, attitudes towards child care and race, style of parenting and interaction with the child, and second, in the child's growing sense of self in relation to parents and the outside world.

The structural relates to the parents' socio-economic status and in relationships with family, friends, and the different racial groups which they come into contact with.

The cultural dimension will emerge in the use of language in the family, accents, meanings and connotations to such words as black, white, 'dark', the music listened to, the toys played with, and so on.

Research into the development of racial awareness and identity is considered in the next chapter but it is already clear that the process by which a child develops a racial identity is very complex. Bibby's statement that: 'Black families are better able to prepare black children for life in what remains a predominantly white society' (Mitchell, 1988, p.2) which is still representative of policy, hides more than it reveals to us. We should rather ask such questions as:

° Are there really such categories as black and white families?

° How do different black, inter-racial and white families differ in the ways they prepare children for the outside world?

° What are the most important aspects of family life which determine the development of children's identities?

It is important to investigate the actual *processes* by which racial identity develops. The simple question of whether a particular type of family is 'good' or 'bad' for black children can be superseded by more complex issues of *how* families affect identity. The situation then becomes less well defined, but perhaps more interesting and relevant to the lives of children rather than politicians (Charles, Thoburn and Rashid, 1992).

The professional debate is characterised by polar oppositions which may hide the real issues for the families concerned. The concepts 'good enough' parenting/bad parenting; black/white; positive identity/negative identity are presented as objective attributes which can be assigned to children and families. Both sides share this view, so that the only issue becomes *which* families fit the particular criteria. Both sides also see identity as a set of cultural traits and social beliefs which are transmitted from one generation to another, especially by the mother.

This debate may be couched too narrowly – children can experience both good and bad parenting, see themselves as black, white or 'mixed-race' in different contexts and feel both positively and negatively about their racial identity. The concepts 'race', 'culture', black, white, 'identity' and 'racial identity', which are taken for granted in the debate, are not self-evident, and need to be further unpacked.

This study focuses mainly on infants and very young children, and considers them mainly in the context of the mother–child relationship. The study was conducted in three stages:

° close observation of two infants

° interviews with the mothers of the two infants and three other mothers

° interviews with parents in nine other families.

All the mothers in the first two stages were white, because I assumed that the task of a black mother bringing up a black child is very different from that of an equivalent white mother. The third stage was undertaken some time after the first two, and both parents were interviewed where possible.

Among the questions dealt with in the first part of the study are:

° Are there any clues to the development of racial identity in mixed-race infants, and how do they manifest themselves?

- What is the process by which these children develop a sense of racial identity?

- How do the conscious and unconscious attitudes of white mothers towards black people affect their children's identities?

- What are the familial, social and psychological factors which determine why some white women choose black partners, and how does this choice affect the relationship with their children?

- What is the relationship between the development of racial awareness and racial identity?

In the third part assumptions underlying some of these questions are challenged, particularly:

- the view that either mother's beliefs or societal norms *determine* either her choice of partner or the identity of the child

- the total centrality of the mother in early identity development

- the unified notion of a 'racial' identity

- the transmission of cultures, beliefs and identity between generations

- the idea that identity development is a continuous, linear process.

CHAPTER THREE

Racial Attitudes and Marginality

Introduction

Studies into the racial attitudes of children go back to the 1930s. The basic questions which they addressed are:

- What racial preferences do children have when they choose potential friends?
- How early do these preferences begin?
- How do they change as children grow older?
- With which racial groups do children identify themselves?

The first major investigations were carried out in the USA by the Horowitzs (Horowitz 1936; 1939), a team who studied the development of racial attitudes in white children. The Horowitzs developed a technique of presenting children with photographs of black and white people and asking them:

- what colour are the dolls (photographs, etc) (racial *awareness*)
- which doll do you prefer? (racial *preference*); and
- which doll is more like you? (racial *identification*).

The authors found that, contrary to common conceptions of childhood, children as young as three years were aware of racial differences and, more important, they showed signs of racial *preference* at this age.

Researchers (e.g. Goodman, 1946; Ammons, 1950; Morland, 1962, 1963) followed the Horowitzs. The body of research which used these methods is referred to collectively as the '"doll" studies'. Although they are methodologically problematic they have produced detailed information on certain aspects of racial identity and their findings have been remarkably consistent in some areas. The importance of the doll studies in relation to white children is that they show that:

- children are able to identify racial differences and display racial preferences at a very young age

- these preferences change over time; and
- the kind of parenting children receive is important in determining their attitudes.

The true significance of these studies is only revealed, however, with the equivalent findings of studies of black children.

The pioneers in the study of black children's attitudes and identity were Kenneth and Mamie Clark, black Americans who worked in the 1930s and 1940s (Clark and Clark, 1939, 1947). The Clarks divided racial identity into three categories, racial awareness, racial preference, and self-identification.

After showing the children the black and white dolls, they asked eight questions to elicit the perception of these three variables. The results were extraordinary, the more so in that they have been replicated many times by other researchers. They found that black children were more racially aware than white, more adept than white children in recognising the colours of the dolls and able more accurately to discern between the dolls even at a younger age.

These findings in themselves are not controversial. One might expect children who are subject to racism to be more sensitive to racial stimuli. The most unexpected results were in the racial preference and self-identification categories. The Clarks found that the majority of black children preferred the *white* dolls, and that a significant number of black children *identified* themselves with the white dolls. This showed that black children internalise society's view of them as inferior at a very young age. By identifying with white dolls, black children rejected their own race and demonstrated the results of damaged racial identity:

> The fact that young Negro children would prefer to be white reflects their knowledge that society prefers white people... It is clear, therefore, that the self-acceptance or self-rejection found so early in the child's developing complex of racial ideas reflects the awareness and acceptance of prevailing racial attitudes in his community. (Clark, 1955, in Wilson, 1987, p.44)

The Clarks found no difference between children from different areas, but older children tended to misidentify less, and lighter skinned children tended to identify more as whites. The Clarks did not differentiate between children from black families and children from inter-racial families, but relied purely on skin colour.

Since the Clarks conducted their pioneering investigations, many other researchers have followed (Brand, Ruiz and Padilla 1974; Aboud and Skerry, 1984) The methods have been refined, for example by matching dolls with subjects in terms of sex and by modifying facial features. Variables such as socio-economic status, inter-racial contact and area of residence have been controlled. Wilson (1987) identifies five main influences on black children's racial identity; sex, age, skin colour, socio-economic status, and parental attitude – positive parental attitude towards blackness tended to foster a stronger black identity.

None of these have overwhelming significance, and there is no consensus amongst researchers about their importance. They added to rather than challenged the Clarks' findings. An important development since the 1960s has been a noticeable decrease in the proportion of children who misidentify. The earlier findings were reliably reported in many studies over a long period of time with differing samples (Brand *et al.* 1974; Wilson, 1987), although they were not universal (Hraba and Grant, 1970; Banks, 1976; Milner, 1983). It seems that misidentification was a widespread phenomenon amongst young black children. By the beginning of the 1970s, researchers such as Hraba and Grant (1970), and Fox and Jordan (1973), were discovering a reversal of the previous patterns.

Milner (1983) explains the change as due to the emergence of black consciousness as a political and social phenomenon. This has allowed black children to feel more comfortable in identifying with black heroes, and therefore to identify with black dolls. Milner and the researchers he quotes do not provide an explanation for the mechanisms by which this change may have taken place. Gergen, Gloger-Tippelt and Berkowitz (1990) believe that historical change affects the reliability of *all* child development studies.

Although the doll studies were relatively reliable, there are serious questions about their validity. Their basic assumption is that the stimuli presented to the children represent real people and that their choices therefore represent the kind of choices that they would make in real life situations. Brand *et al.* (1974) point out, however, that observational studies of trans-racial choice of playmates in young children show little correlation between real choices and preferences expressed in the stimulus selection. Other criticisms have been made of the stimuli, especially of dolls. Black dolls are unfamiliar to most children and could account for the discrepancy.

These criticisms apply to children's racial *choices* and preferences but the studies purport to go further, and be a measure of racial *identity*, concluding that misidentification represents a deep malaise in the identity of black children. The malaise is a result of the introjection of negative societal images of black people (Clark, 1965). These claims depend even more heavily on the validity of the test materials.

Further criticism has been made of this methodology, for example, that presenting only two dolls, one white and one black, restricts the responses (Greenwald and Oppenheim, 1968). Providing a 'brown' doll does not solve the problem, though, because it can be argued that black children are still choosing a lighter, though admittedly more accurate stimulus. The race of the tester (Dreger and Miller, 1968) has also been considered significant, but this finding has not been consistent (Sattler, 1973). The findings suggest that misidentifiation in black children is initially common but decreases with age.

The studies have only a limited value in the explaining of the development of racial identity, mainly because of the difficulty in extrapolating conclusions about *identity* from measurements of *identification*.

This problem is highlighted when the third question 'Which doll is more like you?' is considered. Assuming that black children know the difference between black and white people, and that they prefer whites, there are three possible interpretations of a wrong answer to this question:

- ° black children would like to be white – implying a degree of identification with whites by black children, but not necessarily a problem with identity

- ° black children are confused about their identification and do not really know whether they want to be black or white – implying some degree of ambivalence about being black; or

- ° black children literally believe they are white – implying a significant degree of cognitive dissonance and identity disturbance.

Taken to its conclusion the last interpretation would mean that black children look into the mirror and see a white person.

The conclusions reached, however, have not been as strong as this and have centred around negative self-esteem rather than cognitive disturbance. The third question, therefore, is not necessarily a valid measure of identity but perhaps an extension of the question about racial preference and ideal types. Milner is not claiming that black children literally think they are white. He and those he quotes are using the word 'identification' in the sense of *preference* rather than *identity*. Claims that misidentification in doll tests betrays a confusion in early identity may have to be regarded with a degree of caution.

The doll studies attempt to provide an *objective* measurement for a phenomenon which is largely *subjective*. The method does not address the question of what it means to a child to say 'I am more like this doll than that one'.

Children from age three have been tested using the 'doll' method and theorists have developed a formulation about the development of awareness and identity. There have been no longitudinal studies of development, however, and each study provides a 'snapshot' of a particular sample. Snapshots do not reveal how some children change from misidentifying to correctly identifying while others do not; or even why some may have identified correctly at age three and incorrectly at age seven. It is doubtful whether this method is sufficient in itself to develop a theory about the development of racial attitudes, let alone racial identity.

In Chapter 3, I discuss the problems of investigating racial identity as a separate factor not linked to other personality traits. There are very few studies which link racial identity confusion or misidentification with other evidence of identity problems, Ward and Braun (1972) being a rare exception. Even if there is a link, there is no evidence as to whether these problems cause, or are caused by, other problems of identity.

Despite the evidence in Chapters 3 and 4 that parents play a central role in the early development of attitudes and identity, there are few studies which relate misidentification to either parental attitudes or child rearing practices. The nine independent variables given by Brand *et al.* (1974), and the six by Wilson (1987) do not include parental attitude or child rearing practices. This is doubly ironic because of the many studies (e.g., Adorno *et al.* 1950; Bagley *et al.* 1979) which link *prejudice* to parental behaviour. This may be because sex, age, socio-economic status, and so forth, are more easily measured than subtle parental influences.

The lack of longitudinal studies; the reduction to simple choices; the lack of a subjective perspective; the reliance on verbal responses; the lack of a parental dimension and the isolation of racial identity as a separate variable all have a common methodological theme – the use of a simple quantitative methodology. All these studies provide an overview of a sample of children at a particular moment and relate their responses to various gross social factors. This methodology is useful for predicting responses of groups of people to various social forces, but not really for investigating the meaning of race to individual children.

One way of tackling these problems is to use a more qualitative methodology, concentrating on fewer subjects, but providing more information about them. This approach would enable the researcher to view children in their social and familial context and move towards a subjective perspective. The problems with this approach are not only methodological. Implicit in both the construction of these studies and explanations of the results are assumptions which seriously undermine their value in giving a comprehensive picture of racial identity and its development.

The first assumption is that misidentification has a direct link with low self-esteem. The second, more fundamental, is that an equivalence between 'identity' and 'identification' is assumed.

As regards the first assumption, Tizard and Phoenix (1989) point out:

Self-esteem and mental health do not appear to be necessarily tied to attitudes to race... The belief that there is a 'positive black identity' which must be acquired by black children is over-simplified and presumptive. (p.435)

Even if black children were found to have lower self-esteem than white children the link would still not be established. Only if black children who misidentify were found to have a lower self-esteem than those who identify correctly would any link be shown. Other recent research has confirmed the lack of a relationship between the degree of identification with racial groups and level of self-esteem (Milner, 1983; Spencer, 1984; Jackson, MacCulloch and Gurin 1988). None of the doll studies has tried to establish a more global picture of the individual mis-identifiers and their families.

If racial identity is made up of many subtle components, then the doll studies are very blunt measuring instruments. Admittedly, identification with a group must play a large part in identity, but it surely cannot be the only, or even the defining variable (Aboud and Skerry, 1984). Racial identity must be part of the child's global personal identity and not a discrete set of ideas or behaviours. Identification is only one of the mechanisms by which identity is developed.

Despite these drawbacks, the knowledge gained from the considerable number of doll studies has enabled researchers to learn much about the way children identify with social groups and how their own social conditions determine the way this is carried out.

Other than Wilson's (1987) study, no doll study could be found which considers the identity of mixed-race children. None of the major literature reviews quote studies either partially or fully conducted with mixed-race children. Some studies have discussed skin colour as an independent variable (e.g. Gitter, Mostowski and Satow, 1972; Greenwald and Oppenheim, 1968). The findings of these studies, however, are contradictory. Even if they were not it is difficult to extrapolate from results obtained from light-skinned children both of whose parents are black, to mixed-race children because mixed-race children are likely to have a much greater involvement with white culture. For them identification with white dolls could represent identification with family members who are white. Integrating these results is even more difficult and the doll method on its own is even less valid.

Theories of Racial Identity Development

Goodman

Goodman's (1952) three-stage formulation of the development of racial attitudes proposes that the child first learns about race and how to differentiate between the races followed by the affective or emotional concomitants to this knowledge which are finally elaborated into adult-like prejudices, stereotypes and discriminatory behaviour. These stages are not completely discrete and there is a definite interaction between them.

This was the first attempt at a developmental approach to racial attitude, but the problem is that the theory is too sketchy to be very useful. It is silent on how children become racially aware and how this awareness develops into feelings and behaviour about race. It is also probably wrong. Clark (1955) says:

> The child's first awareness of racial difference is…associated with some rudimentary evaluation of these differences…the child cannot learn what racial group he belongs to without being involved in a larger pattern of emotions, conflicts and desires which are part of his growing knowledge about what society thinks of his race. (in Milner, 1983, p.109)

Katz

A more comprehensive schema is proposed by Katz (1976) involving eight overlapping stages, starting with observation of racial cues before age three and ending with attitude crystallisation, in which attitudes become stable and consistent with environment.

Katz provides a more elaborate view of the development of attitudes than does Goodman, but is heavily biased towards cognitive development. He virtually ignores the emotional and familial factors highlighted by Adorno and others. He emphasises the later stages of racial awareness and is less concerned with its earliest manifestations. His model is a linear model of development and there is little room for attitudes to change or be modified – they simply become more complex and crystallised.

Aboud and Skerry

Aboud and Skerry (1984) contend that racial attitudes develop as part of the general socio-cognitive developmental processes responsible for attitudes. Their model postulates three interacting domains of development: the affective, the perceptual and the cognitive.

Racial awareness is said to begin at about age four. The sequence of development is:

- attitude towards own group
- perceived similarity of self to own group
- perceived similarity/dissimilarity towards others
- cognitive response of classifying/labelling others;

Own-group attitude development is first dominated by the affective domain, but both affective and perceptual domains are necessary in the development of own-group attitudes. At first the focus is egocentric and other group members are only seen as different from the self, but are not themselves differentiated. They are largely related to in terms of how well they meet the child's needs.

As affective differentiation declines, perceptual differentiation increases in the form of own group/other group distinctions, and the child now sees herself as a group member, different from members of the other group.

The focus progresses from the self to the own group to the other group. At the same time the differentiation progresses from the affective to the perceptual to the cognitive domain. This model differs from those previously discussed in that it does not postulate a linear growth of racial awareness, attitude and identity. Racial attitudes are seen to be part of a whole constellation of factors which influence children and their relationship to the world and to other people.

A common factor of these theories is that they are theories of racial *awareness* and *attitude* rather than racial *identity*. Awareness and attitude are essential components of racial identity but, as with identification, they are only part of a larger whole. Because research in this area was precipitated by psychologists and sociologists wanting to know more about the nature of racial prejudice, it tended to focus on the aspects of identity which were most obvious in situations of inter-racial conflict. This gives the research a peculiar bias in that black identity is usually portrayed as only a reaction to white prejudice. The result of this is that the positive aspects of black children's experiences are often passed over. Another reason why awareness and attitude may have been favoured is that they are methodologically easier to quantify than identity and are therefore more attractive for researchers to study.

By not focusing on identity researchers miss out on the inter-racial situation, that is, how black children *experience* their situation. Identity represents the interface between self-perception and attitudes towards others.

None of these theories refers to the development of mixed-race children and how this may differ from black or white children.

Marginal Theory

What kind of person would we expect the child from an inter-racial family to become? Since the late 1930s sociologists and psychologists have been pondering this question. The first to do so was Park who proposed the theory of the 'Marginal Man', first applied to Jews and other immigrant groups in the United States who were seen as being caught between two cultures – their original culture, and that indigenous to the United States. The theory was soon extended to people who were the products of two different *races* rather than cultures. Americans of mixed parentage were seen as sharing a similar condition to immigrants.

Park

According to Park's theory, people who are placed in a 'marginal' situation by society share not only similar social status, but also tend to have similar psychological responses to it. They display characteristic personality traits which distinguish them from the general population. Park (1964) was arguing against contemporary theories and beliefs that racial characteristics are due to inherent differences in 'blood lines'. He accepted that different races have different traits, and even that 'mulattoes' are superior in intelligence to negroes, but he said:

> I am convinced...that what I call the mentality of the racial hybrid...is very largely due to the situation in which his mixed origin inevitably puts him. He is biologically the product of divergent racial stocks, but just because of that fact he is, at the same time, the cultural product of two distinct traditions. He is, so to speak, a cultural as well as a racial hybrid. (p.382)

Park attributed the mulattoes' higher intelligence to the increased 'stimulus' to which they are subjected by their role in society and the internal conflict it engenders. He went on to discuss the 'moral qualities' or personality of mulattoes:

They are...more enterprising than the Negroes, more restless, aggressive, and ambitious... The mulatto and the mixed blood are often sensitive and self-conscious to an extraordinary degree. (p.387)

Park believed that people of mixed parentage have both positive and negative sides to their personality. They are intelligent and sensitive, but aggressive and socially isolated, obsessed by their condition and their ambivalent feelings toward the dominant population whose values and culture they share, but from whose ranks they are excluded. As they are marginalised by society they display 'neurotic' personality traits.

The psychoanalysts are probably right when they say that 'neurosis is one of many ways of meeting various difficulties in his relations with his fellow man', and that the study of these pathological conditions in the individual cannot be undertaken without throwing light also on the inner nature and meaning of the social institutions themselves in regard to which the difficulties have arisen. (p.362)

The most important of these institutions is the family, whose influence on personality development is paramount. Wider societal norms are also important, as they often determine the family's structure and mode of functioning. Because the 'marginal man' originates in a family in which there are likely to be conflicting or confused child-rearing patterns he is likely to develop pathological personality traits.

Stonequist

Stonequist (1937) went even further than Park in emphasising the negative and painful sides of the marginal condition. According to Stonequist the marginal condition is only one of the three stages in the life cycle of people in marginal situations.

THE PRE-MARGINAL STAGE

Children of mixed parentage initially identify with the dominant white group whom they admire and to whom they hope to belong. Unfortunately, this phase is short-lived and they quickly discover that they are not accepted by white society, leading to a crisis of rejection where they suddenly realise that their hopes are bound to be frustrated. This crisis leads to a sense of confusion and feelings of being overwhelmed. This crisis is the transition from the first to the second phase.

THE MARGINAL STAGE

This phase is characterised by intense feelings of ambivalence. Rejected by white society, children of mixed parentage identify strongly with the black population but are still unable to shake off their underlying longing to be part of the dominant group. They see themselves from two conflicting points of view. Their attitude towards the white group alternates between idealisation and denigration and the black community, by contrast, is seen either as a safe family who shares the discrimination against them, or as a hated prison from which they cannot escape. This phase, according to Stonequist, can persist throughout their lives, but it can equally be a short transition to equilibrium.

THE STAGE OF ADJUSTMENT

The final phase comes when there is some sort of accommodation to their condition. This can take one of three forms:

- assimilation into the dominant group
- assimilation into the subordinate group; or
- accommodation between the two.

Of these the first is obviously the most difficult and requires a degree of deception. One way of assimilating into the black community is to become an advocate and leader in black politics so that the internal conflict is resolved by splitting off the hated and envied white part and identifying only with the black part. Accommodation is aimed at by becoming a mediator between the two communities.

Although they started from racist assumptions, the marginality theorists have made an important contribution to the study of race relations in illustrating how the conflicts in the wider society can be reflected in the internal psychological conflicts which affect the most intimate aspects of the personality and personal relationships. They also cite the family as the primary forum in which these conflicts are acted out.

Stonequist's theory is particularly interesting because he postulates a developmental cycle of the marginal condition but there are few longitudinal studies of children of mixed parentage which might have corroborated his thesis. It remains unclear when, why, and under what conditions the transitions to the different stages occur. It is possible that the transition from the first to the second stage happens when the perceptual and cognitive modes take over from the purely affective mode in Aboud and Skerry's (1984) model or the transition from the *pre-operational* to the *concrete operational* stages of Piaget's (1953) theory. The crisis would then occur when the child is able to categorise racial groups. However, it is clear from Stonequist's writings that the crisis occurs in adolescence or even early adulthood and is related to the child leaving home and attaining an adult identity, corresponding to Erikson's (1977) stage of *Identity vs Role Confusion*.

The theory of marginality is also important because it differentiates between the psychological effects of being a member of *both* the dominant and subordinate groups, and those of being a member of an oppressed minority. Essentially, the difference seems to be that minority group members deal with their anger by repressing or introjecting it (Allport, 1979) whereas marginal people act out ambivalence or sublimate it to other activities (Park, 1964). These conclusions are not, however, supported by all the researchers.

The first criticism is that the personalities described are ideal types. Many of the personality traits ascribed to 'marginal men' are equally applicable to members of oppressed minorities. Johnson and Nagoshi (1986), for instance conclude that:

> Stigma is the biggest factor in maladjustment of offspring of inter-racial marriages... Other variables – psychiatric problems of parents, more conflict, identity problems, cultural marginality, that have been claimed to exist...are not significant in. (p.283)

The term 'marginality' has been applied to many types of individuals and groups. Stonequist himself described various groups, including Europeanised Africans, Westernised orientals, American negroes, immigrants, and so forth, as marginal people, and Mann (1973) says: '...More and more individuals and kinds of people have been brought forward to swell a throng that was already dense when Stonequist wrote his book' (p.216).

The second criticism is that of subjective/objective confusion. It is unclear whether marginality is defined objectively as applying to all people in 'marginal' situations or whether it applies to those people who *feel* torn between two cultures or races. As Simpson and Yinger (1985) point out: 'Discussions of marginality do not always distinguish between measures that are used to define the condition and measures that are presumed consequences of it' (p.123). Individuals may avoid the consequences, for example, by identifying totally with one group, but are they still marginal?

A third qualification is that the theory confuses individual and group marginality. There must be a difference between someone who is, for instance, the only Chinese person in a small English village and someone who belongs to the Bengali community in Tower Hamlets. Both are 'marginal' as the term is defined, but their experience of cultural conflict must be very different. To deal with this problem some theorists have proposed the concept of a 'marginal culture', that is, a social structure in which marginality itself becomes a social norm (Gordon, 1978).

The fourth criticism is based on the assumptions which the theory accepts about race relations. It accepts contemporary racist attitudes, that is, the 'superiority' of 'mulattoes', but attributes this to social rather than genetic forces. Moreover, sociologists assume that macrocosmic tensions must be reflected in the individual microcosm (Wilson, 1987). The internal conflict which is seen as the result of social tensions is therefore an assumption by the sociologists rather than a finding of their research. Perhaps, however, an individual can live in the 'marginal area' of group relations and not necessarily suffer severe internal conflict. If both identities are valued and embraced, the conflict between them may be minimalised, but this might only be possible in societies which are relatively tolerant of minorities and differences.

Despite these criticisms of the marginality theory, it remains a powerful conceptual tool and intuitively seems to make sense. It would be hard to imagine that someone who is subject to conflicting social expectations and identities would not have *some* difficulties in resolving them, although this need not necessarily lead to a 'marginal personality'. The theory has been borne out in several studies and is also the main basis for one of the criticisms of trans-racial adoption which was discussed above.

Marginality is largely a theory about internal conflict and its psychological effects as applied to adults. Consequently, it can only portray the consequences for children of mixed parentage when they grow up. Very little has been written about marginality in young children. Only Stonequist has taken a developmental stance regarding the theory and according to him young children of mixed parentage identify exclusively as whites and experience little conflict until much later when they realise that this identification is illusory.

Research has been quoted above showing that many young black children identify themselves as being similar to white dolls. Unlike Stonequist, however, researchers such as Clark (1955) interpreted these findings as indicating *identity conflict* rather than its precursor. This need not be fatal for the theory – it may simply mean that the 'crisis' occurs at a younger age than Stonequist realised. Young children may have the cognitive skills to enable them to understand that they are somehow different from others or from what they want to be. It seems likely that the 'crisis' is more metaphorical than literal and that the awareness of difference from the majority, and the ensuing internal conflict, is part of a complex process rather than a single event.

The theory of marginality and the research into the development of racial preference still fail to clarify whether young children of mixed parentage are in a special category and whether their identity development is significantly different from black children. On the basis of marginality theory it seems logical to hypothesise that it is and that this difference is mainly due to early parental influence.

Inter-Racial Liaisons

One area which marginality theory fails to address is the motivation of people who choose to form relationships with others of a different race. The theory begs the following questions:

- ° Why do people from different racial groups form liaisons which produce children of mixed parentage, given the antagonism between races?
- ° What are the interpersonal dynamics in such liaisons?

There are several possibilities.

'Random Selection'

Adorno and others agreed that there are varying degrees of prejudice in the dominant community and that some people, because of early interpersonal experiences, are less prejudiced than the norm. If these people come across potential partners of a different race, they may well fall in love with them and race would have little bearing on the relationships other than as an external pressure. This explanation conforms with the liberal 'melting pot' view of race relations.

'Love Thy Neighbour'

The theory's hypothesis is that there are likely to be some people in the community whose liaisons across the colour bar are primarily a political statement. Liaisons of this type are largely confined to politically active middle-class people occurring in the radical political movements of the late 1960s (Benson, 1981).

'Love the One You're With'

Historically, white–black sexual liaisons in colonial situations were almost exclusively between white men and black women. They occurred, according to this theory, largely out of expediency because there were very few white women available for these men. In the United Kingdom, however, liaisons have historically been between black men and white women because the initial wave of black immigrants consisted largely of black men.

These demographic or social explanations do shed some light on the reasons for inter-racial liaisons occurring, but they still cannot answer why *some* individuals choose to enter into these relationships and others do not. They also shed little light on the possible outcome for the children.

In order to do so, the role of sex in black–white relations must be considered. In this respect, James Weldon Johnson (1941), quoted in Henriques (1974), asserts that:

> ...in the core of the heart of the American race problem the sex factor is rooted; rooted so deeply that it is not always recognised when it shows at the surface... Taken alone, it furnishes a sufficient mainspring for the rationalisation of all the complexes of white superiority...its strength and bitterness are magnified and intensified by the white man's perception, more or less, of the Negro complex of sexual superiority. (p.80)

The 'complex of negro superiority' is the belief by white people that black people's *intellectual* inferiority is accompanied by a concomitant superiority in their *sexual* abilities. Black women are seen as having increased lubricity, and an unbounded and indiscriminate sexual appetite. Central to it also is the belief that black men have enormous penises and sexual appetites.

The consequence of this myth is that black people are seen not only as an economic threat. The threat is much more personalised and the feelings engendered are more intense. White women are portrayed as chaste and virginal and white men as their protectors against the corrupting influence of the licentious of black men. Black men cannot control their sexual impulses and white women are unable to resist their advances. Black women, however, are seen as seductresses using their sexual abilities to trap white men into bed. Once white women succumb to black men's advances, they are seen as corrupted. They are then seen as part of the black race, to be feared and reviled.

As a result white men have not only treated black men with contempt, but also with fear and envy of their superior sexuality. White women are seen as innocent victims having no choice; they will belong to whichever man is the stronger and more potent.

The myth is not believed by white males alone. Black men's sexuality is also informed by it. Fanon (1968) has eloquently expressed black feelings:

I wish to be acknowledged not as *black* but as *white*.

Now...who but a white woman could do this for me? By loving she proves that I am worthy of white love. I am loved like a white man.

I am a white man.

I marry white culture, white beauty, white whiteness.

When my restless hands caress those white breasts, they grasp white civilisation and dignity and make them mine... (p.91)

There is an element of revenge, in that possession of a white woman punishes white men and whiteness generally. These feelings are very close to the general effects of oppression described by Allport and others. Sexual relations then become a microcosm of the broader dynamics of race relations.

Although black and white men's fears and fantasies have been publicised, the women's perspective is absent. Women are seen merely as objects of fantasy and not as subjects able to make their own choices. However, if, as has been suggested, the myth is all-pervasive in inter-racial sexual encounters, white women must also be influenced by it. This means that the 'random' theory of mate selection cannot be an adequate explanation of white women's choices.

What form does this myth, as held by white women, take? One explanation is that women associate 'blackness' with 'badness' and that these women have low self-esteem (Holland and Holland, 1984). Feeling they are not good enough for white men they turn to black men as their only alternative. Having made the choice they become intensely ambivalent towards white men in a way similar to that described by marginality theory. Another way of coping with the consequences of the choice is for the women to reject white society and culture altogether and to take on the mannerisms and attitudes of their partners' culture. Women may be so low in self-esteem that they choose black partners because they 'know' that black men will take revenge in the sexual encounter and so will fulfil their need to be punished.

Perhaps, however, the choice of a black partner is a positive one. The myth casts white women in the role of chaste, virginal creatures, and to break out of this they may choose black men who represent the uninhibited sexual part of them that cannot be expressed with a white man.

There may be many more explanations for a choice of black sexual partner. The factor common to all is that the choice of a black partner is not random and therefore the partner's race is a significant factor. Race and sexuality combine powerfully. In many inter-racial partnerships the interpersonal relationship reflects aspects of the macrocosmic dynamics of race relations – they become *racialised*. These dynamics can be played out by both partners in unconscious ways so that what is at one level seen as personal conflicts or weaknesses, can be traced back to early childhood experiences and ultimately to unconscious prejudices and beliefs acquired very early in life.

Another complication is that the process can work the other way around, and problems that are ultimately personal are projected into the racial sphere. A woman's anger at her partner's infidelity may take a racist form, for example, 'That is typical of a black man!' Some of the inter-racial couples described by Benson attributed their conflict to racial differences when in fact they were probably largely personal. It is very difficult to separate the personal from the racial elements in these relationships.

Fanon (1968), Hendriques (1974), Benson (1981) and others have shown that relationships between black men and white women are imbued with unconscious and conscious ideas and beliefs about race which are projected on to the partner. This raises the question of how these ideas and beliefs affect the product of these relationships, the children. What unconscious messages about themselves will the children pick up from their mothers?

Stonequist's answer to these questions is that infants will identify totally with the mother and her race until they are able intellectually to understand that *society* does not accept their definition of their identity. Developmental studies of black racial identity also postulate a period, albeit a much shorter one, in which race is not part of the children's identity.

All the theories place enormous emphasis on the mother's influence, most asserting that it begins in the cradle. Perhaps her unconscious attitudes act as a kind of precursor to the children's later development of identity. If so, it is necessary to consider some theories of early intellectual, emotional and identity development which can provide a framework for the study of precursors of racial identity development.

CHAPTER FOUR

Theories of Identity Development

Racial and Personal Identity

Theories on the development of racial identity all postulate that its formation begins between the ages of three and four. Adorno *et al.* (1950), Allport (1979), Aboud and Skerry (1984) and others, have proposed that it is part of a more global personal identity. Many theories of personal identity development state, however, that such development begins in infancy. In this chapter some theories of the development of personal identity will be further explored. There are an enormous number of theories of child development we will only consider here those focusing on the discussion of racial identity and the mother's role in child development.

This chapter presents further argument that racial identity is inseparable from personal identity. It is proposed that it may start very early in a child's life. In the earlier theories children were portrayed as victims or passive recipients of parental and societal attitudes and behaviours. This chapter presents a different picture, in which infants play an active role in constructing their sense of identity. This challenges the simple 'black and white' view of identity and argues that identity development and identity conflict are complex phenomena, dependent on many interrelated factors. It is also argued that children's *identity* development *precedes* their development of *awareness* of social categories.

These theories were used to develop a theoretical background for the first two parts of this study of identity. Post-modernism, on which the third part of the study was based, will be used to show that the conception of 'identity' first developed is too narrow, even though it goes much further than that in the doll studies or current social work anti-racist literature.

Berger and Luckmann

Berger and Luckmann's (1966) *sociological* theory tackles the problem of how individuals become members of a collectivity, and how society affects individuals' knowledge of themselves and the world. This theory starts off with the belief that for humans '…neither their biological make-up nor their environment predetermines the form this (their life) will take' (Berger and Luckmann, 1985, p.21).

Human beings live in an inherently social world and in order to do so the groups they live in must share a common or commonsense reality which all members have acknowledge.

The authors contend that although this everyday 'reality' is *perceived* by all humans as objective it is actually socially constructed. There is no such thing as a separate, objective, reality. All we have are shared meanings and ways of making things explicable to others. Berger and Luckmann set out to answer why this is so and how societies create reality for their members.

Institutions and Roles

Human beings need to live in a predictable and ordered reality because without order the world becomes meaningless. Institutions are created by groups of people to regulate society and make it meaningful to individual members. Institutions are understood by all members of society, although not necessarily in the same way. They set the limits of control, and channel social experience, for example although not everybody in Western society marries, sexual relationships are defined to some extent by the institution of marriage. Similarly, racist beliefs are institutionalised and become part of the social fabric, as has been discussed in Chapters 2 and 3.

Because institutions do *not* have an existence separate from human action, they require ways in which they can be explained and justified or *legitimised*. Legitimation is the set of values, beliefs and norms surrounding all institutions which places them into a larger social order by relating them to other institutions. Legitimation strengthens the normative power of institutions, thus providing:

- ° the 'knowledge' of the institution (e.g., To what race do I belong?); and
- ° the value surrounding the institution (e.g., Is it wrong to marry a member of another race?).

The major legitimising factor in all institutions is language.

Institutions are all-pervasive in human knowledge, action and belief. All social action is performed according to *roles* defined by the institutions. Roles are expressions of the relationship between individuals and the relevant institutions. They are not idiosyncratic to the individual performing them.

Although roles consist of the actions of individual people, there is an interchangeability between actors and roles. On one hand, I am one of many people with the role of 'father' and on the other, acting as a father is only part of my self. Part of the self is *objectified* as the performer of various roles and this part is called the *social self*, which is not the same as the self in totality. The social self perceives others performing roles and as performers these people are experienced as *types* rather than individuals.

The relationship between institutions and roles, therefore, is that when people act in accordance with the rules of institutions, they are acting in roles. Institutions are also:

> ...embodied in individual experience by means of roles. The roles, objectified linguistically, are an essential ingredient of the objectively available world of any society. By playing roles, the individual participates in a social world. By internalising these roles the same world becomes subjectively real to him. (Berger and Luckmann, 1985, p.74)

Thus roles and institutions are not only seen as parts of objective reality, they are also part of people's understanding of themselves and their subjective relations with the world. They are part of identity. The process by which objective social reality is internalised and becomes subjective is called *socialisation*.

Socialisation and Identity Formation

Socialisation is defined as: 'The comprehensive and consistent induction of an individual into the objective world of a society or a sector of it' (Berger and Luckmann, 1985, p.130).

Socialisation takes place largely as a result of *internalisation*, which is the process by which the *objectivated* social world is re-assimilated into individual consciousness. In this way actions of others become meaningful to the self as part of the knowable, predictable world. There are two stages of socialisation:

PRIMARY SOCIALISATION

This starts at birth and occurs within a family context. During it, the parents or 'significant others' present the objective social world to the child, mediated through their own perception of it. The parents' view of the world is not seen by the child as one of various world views she can choose, it is seen as *the* world. The child internalises the parents' reality by (cognitively) learning about it and by (emotionally) identifying with their roles and attitudes. The process of identification is a dialectical between self and others; externalisation and internalisation; and individual and society. Primary socialisation is the process by which a child's identity is formed. Identity is not merely a subjective internalisation of, or identification with, others – it takes on the world of others: 'Indeed, identity is objectively defined as location in a certain world, and can be subjectively appropriated only *along with* that world' (Berger and Luckmann, 1985, p.132)?

The archetypal primary socialisation is language, which is also the mechanism by which the individual links the objectified external world with the internal subjective world. Children cannot but learn the language of their parents (or significant others) and therefore take on their linguistic community. Other significant roles such as gender roles, or class roles are also the subject of primary socialisation where there is no 'problem of identification'. Although children may differ in their reactions and feelings about parents and roles, they cannot choose alternatives.

SECONDARY SOCIALISATION

This follows primary socialisation and is: 'The internalisation of institutional or institution-based...(or) the acquisition of role-specific knowledge' (Berger and Luckmann, 1985, p.138).

Although it is essential for full participation in society, secondary socialisation is overlaid on an already existing self and is taught or 'brought home' rather than being presented as *the world*. Thus reading and writing have to be learned in a way that learning to talk is not – one can decide not to learn to read or write, but one cannot decide not to learn language.

The result of socialisation is a self which is: '...experienced...as a subjectively and objectively recognisable identity' (Berger and Luckmann, 1985, p.50).

Identity is formed by the *dialectical* relationship between the biological organism, the internal reality, the objectivated external world, and societal roles and institutions; biology creates human beings; society is a human product; society is an objective reality; humans are social products. When socialisation is successful the external and internal identities are symmetrical and complementary although there is always some discrepancy between the internal and external reality. When it is not successful there is a 'problem of identity'. Successful socialisation does not imply happiness: A slave may be desperately unhappy with his life yet not see any alternative.

Identity Conflict

When socialisation is unsuccessful identity problems take three forms:

EGREGIOUS INDIVIDUALS

Individual members of society are stigmatised because of individual biological or extra-ordinary social circumstances, such as 'illegitimacy', 'disabled', and so forth. In societies where they are highly stigmatised they are trapped into the socially predetermined roles. Thus the 'cripple', like the slave, may rail against her fate, but there are no alternatives available to her.

This situation can only change when a sub-group of cripples (or bastards, etc) forms and the members glimpse the possibility of a different identity-type for themselves – e.g., as 'leader of the cripples' or 'valued by cripples'. The identity conflict begins to emerge.

UNSUCCESSFUL PRIMARY SOCIALISATION

Separate and/or conflicting realities are presented during primary socialisation.

When acutely discrepant worlds are mediated in primary socialisation, the individual is presented with a choice of profiled identities apprehended by him as genuine biographical possibilities. (Berger and Luckmann, 1985, p.170)

These range along a continuum: at one extreme are hidden part-identities, for example when a child secretly identifies with a nanny's culture. At the other are irreconcilable primary identity splits in which two (or more) incompatible identities and socialised, both equally real to the individual. They render the individual vulnerable to psychological damage.

CONFLICTS BETWEEN PRIMARY AND SECONDARY IDENTITY

When primary socialisation is at odds with secondary socialisation a third kind of identity conflict occurs. The individual, having already been socialised into an identity is presented with alternatives. Such events can have profound consequences.

The secondary identity may become a 'fantasy identity' which is experienced as the true identity, but never acted out, for example an impoverished adopted person believing that she is really an aristocrat. Even if she assimilates aristocratic mores and manners and mixes with the aristocracy, her *identity* will always be working-class and she will suffer from internal conflict.

DIFFERING ROLES UNDER THE INDIVIDUAL'S CONTROL

There are situations where internalisation of separate realities is not accomplished through identification with significant others, but where roles and identities are internalised without becoming 'part' of the individual. Here the different roles and identities are experienced as being 'under control' and the individual can put on different 'masks' in different situations.

Identity conflict therefore covers a number of situations and simply saying of an individual that he has an 'identity conflict' tells us very little. Although individual identities are the result of a dialectic between the person and the society, *identity types* are determined by society. They are seen as part of the larger 'cosmology' of society in general and fit into the commonsense view which individuals have of the world. This implies that stereotyping is an inevitable consequence of socialisation because 'typification' is the necessary precondition for the formation of roles and institutions.

Berger and Luckmann offer an important sociological analysis of personal and group identity. Their model initially explained the relationship between the microcosm of individual identity development and the macrocosmic social structure. Because they attempted to explain how societies perpetuate themselves, their theory is basically a conservative one, which sees society as a stable structure socialising individuals so that they can sustain its functions and structures.

'Nature' only plays a small part. Identity is not static, constant and unified aspect of the self but rather a collection of different selves made up of different roles used in different social contexts and the subjective response to those roles. The roles are sometimes in harmony, sometimes in conflict. Personal identity is an abstraction of the collection of roles. Individual humans outside a social context are meaningless entities which cannot be understood.

This contrasts with previously discussed theories regarding the formation of group identity. Adorno *et al.* (1950) and Park, (1964) take as their basis the assumption that in-group/out-group hostility is a *biological* rather than social trait. The psychoanalytic theories considered below also tend to place more emphasis on biological instincts.

The relationship between socialisation and identity illuminates the discussion of the development of racial identity of children of mixed parentage. Berger and Luckmann confirm that the early identifications, which make up primary socialisation, take place between the infant and the 'significant others' within the family and that these identifications are responsible for the core identity. Secondary socialisation which takes place outside the family is less important to identity formation. This is in accordance with all the major developmental theories discussed so far, but Berger and Luckmann go further in emphasising the two-way nature of. the relationship. They do not see the child as a mere recipient of socialisation but as a *participant* in the development and continuation of societal institutions.

The discussion on identity conflict is particularly salient, but also illustrates some of the limitations of the theory. Berger and Luckmann demonstrate that identity conflict is an inevitable consequence of socialisation because of the inescapable discrepancy between subjective and objective realities. However, the degree of conflict differs greatly between individuals, depending on such variables as temperament, parental attitudes, early experience, social mores and the distribution of knowledge. This implies it is not enough to refer to children of mixed parentage as having 'identity conflict', or as being 'marginal'. These statements beg the question 'What kind of conflict?'.

It is unclear how the different types of conflict can be differentiated in practice. Is mixed-race identity an identity 'type' as has been defined, and as Park (1964) has asserted, or is it a conflict between two identities? How can we tell which is the 'real' and which the 'false'? What part of the identity was acquired during primary and what part during secondary socialisation? The role of parents during primary socialisation is seen here as mediators of societal norms and values. The theory does not explore how the child's relationship with parents affects the way these values are presented to the child and how the child responds.

The emphasis placed on consciousness as a determinant of reality means that the concept of *unconscious* conflict sits uneasily within it. Unconscious conflict is essential to the theory of marginality and most other theories about racial relations. It is difficult to see how socialisation can be fully conscious as many of the assumptions we make about the world are not consciously made, and many human actions are influenced by factors to which there is no conscious access; for example, some white women may prefer relationships with black men because of their own early childhood experiences. It is unlikely that they would all be able to make this link consciously.

The role of language in primary socialisation is also contentious. Language is given the most important place in the process of socialisation, a view that is concordant with Milner and others and is the thinking behind many of the studies on racial identity development. Language, however, only begins in the second year of life and is preceded by other forms of symbolisation.

Piagetian and psychoanalytic theories of development are based on the proposition that much of the core of identity development occurs in the first and second year before language becomes the major symbolic instrument. Pre-linguistic and extra-linguistic forms of symbolisation my be more important in socialisation than Berger and Luckmann acknowledge.

Although the theory does provide a comprehensive sociological perspective on identity development, it does not attempt to deal with the actual process of socialisation itself. The theory does not address such questions as:

- what does the child learn about the world?
- how does the child learn about the world?
- exactly what part do 'significant others' play in socialisation? and
- what is the process of identity formation?

To answer these questions we must leave sociology and address psychology.

Piaget

Piaget's theory of 'Genetic Epistemology' attempts to grapple with the questions of how humans develop knowledge of themselves and the world. Like Berger and Luckmann, Piaget believes that human ideas, beliefs and actions are not genetically predetermined. Humans are born with certain mental structures which interact with the world in the course of development.

Piaget believes that humans have a basic and innate tendency toward maintaining *equilibrium* – a state in which the organism is in dynamic harmony with its environment. As the internal or external conditions change (e.g. by physical growth) the organism changes and reaches a new equilibrium. Thus there is a continuous dialectal relationship between the organism and the environment. To maintain equilibrium humans use two complementary, fundamental processes: *organisation* – a tendency to classify and make the environment predictable, and *adaptation* – the process by which the organism changes in response to the environment. Adaptation is, in turn, made up of two complementary processes: *accommodation* – by which structures are changed to fit in with the environment, and *assimilation* – in which the external phenomena are incorporated into the organism's structures.

Human knowledge is organised into *schemas* which are abstractions of acts, objects, and so forth. Every act of learning involves both processes, but in different ratios. Imitation is mainly an accommodative process because it involves changing according to the person being imitated. Imaginative play, on the other hand, involves mainly assimilation because the external object (e.g. a plank) can be incorporated into a number of schemas (e.g. ship, bridge, bat) without much regard to its objective features. For a fuller account of Piaget's theories see Pulaski (1980); Ginsburg and Opper (1979) or Boden (1979).

Piaget's and Berger and Luckmann's views on human nature and development are strikingly similar in that they assert the primacy of organisation as an underlying and necessary condition for human thought. Both posit a dialectical relationship between human beings and their environment in the process of thought and development. Most important, both hold as a basic tenet that human beings are active participants in constructing their own real world rather than passive recipients of teaching, biological maturation, or other external phenomena.

The nature of the dialectic differs in the two theories and it is not possible to reduce one to the other. Berger and Luckmann see humans as creating society mainly in the collective sense. In Piaget's theory the dialectic lies in the relationship to the inanimate world and between internal processes. He does not deal in any depth with interpersonal relationships nor with the relationship between individual and society, concentrating more on human *intelligence* or capacity for understanding the world (Piaget and Inhelder, 1973). Nevertheless, if Berger and Luckmann are correct and the social world for children is equivalent to the physical world (in that social laws are as real as physical laws) then Piaget's theories on the development of logico-mathematical intelligence should be valid for social intelligence as well (Butterworth, 1982). Indeed, Piaget conducted some of his experiments on the topic of children's concept of nations (Piaget and Weil, 1951). It seems reasonable to believe, therefore, that their ideas are complementary.

Another similarity is the weight both theories place on the roles of abstraction, representation and classification (typification). Schemas and institutions are both built up out of abstractions from phenomena or actions which have been classified and ordered according to a certain 'logic'. Both are ultimately derived from Kantian notions of *categories*.

Piaget's contribution to the discussion of how humans actively create their own reality is that he extends the dialectic to the psychological level and also adds a detailed developmental theory. According to Piaget, development of knowledge takes place in four well-defined stages:

- the *Sensori-Motor* stage from birth to about two years

- the *Pre-Operational* stage from two to seven

- the *Concrete Operational* stage from seven to twelve, and

- the *Formal Operational* through adolescence (Ginsburg and Opper, 1979).

Each stage builds on the capacities gained in previous stages and is characterised by a qualitatively more complex intelligence ordered into schemas which are qualitatively more abstract. Thought develops from being purely *egocentric* and concrete to being *decentred* and abstract.

During the sensori-motor stage, which is essentially the pre-verbal era, infants develop understanding of how their senses and actions affect, and are affected by, the immediate outside world, for example that an object hidden under a cloth is found by removing the cloth. Piaget shows that this 'simple' deduction is in fact the result of complex thought processes which are only to be acquired over time. Thought in this phase is 'egocentric' because the child initially has no concept of 'object-constancy'. When an object is removed from its immediate sensory environment the child has no way of knowing that it still exists – its world consists of the immediate moment and location. By the time language is acquired in the second year, the child has a sophisticated knowledge of its place in the immediate world and an ability to 'represent' – to classify and remember objects in the environment.

For Piaget language plays a relatively minor role in the development of knowledge, being only one, rather late, form of representation. Piaget does believe, however, that representation itself only begins in the second year, a view hotly contested by other theorists. Some fairly sophisticated representations of the self may manifest in a pre- or non-linguistic fashion. This has major implications for the study of racial identity where all the investigations have assumed some degree of verbal sophistication preceding any development of racial identity. Much early primary socialisation is not necessarily verbal and the rudiments of the later, more sophisticated notions about racial groups, may begin very early.

Piaget does not deal directly with the development of identity. He does, however, deal with the development of knowledge of the self and its relationship to the world, which is a major and necessary component of identity. The notion of development from almost total egocentrism, in which the infant has no sense of a separate self, to decentred modes of thought is crucial in any discussion of identity development.

The theory of *genetic epistemology* is generally recognised as the most comprehensive existing theory of intellectual development (Donaldson, 1978), although it has received severe criticism. The basic concept that development progresses in defined and invariant stages has been challenged. Many of the capacities which Piaget assumes occur only towards the end of the sensori-motor period apparently occur much earlier.

The challenge to Piaget with which this book is most concerned is that he places little emphasis on the role of emotions and relationships in the process of human development. Although he acknowledges that they influence development, he differs from Berger and Luckmann who stress the central role of 'significant others' and the child's identification with them in the process of development. Piaget often portrayed people as objects of knowledge for infants, similar in principle to inanimate objects. Ironically, Piaget's initial subjects were his own children and his descriptions clearly show how closely he was involved in their development.

In order to complete the picture of how identity develops in children, the area of emotional development and the development of relationships must be addressed. The theories most associated with them are psychoanalytic. Although psychoanalysis contains an enormous body of knowledge, relatively little has been written specifically about identity development.

Erikson

Erikson formulated one of the most important psychoanalytic theories of the development of identity. It was basically Freudian but, unlike Freud, Erikson believed that development of the personality does not end after the Oedipus Complex has been resolved. Each of the eight stages of life, from birth to old age, presents a crisis for the individual which has to be resolved. Each stage must be lived through and its particular crisis resolved before the next stage can be reached. Erikson believed that identity development is finally achieved (or not achieved) during adolescence, but that the prototype of identity is already discernible during the first two stages – *basic trust vs mistrust* and *autonomy vs shame and guilt*.

During the first stage an infant's world is dominated totally by bodily needs and their satisfaction by the mother. The infant must be able to develop a sense of trust in its mother before it can continue to function when the mother is absent.

The dialectical relationship between individual and society is also a vital part of Erikson's (1980) view of identity:

> From a genetic point of view, then, the process of identity formation emerges as a process of *evolving configuration* – a configuration which is gradually established by successive ego syntheses and re-syntheses throughout childhood; it is a configuration gradually integrating *constitutional givens, idiosyncratic libidinal needs, favoured capacities, significant identifications, effective defences, successful sublimation and constituent roles.* (p.125)

This dialectic is repeated in all eight stages, with the individual's contribution becoming more and more significant until adulthood is reached. The dialectic between the individual and the outside world is a backdrop to the internal tensions and conflicts which must be resolved at each stage if the individual is to maintain psychological growth. Erikson, like Piaget, sees most of the real impetus for growth in these internal conflicts and their resolution.

Erikson believed that a mother's patterns of care, even during the earliest stage of life, are carried out within a cultural context. The personal identity or sense of self which emerges as a result of the mothering pattern is seen as a *social* as well as a *personal* construct, and cannot be understood outside the socio-cultural milieu of the family. This approximates to the spirit of Berger and Luckmann's idea of the social construction of identity. The basic sense of identity precedes awareness of the societal influences which determine a mother's actions and with which the child will interact to form an adult identity. This may mean that the development of a child's racial identity begins as soon as the child becomes aware of herself as a social being long before any awareness of racial differences is possible.

Winnicott

Although Erikson acknowledges the role of the mother in the first stage as the primary provider of both physical and emotional nurturing and as the primary object of the child's identifications, he views development primarily as an internal struggle between opposing forces within the child. In this respect he is true to the Freudian tradition. The *Object Relations* school of psychoanalytic thinking, developed by Melanie Klein, challenges some of these basic Freudian assumptions about human development (Segal, 1979). Klein and her followers placed much more emphasis than Freud on child development in the first year of life contending that much of the basic personality structures are in place by the second year and on the mother's role in development. In Kleinian theory the real mother is relatively unimportant as the child's emotions are largely directed towards an internal fantasised 'object mother'.

One object-relations theorist, however, who stressed the importance of the real mother was DW Winnicott who held the dictum: 'There is no such thing as a baby' (1975, p.99).

By this he meant that during the first part of an infant's life she cannot exist without the mother either physically or emotionally, and cannot be fully understood without reference to the mother. The process of identity development or development of the 'self' is that by which the infant slowly moves away from absolute dependence, through relative dependence towards independence.

Winnicott maintains that normally, during the last few weeks of pregnancy and the first months after birth, the mother is in a state of *primary maternal preoccupation*. This means that she is 'given over' to the needs and wishes of her child. She has an almost supernatural sensitivity to the child's needs and can satisfy virtually all of them. She provides a *facilitating environment* for the infant which allows the latter's capacity for psychological growth to realise itself. During the first months the mother is not only part of the environment, she *is* both the inner and outer environment and at this stage the father has a secondary role of supporting the vulnerable mother.

The infant is in a state of *unintegration* – there is no differentiation between the 'me' and 'not me', the inner and outer world, self and mother, or even parts of the self. Unintegration differs from *disintegration*, the latter occurring only *after* a degree of integration has been achieved.

> ...cohesion of the various sensori-motor elements belongs to the fact that the mother holds the infant, sometimes physically, and all the time figuratively. Periodically the infant's gesture gives expression to a spontaneous impulse; the source of the gesture is the True Self, and the gesture indicates the existence of a potential True Self. (Winnicott, 1965, p.145)

Development of the self therefore starts at this very early stage, although in the very beginning the True Self is a potential. The True Self is the infant's sense of aliveness which is the precursor of the sense of creativity, the hallmark of successful development. The infant experiences a sense of *omnipotence* because all desires and fantasies are being satisfied. She is not aware of any outside limits. If all is well, the infant is *going-on-being* 'a kind of blueprint for existentialism.' This going-on being constitutes the most primitive precursor of identity.

The going-on-being depends on the mother adapting the environment to meet the infant's needs. If this is done satisfactorily, the mother prevents impingements from interfering with the sense of omnipotence and the True Self can develop relatively unimpeded so the mother is a *good enough mother*. If she is not 'good enough' and cannot meet the child's needs, the going-on-being is disrupted by impingements. The sense of omnipotence is thwarted and the True Self is threatened. The most damaging kind of mother is one who, through inconsistency, tantalises the infant by developing an expectation of care which is not fulfilled. The infant feels 'let down' and in extreme cases the True Self is disintegrated. In order to protect the True Self from impingement, a False Self begins to develop whose main characteristics are compliance, lack of creativity and a sense of not being 'alive'. Winnicott (1965) proposes a classification of False Self organisations as follows:

- ° the individual presents as normal, but there is always 'something lacking'
- ° the False Self defends the True Self, which only has a 'secret life'
- ° the False Self searches for conditions in which the True Self can survive
- ° the False Self is built on identifications with others (e.g., a nanny); and
- ° the False Self represents a social attitude, and protects the privacy of the True Self which is available to the individual. (p.144).

When the infant's going-on-being is strengthened by many repetitions of needs being met, the inevitable impingements do not destroy the self, but they force the infant to become aware of the environment. With this awareness comes the second stage, that is, *relative dependence*. The mother, who hitherto has not been differentiated from the self, has been a *subjective object*. The infant becomes aware of her caring and she becomes an *object, objectively perceived* – she begins to be a separate self. The infant can now have a capacity for *concern* and with this a capacity for real object relations. If all the infant's needs are met at this stage, omnipotence continues and she will be unable to develop object relations. Frustration is therefore a necessary part of development.

The third stage is the transition 'towards independence'; in which the infant develops a capacity to be alone (i.e., separate) in the mother's presence. She has to be available when necessary, but to let go when this is required. The concept of *transition* is crucial for Winnicott and transitional phenomena include play, language, culture and *transitional objects*. The use of transitional phenomena represents the infant's struggle to: '...relate subjective reality to shared reality which can be objectively perceived' (Phillips 1988, p.117).

In play the objects, although they exist independently, are created by the infant to suit its needs. Similarly, although words have an objective and intersubjective meaning, they are used to convey a purely subjective reality. Transitional objects, toys, blankets, and so forth when shared become meaningless. The special meaning slowly recedes as the child becomes more independent. (For a fuller description of transitional objects and the role of play see Winnicott 1974, p.60).

The third stage is never fully completed, but when the development is successful the individual is able to reach maturity and is successfully socialised. The healthy individual:

> ...is able to identify with society without too great a sacrifice of personal spontaneity; or, the other way round, the adult is able to attend to his or her own personal needs without being antisocial, and indeed, without a failure to take some responsibility for the maintenance or the modification of society as it is found. (Winnicott, 1965, pp.83–84)

Winnicott's theory of early development is not dissimilar to Erikson's, despite their different schools of psychoanalytic thought. With Piaget they postulate an innate drive towards creativity and spontaneity which is at variance with both Freud and Klein's. Creativity for Freud is a sublimation of id drives, whereas for Klein it is a reparative activity (Segal, 1979).

Winnicott lacks Erikson's sociocultural dimension and his theories are very culture-bound in their assumptions about gender and family roles. Nevertheless, Winnicott's contribution to the understanding of the origins of identity development is his description of the centrality of the early mother–infant relationship and its vicissitudes. He has been accused of over-emphasising the mother's role at the expense of the father's because he does not see fathers as having any direct role in early development. Clancier and Kalmanovitch (1987), however, dispute this point.

Winnicott's description of the state of unintegration and the development towards integration is similar to Piaget's move from egocentric to decentred modes of thought. In both formulations the neonate has no boundary between the self and the world, and object relations only develop when the child has a symbolic representation of the object available. For Piaget object-constancy is only fully developed in the second year towards the end of the sensori-motor stage when memory has formed and language begins. For Winnicott, object relations is a relatively early phenomenon and begins with the capacity for concern around the sixth month. Piaget does not even contemplate the role of *part-object relations* which is crucial for Winnicott and begins even earlier in life. Part-object relations are somewhat akin to Berger and Luckmann's definition of *roles*, because the relationship is not with a *person*, but with one aspect of that person's behaviour. In early infancy the nurturing mother is seen as separate from the withholding mother, and even earlier the relationship is with the nipple, which is separated into the 'good breast' and the 'bad breast'.

The similarities are nevertheless more striking than the differences, for example the transition from relative dependency towards independence, and from the sensori-motor to the pre-operational stage. In both descriptions the capacity for play is central because play demonstrates the ability to use objects as symbols or representations of other things, and because it is one of the first signs of creative thinking in which the world can be 'taken in' in a non-threatening way. Winnicott (1974) acknowledges Erikson's contribution, saying that the capacity to play is contingent on basic trust.

The work of Winnicott focuses on emotional rather than cognitive development, and adds the dimension of the mother–infant relationship in the consideration of identity development. It goes some way towards explaining the infant's motivation in the development of identity – the area with which Piaget has most difficulty.

Winnicott's contribution to psychoanalytic theory was formulated to re-introduce the importance of the real mother in development. He gives the mother a relatively passive role, at least from the infant's point of view. He de-emphasises the infant's adaptation to the mother, while emphasising her adaptation to the infant. Although he shares the view that infants create or construct their worlds, he tackles in very broad terms the world's (i.e., the mother's) role in constructing the infant. What he does give us – the concept of the 'good enough mother' – provides a framework for considering the different ways mothering can influence identity development.

From the infant's point of view, mothering influences formation of the False Self. The idea of 'degree of False Self' parallels Berger and Luckmann's continuum of identity conflict, and confirms that it begins very early. Interestingly Winnicott does not postulate a condition in which there can be two 'True Selves' competing for ascendancy, rather he sees the relationship between the True and False selves as complementary, not conflicting, perhaps because his theory was a reaction to the paramountcy of internal conflict advocated by Freud and Klein.

Stern

Stern (1985) claims that the *self* is the most important organising factor in development. This theory is an attempt to integrate the psychoanalytic and experimental views of the development of interpersonal relationships (see also Brazelton and Cramer (1991) for a more recent and perhaps more cogent synthesis). Stern believes that there are no stages of development as such, but that the infant moves through *domains of relatedness* which are characterised by *senses of self*. Stern believes that although the domains arise sequentially, the infant, and even the adult, can move from one domain to another. Stern's senses of self are *Emergent, Core, Interpersonal,* and *Verbal.*

He believes that an important part of development is temperament, which is genetically determined. The infant's temperament interacts with the mother's and the resultant *fit* or *contouring* has a crucial effect on the pattern of their relationship and ultimately the infant's sense of self. A pattern of largely unconscious mismatches between the infant's temperamental capacity for stimulation and the mother's expectations can lead to serious and damaging psychopathology in later life. The sense of self is built up during everyday interactions with others and not through any exceptional or traumatic events in her life. The mother's own experiences in infancy, her sense of self and feelings and expectations about the child subtly influence her responses which may be more sensitive in one domain of relatedness than another, as may the infant's. The mother's personality and her attitude towards the child are crucial to the child's development.

Stern extends Winnicott's view of the mother–infant relationship to include the inner world of the mother and the biological predispositions of the infant, showing that both the objective and subjective aspects of development can be taken into account by the theoretical framework.

The Structural-Developmental Theory

Reductionism

Before discussing an overview of these theories, it is necessary to give a caveat about the danger of *reductionism*. None of the theories presented here can, on its own, answer the questions about identity development. Even when combined they can only point to the kind of theory which would have to be developed to give a really comprehensive picture of the subject.

It would be tempting to reduce sociological theories to psychological or biological ones and *vice versa*, and to conclude that the different theorists are really saying the same thing, or that one level of discourse can explain the other. The problem is compounded when discussing identity because it is inherently both a psychological and a sociological phenomenon – see Berger and Luckmann's differentiation between individual identities and collective identities. White racists are an identity type, sharing many social attributes; they are also individuals with personal histories and motives. Depending on what stance the observer takes, the type or the individual will be more salient. Devereux (1978) argues that all facts about humans can be explained fully either psychologically or sociologically. These explanations are complementary and not contradictory, but they can never be *simultaneous* – there cannot be a coherent psycho-social explanation of human behaviour.

Even if it is, however, impossible to create one composite 'psycho-social' theory, can one dovetail these theories to provide a more holistic theoretical background for the study of the early development of personal and racial identity?

Definition of Identity

No common definition of identity encapsulates all these theories but a working definition could be:

The ongoing interaction between and the sum total of:

- ° the biological make-up of individuals, including their physical attributes, particular abilities and temperament
- ° their conscious and unconscious beliefs, opinions and ideas about themselves
- ° their relationships to significant other people and groups, and
- ° the roles and status afforded them by these people and groups.

This 'structural-developmental' definition takes into account the sociological, psychological and biological levels, as well as the role of unconscious processes. It shows identity as a dynamic process capable of change and development.

Development of Structures

The theorists discussed above believe that identity formation involves the establishment and elaboration of internal structures which enable the infant to develop an increasingly complex ability to make meaningful the internal and external world. Humans are born with some innate mental structures such as rudimentary schemas of sucking and the capacity for behaving socially. Other structures, for example internal mirror-images of roles and institutions which infants encounter, such as the internalised *object mother*, are developed later. Each child is born with a unique set of capacities and a unique temperament (Stern, 1985) into a unique environment. Although some structures may be common to all everyone, and some to particular cultures, each person's structures have different *content*. People assimilate the world which they fit into the structures which in turn are affected by new material. The structures are determined by meta-structures. Roles are determined by institutions, schemas by adaptation, and object mothers by introjection.

Identification

Identification is one of the primary means by which an infant assimilates the outside world. By identifying with people, roles, actions, attitudes, beliefs, and so on, an infant slowly develops a sense of self as separate but related to others actions and ideas. Psychoanalytic theories claim that identification with other people is preceded by *projective identification*, which involves part-object relationships. Laplanche and Pontalis (1983) and Klein (1955) provide definitions and discussions of projective identification.

Mother's Role

All the theories assert the mother's paramount importance as a social object in the infant's life. In the first few months she *is* her child's social world, the first and most important object of identification for her child and thus the focus of early socialisation.

The mother is not merely an *object*, however, she is also a *subject*. The way the infant presents herself to the mother affects her parenting. Sociologically, the mother is seen as the mediator of social knowledge who filters social facts to present them to her child, thus perpetuating the social order. Psychologically this means that the mother brings her own experiences of being parented and both conscious and unconscious beliefs and attitudes into the relationship. They are shaped by cultural attitudes and individual experience of pregnancy and childbirth. A mother does not simply respond to her infant's behaviour. Her response is mediated by the social context and by elements which she *projects* onto her child.

The infant also brings into the relationship her own temperament and disposition and this in turn affects how the mother responds. Thus primary socialisation is not simply a matter of transferring attitudes from one generation to the next. Socialisation consists of a series of complex interactions characterised by *reciprocal* projection.

The Dialectical Nature of Development

The way in which mother and infant project and introject parts of each other constitutes a *dialectic*: the mother projects fantasies about how she believes her child is (or should be) and acts accordingly. The infant reacts by either *introjecting* the fantasy and responding accordingly and/or by projecting feelings back on to the mother who in turn introjects them. This dialectic between unconscious internal structures and social interaction is only one level on which the dialectic operates. There are also dialectical relationships between the individual and groups, such as the family, and society (Berger and Luckmann), between internal objects and structures and between those structures and the physical environment (Piaget).

Through continuous interaction with the environment the infant develops an increasingly sophisticated sense of her own place in the physical and social cosmos. This sense is the precursor to full identity development.

The Active Role of the Infant in Identity Formation

All the theories postulate the infant as actively participating in the construction of her own reality. Although the parents, especially the mother, present their own constructions of reality to her, the infant filters this reality in the process of internalising, and acts upon it.

Identity is partly a social construct, but it is also inherently subjective, and to be fully understood the subjective quality must be considered. To say to someone 'You are a black man' is coherent. To say 'You have a black identity' is not.

Identity and the Social Context

Personal identity and its development is only meaningful within the socio-cultural context within which it takes place. In the first months, society is represented to the infant by the mother. Much of identity development consists of internalising the roles and institutions of society so that society becomes a subjective reality for the growing infant. The process by which a person becomes part of society is *socialisation* and, when successful, the subjective world of the individual; 'Who am I?' corresponds with his objective place in society: 'Who you are?'. Socialisation begins at birth and continues throughout life.

Preverbal Experience

The first two years are enormously important in identity development. The basic structures of the personality are formed and the basis of later identity structure, in other words the separation between *me* and *not me* (Winnicott, 1988) is normally achieved. There is a conflict, however, between the Piagetian and the psychoanalytic views regarding the development of the capacity for *representation*. Piaget believes that the infant's ability to represent absent objects is usually achieved in the second year, when the child has demonstrated *object constancy*. Object relations theorists, however, believe that representation, for example of the nipple, occurs very much earlier perhaps at birth. All agree nevertheless that representation and symbol formation is a pre-linguistic achievement and therefore that some kind of abstraction of a self occurs by the end of the second year.

Identity Conflict

Identity conflict and identity diffusion result from a failure of socialisation. All humans have some identity conflicts but they become pathological when they severely restrict people's ability to relate to others or to fulfil their adult potential. Identity conflict ranges over two continua:

CONFLICTS BETWEEN DIFFERENT STRUCTURES WITHIN INDIVIDUALS

Infants who are given *good enough* parenting in their first years will tend to see themselves as separate individuals who have a stable 'inner core' or *True Self* (Winnicott). Their relationships with the world will be characterised by *basic trust* (Erikson), and the different aspects and identifications in their personalities will largely be integrated. Conversely, those not given good enough parenting will tend to have a diffuse sense of being separate and autonomous. They are unlikely to developing a coherent sense of self and may find difficulty integrating the different parts of their personality, being constantly confronted with the fear of *disintegration* (Winnicott). They will tend to over-identify with others or be unable to make appropriate identifications. Their personality will be characterised by *False Self* organisation and their relationships by a basic sense of *mistrust*. When their identity is put under stress later in life, these people will need to use extreme measures to defend themselves from disintegration. They may repress whole aspects of their personality, act out the conflict by destructive or self-destructive behaviour. They may even regress into psychosis.

CONFLICT BETWEEN THE VIEW PEOPLE HAVE OF THEMSELVES AND SOCIETY'S VIEW OF THEM
This corresponds to Berger and Luckmann's conflicts of secondary socialisation. Even if people have achieved a coherent sense of self, their self-concept may be challenged by society. This can also have severe consequences for identity development, but is unlikely to lead to disintegration. Individuals can play different, and even sometimes contradictory, roles if their primary identity or true self is intact.

Racial Identity

The ideas about Self, in particular of False Self organisation of the psyche, are crucial to the discussion about mixed-race identity development. They confirm that the pathological identity dysfunction in children can begin long before any truly racial or sociocultural factors become part of consciousness. If early mothering is adequate and the child develops a largely True Self sense of identity then later racism need not lead to fragmentation or breakdown. However, racism may be one of many social, psychological and interpersonal forces which confront the child, and there are therefore many opportunities for the child to form both positive and negative identifications with the mother or with other people. The concept of False Self is consistent with the analysis of the marginal theorists who portray the marginal individual as having an inner core which is white, but being forced to live the life of a black person. One interesting difference is that Park proposes that the marginal man's creativity derives from internal *conflict*, whereas Winnicott sees creativity as deriving from psychological *health*. He would probably see marginal people as less creative than those who attain 'maturity' and whose inner and outer selves do not conflict. Another difference is that the False Self organisation is typified by compliance, which Park claims is the trait of 'fully' black rather than marginal people of mixed-race. Perhaps compliance is linked to low self-esteem rather than identity conflict, or is a response to political or individual oppression. Perhaps there is not a rigid definition between 'true' and 'false' aspects of the self, and that what is true or false may depend on the political, social or interpersonal context in which individuals see themselves.

The implications of the views of Berger and Luckmann and Winnicott on identity conflict are that it becomes very difficult to make generalised statements about any group's reaction to identity conflict. Even if all mixed-race people are categorised in the same way by society, their reaction to this must be determined to a large extent by their early parenting and by the meaning which they attach to racist actions. Thus both those theorists who claim that mixed-race people are bound to suffer from severe identity conflict (Stonequist, 1937; Park, 1964; Benson, 1981) and those who claim that they do not (Wilson, 1987), are generalising. Unless it can be demonstrated that a group of children of mixed parentage have received a similar pattern of parenting, and attach similar meanings to the racialised aspects of their environment, these generalisations are invalid. They also focus on one aspect of a multi-factorial phenomenon.

If the multi-factorial nature of identity development is accepted then all theories which view racial identity and its development as an essentially unidimensional process are arguable. Even theories which acknowledge complexity, but see development as a more-or-less straightforward process by which feelings and beliefs become more complex and mature, cannot do justice to the heterogeneous nature of identity. Recent theoretical developments in sociological theory based on post-modernism would therefore seem to provide a more adequate basis for investigating the identity of mixed-race children.

The third part of the study was based on the findings of the first two parts together with advances in anti-racist theory and research methodology informed by post-modern philosophy. The changes in theory and methodology reflect an acknowledgement of the diversity of parenting styles as they relate not only to race, but to other constructs such as class, gender and culture which were fundamentally important in structuring the way mixed-race children are raised. These innovations also led to a new formulation of identity and identity development.

Post-Modernism

Although the definition of post-modernism is controverted (Bernstein, 1991; Steuerman, 1992), it is a way of seeing the world which has entered the discourses of disciplines such as architecture, art, literature, philosophy and sociology but has limited influence in social work (Rojek, Peacock and Collins, 1988; Parton, 1995). I will be focusing on the philosophical and sociological implications.

Post-modernism can be seen as a way of considering reality. It is a reaction to Pre-modernism in which reality is revealed (by God, magic, religion) and Modernism in which reality is discovered (by science, psychoanalysis, Marxism). In Post-modernism 'reality' is created (by social interaction, writing, interpretation).

The most commonly used definition is provided by Lyotard (1984), who defined the post-modern as: '...incredulity towards metanarratives' (p.xxiv).

Harland (1987) contrasts (Modernist) Structuralism with Post-Structuralism:

Post-Structuralism does not counter superficial social conformity by invoking deeper necessities of biological nature, nor does it counter external social impositions by invoking a free will that comes from within... Post-Structuralists distinguish between two possible modes of functioning for the Sign. On the one hand there is the conventional mode where the sign works rigidly and despotically... On the other there is the unconventional mode where the Sign works creatively, anarchically and irresponsibly. This is the mode that represents the real being of the Sign. (pp.123–124)

Using these notions I will return to the original theoretical basis of this thesis, that is, the Marginal theorists (Berger and Luckmann, Erikson, Piaget, Winnicott, the doll studies and social work anti-racists such as Small and Dominelli) and argue that these very different theories are all 'modernist' social and psychological accounts, and that they provide limited insights about racial identity development.

I will focus on particular elements of the post-modernism analysis, on the meta-narratives of development, maturity and anti-racism. The 'Signs' I will be concentrating on are 'Race', 'Culture', 'Ethnicity' and 'Parenthood'.

'Modernism' is viewed by post-modernists as the theories, philosophies and political beliefs which are the legacy of the Enlightenment. Enlightenment is a way of seeing the world which is characterised by 'grand-narratives' or 'meta-narratives'; explanations of the world which try to unify and explain all human experience and look for political systems which will liberate all humans from oppression or which will explain all scientific and natural truths. These meta-narratives include the philosophies of humanism, Marxism, positivism, and Christianity (Lyotard, 1992). Although these theories are very different they share some things in common:

> *Totalisation* – they are holistic, and attempt to explain the whole human condition or the condition of whole societies either philosophically, psychologically or socially, emphasising 'sameness' rather than 'difference'.

> *Teleology* – they see societies, individuals and theories progressing towards an ultimate goal such as liberation, emancipation or maturity. Individuals and/or society start from some form of primitive existence and progress through stages to a higher level of being.

> *Essentialism* – the belief that people, cultures, and society as well as natural phenomena have an 'essence' or true nature which, with the right theoretical and practical tools is, in principle, able to be discovered by 'Science'.

> *Logocentrism* – the belief that scientific rationality provides the absolute truth about the world, and that reason (i.e. western thinking) is the highest form of knowledge and understanding. *Logocentrism* is equated by post-modernists such as Derrida with *Phonocentrism* – the belief that the spoken word is the ultimate communication and *Phallocentrism* – the belief that male ways of viewing the world are primary (Kearney, 1986).

Post-modernism and post-structural theorists attack these tenets. They see totalisation as having a 'hidden agenda' of terrorism or totalitarianism. Thus Stalinism and Nazism are not aberrations or retreats from modernism but the consequences of a view of the world which can easily move from describing people's similarities to forcing people to be the same.

Totalisation is therefore seen as operating in two ways, either by incorporating 'the other' into the 'the self' or by excluding 'the other' from 'the self'. Western philosophy, especially Humanism, is attacked because it assumes that humans are all basically the same (Barthes, 1973; Young, 1992). All humanist philosophies have a hidden implication that people who are not part of the 'good society' become identified with 'the other' and therefore become dehumanised.

Instead of celebrating sameness and unity, the post-modernists celebrate difference. Teleologies are attacked by post-modernists because of their tendency to totalise. Teleological theories aim at a future in which human beings will all be the same, and their essence revealed, whether the goal or *telos* is the liberation of man, the coming of the Messiah, the dawning of a new socialist age or a society in which people are all mature and rational.

They view the past as merely as a precursor for the inevitable historical achievement of the telos. The problem is that each telos, and the totality it implies, is seen as the only truth and the right way forward. In modern thinking the goal has usually been the reproduction of western bourgeois, logocentric and phallo-centric ideals. Those with different ideals are seen as resisting the inevitable advance of history and of being irrational, immature or marginal. They become part of the dehumanised 'other' who needs to be resisted and eliminated.

Essentialism is attacked for similar reasons. According to post-modernism, modern theories of the truth or essence of human beings, society or nature all rely on a view of truth which claims to be universal and everlasting. Post-modern theorists believe that this version of 'truth' is a construction of western society, imposed by violence on other cultures or dissenters. In modernist western thought the biological is seen as prior to and more fundamental than the social, the individual is valued over the collective, and the conscious 'self' is valued over the unconscious or the group. Post-modernists see truth as bound by culture, time, and place, and accuse modernist beliefs of legitimating the Eurocentric, logocentric power relationships in society.

Post-modernism views societies and cultures as conflictual, irrational and changing. Their development is contradictory, discontinuous, and agonistic. The totalising beliefs which hold societies, cultures, individuals and families together are seen as myths and meta-narratives which need to be constantly deconstructed to uncover their role in legitimating power structures. Rutherford (1990) contrasts this notion of 'difference' with the modernist notion of 'diversity' which exalts the diversity of cultures, but sees culture as a superficial addition to essential human nature. Post-structuralists deny that there is a human nature. All discourse about humans, including the idea of human nature, is seen as being socially constructed. Human nature is a product of culture rather than cultures being different ways of expressing human nature. This view of difference is carried into the post-structu-ralist critique of social science. Post-structuralists attack both absolutism and relativism as false dichotomies created by modernist philosophy.

This brief overview points to some of the criticisms which may be levelled at the theories which were used to underpin the original part of the study. The theories of Berger and Luckmann, Erikson, Winnicott, and Piaget which formed the basis of this study can be subjected to post-modernist critiques. Consider Erikson's concept of identity:

> The creation of a sense of sameness; a unity of personality now felt by the individual and recognised by others as having consistency in time; of being, as it were, an irreversible historical fact. (Erikson 1963, p.11, quoted in Banks, 1992a, p.22).

His use of eight stages, each dependent on the successful completion of the previous one, demonstrates his conception of identity as essentially continuous, individual, progressive and aimed at the ultimate goal of a 'maturity' which involves a homeostasis between inner and outer reality. Winnicott's view is of a child moving from dependency to independence and the process of identity formation being a struggle for autonomy. Successful identity development or socialisation are seen as producing an individual who is happy, productive, has high self-esteem, is mature and viewed with respect by members of the community. A positive identity is seen as a stable entity in which the internal and external realities of the individual are matched or complementary. These theories are based on a teleological view of identity development.

This position has been attacked by Lacan (1977) and other post-structuralist thinkers such as Foucault (1987). Lacan's criticism is that the view of development and maturity as autonomy is narcissistic, culture-bound and dependent on a specifically Anglo-American conception of adulthood in which the 'good citizen' is seen as productive and conforming. The ego psychologists view society as benevolent and nurturing, and the task of individual development as successfully integrating into society. Society, socialisation and therefore the super-ego are something added on after the basic individual has been constructed. Lacan claims that this view, too, is culture bound:

> ...in the grand old Anglo-Saxon tradition, what's basic is what's individual...but in the unconscious...society and the 'other' have already preceded individuality and the self. Far from being a healthy growth or natural extension, individual selfhood is thus a meconnaissance, imposed and extraneous. A paranoid construct...something to be overcome. (Harland, 1987, pp.37–38)

Foucault says that:

> Maturity would consist in at least being willing to face the possibility that action cannot be grounded in universal, historical theories of the individual subject and of writing or in the conditions of community and speaking, and that, in fact, such attempts promote what all parties agree is most troubling in our current situation. (Dreyfus and Rabinow, 1986, p.118).

Walkerdine (1985) using concepts derived from Lacan and Foucault attacks Winnicottian views of education and parenting which she claims:

> ...aim to produce citizens who would accept the null order by choice and free will rather than either by coercion or through overt acceptance and covert resistance... [Central to those theories] is the idea of an autonomous agent, who attributes feelings to him or herself and does not feel an excess of passion or conflict. Such an agent is a citizen who, as in the humanist dream, sees all relations as personal relations, in which power, struggle, conflict and desire are displaced and dissipated. (pp.206–207)

I have quoted these criticisms of ego psychology because the ego psychological view of identity is so entrenched in our conception of human beings that it seems to be natural and commonsensical rather than a social construction, and this assumption should be questioned.

Previously Berger and Luckmann's and Winnicott's theories were used as the basis of the social dimension of identity development. As structuralists Berger and Luckmann anticipate many of the post-modernist arguments, especially the primacy of society over biology in constructing human nature, the role of legitimation in maintaining society, the view of ideology as being determined by everyday knowledge and the primary role of language in the construction of reality. Their denial of a unitary 'self' in favour of a collection of 'selves' constituted of externally validated social roles anticipates the 'decentring of the subject', especially if the psychoanalytic emphasis on unconscious processes is added to the role of consciousness in their theory. This 'decentring' is a core post-modernist tenet. Nevertheless, there are some crucial differences which are important in the discussion of racial identity.

The Berger and Luckmann view conceives of societies as autonomous entities evolving slowly over time. Power relationships are maintained through mutually re-enforcing and legitimating institutions which are relatively stable, monolithic and coherent. Post-modern societies, however, are characterised by conflicting institutions which may undermine as well as re-enforce each other. Furthermore, the relationship between the signifier (language) and the signified (the institution) is 'slippery'. For example the institution 'race' need not imply a set of fixed concepts (or 'markers') shared by all members of a society, nor a set of fixed social (power) relationships which position all members of the society.

Another contrast is the different conception of the relationship between social groupings. Berger and Luckmann adopt an essentially Marxist stance, which sees the primary groupings in terms of class. Post-modernists see power in a much more diffuse way than simply as class, gender or racial hierarchies, regarding it as a 'network' or as being 'fractured' across race, class and gender.

Post-modernists deny that identity formation is a continuous process starting with primary socialisation, moving onto secondary socialisation and then developing a more or less stable adult identity. Identity is being continuously reconstructed and re-evaluated like a text being re-read or a story being re-told.

This poses a problem for the concepts of 'primary' and 'secondary' socialisation on which Berger and Luckmann's model is based. These notions are founded on the same basically conservative view of identity adopted by Erikson and Winnicott. If identity is seen more as an ever-changing and sometimes conflictual process then the concepts of 'primary' and 'secondary' socialisation, and of 'true' and 'false' self, become contextual rather than essential. Therefore parents are not seen as 'filters' or 'mediators' of pre-existing societal norms and values, but involved with their children in continually negotiating the meanings of societal forces, and reconstructing and re-interpreting these institutions. Parents' responses to their children would not be seen as a reflection of social values, but are themselves a process by which parents create meanings for their own lives. This process is informed by how the parent is positioned in terms of class, race, gender and culture.

In the case of racial or ethnic identity an adult may well re-interpret not only her identity in the light of current situations, but also the relationships on which the identity is supposedly based. This does not deny the fundamental importance of early parenting. The post-modernist view of identity would not challenge Adorno's view that racial identity and attitudes are formed as part of family functioning, but it would claim that this functioning itself is an interpretation informed by current social theories and ideologies, rather than as a historical fact. It also means that early parenting and attachments do not create or determine later identity in a simple cause–effect relationship; early parenting may be a creation of later 'identity' rather than 'identity' being the product of parenting patterns.

In summary, post-modernism argues against conventional modernist and psychoanalytic views of racial identity because:

° they see society as a monolithic structure, 'internalised' by infants

° they tend to totalise, seeing all black people as having the same concerns.

They share a teleology which sees identity development as a linear process in which set structures are developed in a similar way for all individuals, and determined by early experience. The ultimate aim is a conventional notion of 'maturity'.

They essentialise racial identity, seeing it as a 'core' identity, formed at an early age, and separable in principle from other aspects of personal identity. Those aspects of the self which develop earlier are seen as the most fundamental and immutable parts of identity. This makes them confuse the description of the way individuals construct their identity with the prescription of a pre-decided 'positive' racial identity to which individuals are expected to conform. 'Positive racial identity' is part of a conventional and prescriptive view of maturity in which the basic structures of society are not challenged.

It is these post-modernist ideas that informed the third part of the study, and led to the development of the notion of 'narrative identity' (discussed more fully in Chapter 11) as an alternative to the 'structural-developmental' view.

CHAPTER FIVE

Methodology

Introduction

Previous studies of the development of racial identity have relied mainly on the methods of the 'doll' studies, with some variations and developments. Here I will look specifically at some of the *methodological* problems they pose. Informed by this discussion the methods used by the child development theorists will be further explored. In considering these methods I will develop a methodology. The difficulties encountered are considerable, and some will be discussed.

Methodology of Previous Studies

Many studies have been carried out on racial attitudes, awareness and identification. Virtually all of them have used the 'doll' technique (see Chapter 3), or a variation of it (Brand, Ruiz and Padilla, 1974; Milner, 1983). To recapitulate, this technique involves showing a sample of children from age three upwards a black and a white doll, drawing or photograph.

Alternative Methodologies

In order to look at the subjective experiences and intimate relationships of very young children, one must turn again to developmental psychology and psychoanalysis, and the methodologies of some of the theorists discussed in Chapter 4.

Stern (1985) contrasts the two main methodological paradigms used for the investigation of child development, that is, developmental psychology and psychoanalysis. Stern contends that these two approaches provide different pictures of the infant which are sometimes complementary and sometimes contradictory. The methodologies use different technical languages; describe different phenomena; publish in different journals and seldom refer to each other. Stern argues that most of the findings can be compared and a synthesis developed.

Developmental Psychology

Stern says developmental psychology provides a picture of the *observed infant*. The methods used by developmental psychologists consist of direct observations of infants by trained personnel. The methods employed vary considerably and can involve classical experimental situations or qualitative methodologies (Brazelton and Cramer, 1991). Videos have been used and sometimes measures of physical changes, such as electrical resistance in the skin, have been employed. Most studies have as their subject the development of physical and cognitive capacities of children at different ages, but recently Stern and others have used this methodology to study more social and subjective phenomena. Developmental psychology is the basis of much of our contemporary knowledge about identity development, and its methods have provided both reliable and valid results. These methods do have limitations when the subjective viewpoint is sought. Stern (1985) says:

> ...at best, the observations of an infant's available capacities can only help to define the limits of subjective experience. To render a full account of the experience, we require insights from clinical life, and a second approach is needed for the task. (p.14)

Psychoanalysis

Psychoanalysis is the second paradigm used to study infants and provides the picture of the subjective or *clinical infant*. The psychoanalysts employ the method of *clinical reconstruction* of infantile experiences, which is always conducted in the course of a series of clinical consultations. Patients, usually adults, are encouraged to *free associate*, that is, to say whatever comes into their minds, and the analyst offers interpretations which enable the patients to make sense of their experiences. Patients provide material about their childhood and also relate to the analyst in infantile ways, *transferring* some of the primal feelings which were held towards their parents on to the analyst. Using a combination of the patients' recollections and transferences the analysts can use their theoretical training as well as their own *counter transferences* to construct a picture of the patients' infantile emotional development. For a fuller account of the clinical psychoanalytic process see Klein, Heimann and Money-Kyrle (1955), Racker (1968).

This process, however, is not an *objective* way of quantifying *subjective* experiences of infants, but a mutually constructed dialogue between two people informed by the particular theoretical stance of the analyst. The method is not based on any 'objective' observations of the patients and no verification of what is reported in the sessions is undertaken. Distortions of the truth, and inconsistencies, are seen as simply adding a further dynamic to the dialogue rather than undermining the analysts' reconstructions.

Psychoanalytic reconstructions of infants have been criticised because they are very difficult to confirm or deny in any scientific way. They do not generate hypotheses which are refutable. Philosophers of science such as Popper (1972) label this methodology as *metaphysical* rather than scientific because different psychoanalysts can make different interpretations of the same material. Popper (1972) attacks psychoanalysis and especially the use of 'clinical observations', arguing that since both Freud and Adler are able to provide different but irrefutable explanations for every human action, their claim to scientific status must be specious. The validity of this method has also been criticised by behaviourists arguing that inferences about subjective states cannot be made from observations of behaviour (Eysenck, 1986).

Wolfenstein (1991) argues that clinical and applied psychoanalytic methodologies have different epistemic statuses, and both are different from natural or social sciences. Nevertheless, psychoanalysis has few rivals in providing a subjective view of an infant's inner life. Perhaps there is no 'scientific' method which can provide such subjective data.

Piaget relied on naturalistic and quasi-experimental observations of his own three children. He carefully noted down the behaviour of the children and conducted informal experiments to confirm or illustrate particular points. He has been severely criticised because of the smallness of his sample, lack of corroboration, the difficulty of demonstrating cause–effect relationships from naturalistic observations, and the known unreliability of parents as observers (Ginsburg and Opper, 1979; Maier, 1969). He is subject to many of the criticisms levelled against psychoanalysis, especially in his assumption that a detailed analysis of a small sample will provide universal information.

Despite these criticisms this method does have very powerful advantages, and his theory is one of the most influential in developmental psychology. The criticism that his methods are unscientific can only be made by employing a very restrictive view of science. Nevertheless, Popper's criticism of Freud can equally apply to Piaget. Given the explanatory power of both theories perhaps Popper is being too restrictive.

Winnicott, like Piaget, was a very acute observer of children's behaviour, and his observations were combined with clinical work in the development of his theory. He did not develop a method of observation nor give any clear statement about the nature of his technique. Three of his papers were based on direct observation (1941, 1951, 1957) and he provided only a sketchy outline of the techniques he used.

Despite his rather haphazard methodology, Winnicott was one of the few early psychoanalysts who seriously regarded direct observation as a valid investigative tool. Combined with his insistence on taking case histories (which gave him a perspective on the context in which problems developed) this technique allowed him to transcend the *clinical infant* as the sole source of his theorising. Winnicott (1957) said of the role of direct observation:

> ...psychoanalysts were liable to say things which were true in analysis and yet untrue when applied in a crude way to the psychology of childhood. (p.112)

and

> It will always be the direct observers who are telling the analysts that they have
> made too early an application of their theories. The analysts will continue to
> tell the direct observers that there is much more in human nature than can be
> observed directly. (pp.113–114)

There have been other attempts to combine the two methodologies which use a
more systematic approach than Winnicott's, but rely heavily on psychoanalytic
insights for their conclusions (Stern, 1977; Escalona, 1968; Bentovim, 1979;
Lichtenberg, 1983; and Brazelton and Cramer, 1991). The most celebrated study
of this nature was conducted by Mahler and her associates during the 1960s
(Mahler, Pine and Bergman, 1975). She used a set situation and employed trained
observers who cross-checked their observations. Over the ten-year period in which
the study was conducted, the methodology developed *organically*. This meant that
the setting, methods of data collection and analysis changed as the research lead
the team into different areas of enquiry.

Mahler's approach to methodology was both original and creative, offering an
avenue for exploring child development which has seldom been followed.

Ethnography

One perspective on the problem of obtaining data about the internal states of
preverbal infants is to conceive of the problem *ethnographically*. This means that
infants are perceived almost as if they were members of a culture whose language
is not understood. Ethnographers placed in such a situation become participant
observers in the cultural life, and rely on observation of behaviour patterns. They
would also have to be aware of their own experiences and feelings during the
participant observation and extrapolate from these to the experiences of the
subjects.

Ethnographic research is in a different tradition from psychoanalysis or
developmental psychology, and yet the methodology combines many aspects of
both. Many ethnographic studies use a similar 'organic' approach to Mahler's,
employing a basic methodology but using different techniques as and when they
are appropriate to the data (Hammersley and Atkinson, 1983). Devereux (1978)
believes that psychoanalysis and anthropology are 'complementary frames of
reference'; that the two disciplines inform each other. Freud (e.g. 1913, 1930) also
believed that psychoanalytic thought had relevance for anthropology.

Infant Observation

Although direct observation has only occasionally been used by psychoanalysts
as a method of research, infant observation has, since 1948, been part of
psychoanalytic *training*. Every trainee analyst and psychoanalytic psychotherapist

must observe an infant for one or two years. The method of infant observation was pioneered by Esther Bick.

Bick (1964) describes the basis of her method:

> The child psychotherapy students visit the family once a week up to about the end of the second year of the child's life, each observation normally lasting about an hour...[the observer is able] to compare and contrast his observations with those of his fellow students in the weekly seminars. (p.558)

Bick believes that this method enables students to have an insight into the intensity of the infant's experience and behaviour, the mother's feelings and the relationship between them.

The observations are held in the family home and the observer is offered a weekly 'slice' of the infant's development. The infant may be sleeping, alert, alone or with other people. The mother is encouraged to carry on as far as possible with whatever she would have been doing.

The observer takes no notes during the session because it interferes with *free floating attention* and prevents him/her from responding to the mother's emotional demands. For the same reasons tape recorders, video cameras and other technical equipment are not used.

The observer should:

> ...feel himself sufficiently inside the family to experience the emotional impact, but not committed to act out any roles thrust upon him, such as giving advice or registering approval or disapproval. (p.559)

This balance is difficult to maintain. Mother–infant relationships are powerful and it is easy for an observer to be sucked into the family dynamics. It is precisely these emotions and dynamics, however, that are being studied and too much detachment stops the observer understanding the quality of the relationships. The observer must be very sensitive to the mother and allow her to fit him into the household in her own way.

The most powerful feelings for the observer are the *transferential* feelings of the mother towards him, and his *counter-transferential* responses. Bick warns observers to resist being drawn into roles involving transference, especially during a mother's post-natal depression. I will discuss transference and counter-transference in more depth below.

Other than this short adumbration of her method, Bick wrote nothing further about it. Her one other publication (1968), is based on this method, but offers no explanation. Of the few other studies explicitly based on this method, e.g., Call (1964), Piontelli (1985), Talberg, Couto-Rosa and O'Donnell (1988), only Miller *et al.* (1989) provide details or discussion of the method. Rustin (1987) discusses the method but does not use it for research.

The Method in Operation

Observers are expected to find their own subjects and usually select 'normal' families, in other words where the mother seems to be relatively stable and mature, and where the baby is expected to be normal. The families tend to be middle-class and white. Inevitably appearances can be deceptive and sometimes major pathology becomes evident during the observation.

Discussion seminars lasting for two hours and usually consisting of five to seven observers and a seminar leader. Observers take turns in presenting observations to the group, while a colleague takes notes of the discussion. The notes of the previous discussion of the case are read out before the presentation.

The seminar leader focuses attention on relevant aspects of the situation and offers support and advice, for example when particularly strong feelings are being expressed by mothers, or when the observers find themselves out of role, caring for the infant or a sibling. The discussion may range over the whole presentation or focus is on a particular sequence of actions or interactions.

The observer's task is to experience and memorise as much as possible during the observation with as little effect on the mother and infant as possible. This involves not only sequential awareness but also the emotional 'flavour' of the interactions and his own emotional responses. The observer must be friendly and accommodating, while maintaining a distance. Generally the observer will remain passive, only responding when directly addressed. He avoids taking care of the infant. If the infant is in a different room from the mother, the observer will try to go with the infant rather than stay with her. Her wishes must be respected, though, and if she prefers the observer to be with her the observer will comply.

Ideally, the observations should take place at a set time, preferably when the infant is feeding or otherwise active, and the mother is present. Sometimes observations will take place while the infant is sleeping but the observer will continue to observe.

No notes are taken, but the observer will subsequently write as full an account of the session as soon as possible, including the date, time and location, those present and the infant's age. A detailed report follows concentrating on the infant's activity – the interaction with mother, and the observer's own responses to specific events. To preserve confidentiality, initials, first names or simply 'mother', 'baby', are used.

The record does *not* contain a theoretical explanation of the behaviour. The observer is encouraged not to use any preconceived theoretical framework but to try to have as immediate an experience as possible. Theoretical explanations are given at the seminars after the account has been completed. The observer presents a annual summary of the observation to the seminar when the patterns of development are pointed out and again observation is related to theory.

Transference and Counter-Transference

Bick (1964) warned observers about becoming overwhelmed by transference and counter-transference during the observation. Transference is defined as:

> The experiencing of feelings, drives, attitudes, fantasies and defences towards a person in the present which do not befit that person but are a repetition of reactions originating with regard to significant persons of early childhood, unconsciously displaced on to figures in the present. Greenson (1967) (in Mattinson 1975, p.33)

In the context of observation this would involve mother responding to the observer as if he or she was a punitive, judgmental parent looking for her to make mistakes, or a helpful and nurturing parent helping her to look after her child and relieving her of anxiety, or a competitive sibling vying for her attention.

It is often difficult to distinguish maternal concern from transference. Part of the observer's job is to recognise transference and deal with it appropriately. This does not mean interpreting it as an analyst would do, but acknowledging it or changing behaviour to minimise it. Transference reactions by the parents can provide data for the observer, revealing things about their relationships which would otherwise remain hidden.

Laplanche and Pontalis (1983) define counter-transference as: 'The whole of the analyst's unconscious reactions to the individual analysand – especially to the analysand's own transference' (p.92).

Counter-transference is a less discussed and more controversial topic in psychoanalysis. The social science equivalent is the effect of the experimenter's personality or beliefs on the outcome (the 'halo effect') which is countered by means of double-blind and other methods which attempt to exclude it as a variable in order to increase the validity of the results. On the other hand, ethnographic and other more 'naturalistic' methods incorporate the reflexivity of the experimenter as a factor and try to utilise rather than neutralise it. Devereux (1978) goes much further in asserting: 'The counter-transference of the observer is the fundamental datum of the behavioural sciences' (p.95). By this Devereux means that an observer has no access to any *objective* facts about subjects, but makes sense of his perceptions which result from his own counter-transferential responses to subjects.

This assertion of the importance of counter-transference is resonant of Piaget's view of the formation of schemas and is indeed couched in similar language. It implies that counter-transference is a dynamic and dialectical process between observer and subject and that acknowledgement of the counter-transference is essential in *any social scientific endeavour*. Devereux's view implies an even wider definition of counter-transference than Racker's or Mattinson's, in that it could include all idiosyncratic responses of the observer (see also Hunt, 1989) and seems to show that the usefulness of counter-transference extends beyond the context of the patient–analyst relationship.

But how do we know that a particular account does not say more about the observer than the subject? This question underlies much of the criticisms of psychoanalysis mentioned above. The answer must be that it is only through the observer that we know the subject, and there need not be a conflict between subjectivity and validity. Validity in this context depends on the extent to which the observer is able to give an accurate account of the events and the process of thinking about what happened. It is the observer's ability to *think* creatively and to convey these thoughts that ensures the validity of the account.

This formulation is based on Bion's theory of thinking (1984a and b; Barker, 1982). Bion believes that learning from *experience* rather than applying 'facts' to a preconceived theoretical framework is the most valid form of knowledge and that lines of creative thought should be followed through even if they experience later prove them wrong. Bick's insistence that the observer excludes theory in order to experience the intensity of the situation derives in large part from Bion but she makes no acknowledgement.

For the account to be valid, a record of the observer's responses must be kept, supplemented by a statement of the observer's point of view and the factors which have influenced it. An observer must show how particular patterns were noticed and how the conclusion was reached from the observation. Any pretence at 'scientific' objectivity is a distortion of the validity of the information because it denies a vital component in the dynamic of the observation.

Isaacs (1952) offers three methodological principles to enhance the validity of infant observation:

- attention to details
- observation of context; and
- the study of genetic continuity.

If attention to the observer's counter-transference is added, there is a good argument for the validity, and even reliability, of infant observation as a viable method of developmental research.

Having pointed out the usefulness of Bick's method of infant observation for research into child development there are nevertheless a number of criticisms which can be made they are based on my own experience – there is a lack of critical discussion in the literature.

DIFFICULTY WITH THE SEMINARS

In my experience genetic continuity was not adhered to very tightly. Interpretations of behaviour were to be made regardless of the age of the infants – for example, a grasping motion by the infant would invariably be interpreted as a symbolic holding on to the nipple. At one level this may be correct, but it misses the point of how the representation of the nipple changes from a neonate to a toddler.

RESTRICTIVENESS

The passive stance of the observer is intended to ensure maximum free-floating attention and minimalise counter-transference. It reflects the stance of psycho-therapists who only respond to what is brought into the session and not the 'reality' outside. I believe that this stance is restrictive and prevents pertinent questions being asked and other sources of data being obtained resulting in a very unrepresentative view of the infant–mother relationship. For teaching purposes this may not matter, but for the purposes of this research it was important to incorporate as much of the context as possible.

Observers are told to reveal as little as possible about themselves and the purpose of the observation so that they do not burden mother with their own agenda. This decreases the chance of mother acting in a way she thinks the observer would like.

In this study two infant observations were undertaken. The methods used in these observations varied in some respects from Bick's method. The main differences were:

AGE

Because racial identity is a social phenomenon I believed that it would be more cost effective to begin the observations when the infant became socially aware and I wanted to start the observations at about six months. Only the first observation started when the infant was this age; however, the second began at six weeks.

INFORMATION

Both mothers were informed of the broad outlines of the study early in the observations.

After completing observations were supplemented by semi-structured interviews with the mothers.

With these exceptions, I followed Bick's method as far as possible.

ACCESS

The main practical problem was gaining access to suitable subjects. The criteria for suitability were:

- mothers had to be white, preferably British, and fathers black
- infants had to be between birth and nine months old, preferably around six months
- in the health visitors' estimation families had to be reasonably stable, i.e., not in a state of crisis or with major chronic problems
- the families had to be able to be observed weekly over a period of time
- the families should not be current cases of the social services department; and

∘ mothers had to agree to the observations.

White mothers were chosen because mothers are the primary caregivers, and the inter-racial debate is invariably couched in terms of white families with black children. Black mothers raising black children would not face the same conflicts as white women, because they have experienced being parented by a black mother themselves. I also believed that my presence as a white observer would have less effect on the mothers' responses if they were also white.

It took six months of intensive lobbying to find the first family, and another six months to find the second. This involved talking to personal contacts and writing to health visitor managers in two Inner London boroughs to ask for assistance.

Further difficulties arose over how I would approach the mothers. I expected that my being a white male could make it more difficult for the mothers to accept me into their homes to observe and talk about very intimate subjects.

I first briefed the health visitor who then discussed the observation with the mother. If the mother was agreeable I contacted her myself (either by telephone or letter). I gave the minimum amount of information about myself and the purpose of the observation, saying that I was a student looking into child development in mixed-race infants and that I would like to observe them once a week for an hour over a period of a year. I gave them my work and home telephone numbers in case they had to cancel at short notice.

Interviews

The second element of this study was based upon more conventional methodological lines. I conducted fairly lengthy semi-structured interviews with both mothers, and three other mothers of mixed-race infants.

Purpose

My purpose to explore what a mother brings into the relationship with a child of a different race and specifically the relationship between the mother's past family history and her feelings about race, relationships and child care. I wanted to relate these to her ideas about the racial identity of her children.

For the two subjects of observation, these responses were contrasted with the results of the observations. I hoped that by studying both the infants' development and the mothers' attitudes and histories, I would have a wider picture of the infants' identities, encompassing the subjective, the intersubjective and the social context in which they were developing.

For those mothers whose infants also had not been observed, this full picture could not be obtained. Nevertheless, the information I obtained was also important in elucidating some of the relationships between mothers' attitudes and responses to their infants, and the infants' identity development.

Another purpose for supplementing the observations with interviews was to obtain a validity check. Kirk and Miller (1986) argue that validity is increased by *triangulation*, i.e. using a number of different methods to obtain data, each with its own characteristic strengths and weaknesses. Different methods complement each other.

The validity check is particularly important in studies such as the present one, where only one person is collecting the data and is therefore unable to cross-check it with a fellow observer.

Semi-Structured Interviews

Semi-structured interviews were used for the first set of interviews to test out initial assumptions and hypotheses. The semi-structured format allows for free expression on the part of the subjects, but also allows the interviewer to concentrate on particular areas of importance (Bernard, 1988; Patton, 1990; Sudman and Bradburn, 1982). The idea was to enable the mothers to talk as freely as possible about themselves. The questions were posed chronologically, starting with the family of origin and the relationships within it, and moving on to friends and sexual relationships. Finally ideas and relationship to their infants were explored. Within each question, the *funnelling* technique was used; questions were posed in a broad fashion and then specific answers were probed for (Sudman and Bradburn, 1982) The questions were not asked in strict order and mothers often returned to previous topics or pre-empted questions.

The semi-structured format was used because it is the most germane for obtaining sensitive information and disclosures, while also focusing on specific areas of interest. Structured interview schedules, although they produce more reliable results, only elicit responses to pre-set stimuli, and do not allow for spontaneity. In this study each interview was subtly different from the previous one, in response to the individual replying to the questions. Some mothers found it much easier to talk about certain topics than others, and so different information was gathered from their responses.

Another factor contributing to differing responses was my reaction to the mothers and theirs to me. The different context and venues must have influenced the way the questions were framed and responses elicited. Another factor was that I tended to stress certain aspects which seemed likely to provide the information I was seeking. The interview schedule was used 'organically' (in Mahler's sense) and evolved over a period of time in response to the information given.

The Biographical Method

Although the first set of interviews provided much information about mothers' histories and their attitudes toward their children, I felt on reflection that the semi-structured approach had been too restrictive in some respects. The main limitations were:

- The attempt to provide it proved impossible to make causal links between mothers' early experiences of being parented and their own parenting style.

- The first interviews confirmed that identity was probably a much wider phenomenon than the 'racial identity' whose character I had set out to discover. I felt that the real issue was how families dealt with 'difference' rather than how they dealt with 'race'.

- Pre-set topics, even in a semi-structured interview, tended to 'frame' the interviews so that the information gained was determined too much by the interviewer's assumptions, and not enough by the mothers' own constructions of their reality.

- The restriction of the interviews to mothers only meant that the black perspective was given third hand. The observations and interviews showed that fathers played a crucial role in the identity of their children, and it was therefore felt that the next set of interviews should include both parents where this was possible. It was also decided to include families with a black mother and white father to see if the issues were very different.

The second set of interviews were therefore based on a somewhat different method from the first. Fortunately, there have been developments in social research based on the 'oral history' movement which are designed to elicit how individuals and families make sense of their lives, and how this relates to their social and cultural context. This approach is called the 'life history' or 'biographical' approach (Bertaux, 1981; Denzin, 1983). The biographical approach is concerned with obtaining stories from people about their experiences and identifying themes which run through those stories. It does not look for causal links between earlier and later events, rather it tries to identify the continuities and discontinuities in people's accounts of their lives, and to uncover the 'scripts' or 'myths' by which they live.

The methodology I used was unstructured interviews with both parents or with one parent where there was no partner in the house or the partner refused to be interviewed. I used this approach so that parents could give their own account of their lives and tell their life stories spontaneously with the minimum of prompting.

I felt that this method (described more fully in Chapter 8) would provide both the relevant material and the appropriate analysis to broaden and deepen the findings in the first two phases of the study. Nine sets of parents were interviewed in the third phase. The 'ethnic' breakdown of the families was:

- three where the father was Asian and the mother English

- one where the mother was Jewish and the father Ghanaian

- one where the mother was an Australian and the father a South African Muslim
- one where the mother was African Caribbean and the father American
- one where the mother was English and the father African Caribbean (father not interviewed)
- one where the mother was Norwegian and the father (not in the household) was half Afro-American, but adopted by a white English couple
- one couple where the mother was Ghanaian and the father English.

The youngest children in the families ranged from four months to almost four years.

Conclusion

The spirit behind both the observations and the interviews was to try out the methods to see how well they would provide the information I was looking for. It was in this spirit that the methods developed over time, and were able to provide a 'feel' of how these families functioned and dealt with the issues around identity development. The methods were informed by the theoretical basis on which the research was established. The methods themselves, and the information derived from the various components of the fieldwork, served in turn to adapt the theory. These methods complement quantitative approaches such as the doll studies. They were certainly not seen as the only 'right' methods for studying racial identity development.

This study can be seen as an exploration of how much light these methods throw on the subject, perhaps providing a glimpse of how future research may be able to address it.

CHAPTER SIX

The *A* Family

Introduction

Here and in the next chapter I will present the results of the two infant observations. The two families were observed concurrently in 1986 and 1987. There were altogether 63 observations: 37 for the A family and 26 for the B family. The observations generated large amounts of raw data and, in presenting the results, I will try to give a picture of the infants and their environments and to examine the clues the observations provided to an understanding of the development of their racial identity.

My observations of the A family formed the major part of this study. The family composition was:

Mother (Tracy)	age: 25 yrs	
Father (Norman)	age: 26 yrs	
Sister (Roberta)	age: 3 yrs	D.O.B 1/1983
Subject (Cathy)	age: 7 months	D.O.B 7/1985

The family were described to me by their health visitor as being 'Rough and ready and very warm'. She said that when she had approached the mother she had asked whether Norman would mind about the observations and Tracy had replied 'It's none of his business'. She also told me that although they were not married, the couple intended to marry soon, and that they had a three-year-old daughter as well as the baby. Other than this I had no information. Perhaps the best way of providing an initial description is to quote my observations after the first visit (25/2/86).

Physical Environment
THE FLAT

The A's live in a small ground floor flat in a large housing estate. The block, probably built in the early part of this century and typical of this rather deprived

67

inner London area which has a high proportion of people from ethnic minorities, notably of West Indian and Moroccan origin.

The flat consists of a small living room, a kitchen, bathroom and two small bedrooms. The living room is heated by a single gas fire has a sofa, an armchair and an upright chair. A large black and white television sits on a trunk against the wall. There is a thick pile carpet on the floor. The furniture is rather tattered, and the room has an atmosphere of untidiness and cosiness, but also of poverty. The curtains were almost fully drawn though it was mid-afternoon. There were many toys scattered around, both hard and soft, and some children's books (but no adult ones).

The parents' bedroom leads off the living room, and is separated from it by a curtain, as is the tiny kitchen. The children's bedroom leads off the hall, and has two beds, two cupboards and a chest of drawers, with room for very little else. Generally the flat seems rather grubby and there is a noticeable smell from the family's two dogs.

The physical environment became an important part of the observation. The family were very unhappy in the flat and during the course of the observations they changed the layout of the living room several times, buying and selling furniture, televisions and other equipment. One constant factor was that the curtains were almost always half shut.

Family Descriptions
BABY (CATHY)

Cathy is a coffee-coloured girl of seven months. She is rather chubby and has black, wavy, wispy hair. Her largish ears are adorned by gold earrings. She has a habit of staring intently for minutes at a time with her black and slightly squinty eyes. She seems to be a calm baby who does not cry much. She is responsive to her mother's attention.

Cathy enjoys playing with toys, especially cuddly ones, and can sometimes become quite engrossed in this. Mother also told me that she has recently started eating the same food as the family and she that she really enjoys her food. Cathy sleeps in a bed because when she was smaller she got her hand caught in a cot. She shares a room with Roberta, and has no difficulty sleeping through the night. All her milestones are normal, but she is slow to begin crawling.

MOTHER (TRACY)

Tracy is a tall, plump woman in her early thirties. She has shoulder-length black hair in an untidy style, and a round, pale face with small brown eyes. Her nose is straight and sharp and she has a small mouth with a mole just above her upper lip. Tracy speaks in a quick staccato manner with a working-class

London accent. Her manner is seemingly relaxed and outgoing, but at times she becomes tense and ill-at-ease.

During this visit she wore old grey trousers and a cardigan over her white cotton blouse. Tracy spoke confidently about her mothering, and gave the impression of being in control of the children, but not rigidly controlling them.

FATHER (NORMAN)

I only saw Norman very briefly during this visit. He is a tall thin black man with his hair in dreadlocks. He looks to be in his late twenties. He speaks with a pronounced African Caribbean accent. He seems slightly to resent my visit. Tracy told me he has just started 'shift work.'

SISTER (ROBERTA)

Roberta is a four-year-old girl who has similar features to Cathy, but is skinny for her age. She also has much curlier hair in an 'afro' style. Roberta is a very lively girl who likes to be the centre of attraction. During this visit she constantly tried to distract my attention from Cathy, whom she ignored most of the time, concentrating her attention on the adults and the two dogs.

Although these notes are first impressions, they preface many patterns which later emerged in the observations, for example:

- ° Tracy's casual and rather grubby dress
- ° Cathy's tendency to stare fixedly for long periods
- ° Cathy's ability to immerse herself in repetitive play
- ° Norman's hostility towards me
- ° Tracy's wavering from relaxation to tension, and
- ° Roberta's constant struggle to divert my attention from Cathy to herself.

Family History

During the observations, I learned the history of this family, mainly from Tracy.

Tracy comes from a working-class Irish background. Her parents moved to London before she was born and she grew up on a West London council estate. She has two sisters and a brother, and described her childhood as 'happy enough'. She was close to her parents, but as a teenager became rebellious and independent. When she was younger she thought she was attractive and had several boyfriends – all white. Norman was her first black boyfriend. Initially her mother was very disapproving but later accepted him. Tracy continues to have close links with her family. Having come from the neighbourhood, and being a gregarious person, Tracy has many friends locally who offer her support.

Norman was born in the West Indies and came to London while still a young child. He is the eldest of five siblings and half siblings. He grew up in an estate near the one where Tracy lived. Norman said his upbringing was very strict and his mother 'ruled the roost'. He lost contact with his father when he was in his teens, but still maintains contact with his mother and siblings. He, too, has had many girlfriends, some of them white, but Tracy was his first long-term relationship.

The couple met at a party and began living together soon afterwards. They moved to a flat in East London, but were evicted before Roberta was born. After the birth Tracy was placed in a mother and baby home for a few weeks and Norman was not allowed to stay overnight. They were then offered their current flat by a housing association, and took it because they were desperate. They do not like the flat because it is cold, small and on a rough estate.

Children's Histories

The two children had very different births: Tracy told me that her labour with Roberta lasted five days and was very painful. Nevertheless she described it as a 'wonderful experience'. Norman was not present at the birth. By contrast, her labour with Cathy's had only lasted three hours but she described it as 'agony'. She had to have an epidural and was so sedated that she was hardly aware of the birth, which made her feel disappointed and bitter. Norman had been present at Cathy's birth. Tracy had given birth to stillborn twins between Roberta and Cathy's births, after which she and Norman quickly tried for another child to make up for the loss.

Tracy said that she had found it relatively easy to bond with Roberta because they had been alone in the mother and baby unit after her birth. Since then Roberta has been 'her' baby and they are very close (Obs 2). Because Norman was at Cathy's birth, she believes he has always been closer to her. Tracy described how, after Cathy's birth, she had given her to Norman and said 'Take her, she's yours'. Tracy feels that she was not able to bond well with Cathy because of the traumatic birth and also because she did not want a girl. Her only explanation for not wanting a girl was that the council would only rehouse them if they had children of different sexes. Another factor was that she did not breast-feed Cathy because Cathy would not take her milk. She did say to me that by the time I had started observing, their relationship had improved, but Cathy was still Norman's baby (Obs 1). Tracy also expressed some irritation at Cathy's slow progress. Cathy had been a small, five pound baby, and was late in reaching her milestones. Tracy's first descriptions to me of her relationship to Cathy were mainly negative. In summary they were:

- ◦ the difficult pregnancy
- ◦ the traumatic birth
- ◦ the lack of a settled home in the first weeks
- ◦ Cathy's refusal to take breast milk

- ° her wish for a boy
- ° Cathy's small size and slow development
- ° Cathy's birth was very soon after Tracy had lost the twins; and
- ° Tracy gained a lot of weight during the pregnancy and did not lose it again after the birth.

Context and Patterns

Below are some of the major patterns that occurred during the course of my observations of the A family. Later I will deal more specifically with the patterns of behaviour and relationships which emerged during the observations. The context is important for two reasons:

- ° the physical environment was important in the A family's relationships and Cathy's development; and
- ° the context of the observation affects the observer's own feelings and therefore the outcome of the study.

Patterns

The observations quickly developed a character of their own, and patterns emerged which were to become typical of my encounters with the A family. The most obvious were:

- ° The regularity with which the family was absent when I arrived for the observation – despite the fact that the times of the observation were fixed. Even when they were present, I was often greeted with a surprised look, or confronted with the family about to go shopping.
- ° The parents never learned my name, although I repeated it very often, and even wrote it on notes. I became known as 'Cathy's friend'.

Observations were made difficult by constant distractions; often people came in and out of the flat and the TV and/or stereo was usually on, Cathy was often taken out of the room; and Roberta constantly tried to attract my attention.

The furniture and layout of the living room was changed every few weeks. During the months I visited three different TV sets, two sofas and several other pieces of furniture were acquired, which were rearranged almost every week. The living room curtains were nearly always drawn, sometimes the light was on, at other times it was off.

Often the flat was not very clean or in a good state of repair. For example, the door was broken around the time of my sixth observation, but had not been mended by the time my observations ended. As they progressed, it became evident that the lack of *physical* boundaries (doors) within the flat reflected the lack of *psychological* boundaries within the family.

Information

Other than two major family events about which they were very reticent and which I could only guess at, both parents were reasonably candid about their feelings. The two events were Tracy's miscarriage, which happened towards the end of Cathy's second year; and Norman's leaving the home, which followed shortly afterwards. Tracy hinted that Norman had been 'forced' to leave by the social services because he had been 'molesting' Roberta and also hinted that he had not left altogether. Both these events were obviously traumatic for the family, but I could only infer their effects in terms of the family dynamics.

Overall I felt that family life had very little regularity or predictability. Sometimes a pattern would develop for a few weeks, for example, when one of the parents found a job, but this soon changed – the job would be lost or given up and the pattern would change again. The chaotic nature of family life became, in fact, the most predictable and characteristic aspect of the observation.

My observations of Cathy were rather 'chaotic' from the beginning, and remained so throughout. They almost ended after the first one. On the second visit I was greeted by a very hostile father who questioned me about what I was doing and insisted that I bring him my notes. (Obs 2) Contrary to normal procedure in infant observation I conceded, largely because of my desperation in trying to find a suitable family. Also, I felt that they had a moral right to see my material although it was against normal practice. After a cursory glance at them he returned them and from then on was relatively friendly towards me. Tracy also showed some ambivalence – although she was never overtly hostile, the way she organised the observations (e.g. by not being there) and her rather offhand matter made me feel unwelcome.

Cultural Patterns

In the A family although culture was not generally talked about there were many signs of cultural influences on the family.

Very often there was music playing when I was observing. The music was almost invariably either Reggae or Rap. Norman said that he played drums in a Reggae band. He had a large set of amplifiers and speakers in the bedroom which had 'Black man music' painted on them. Tracy also enjoyed listening to this music.

The food was almost exclusively what I expected a white working-class family to eat, for example fish fingers, sausage and chips, lots of Coke. There was no evidence that the children were given any 'ethnic' Jamaican food.

There was a map of Jamaica in the hall, but otherwise there were no pictures, although there were a number of photographs of the family around the flat. One striking thing was the complete absence of adult books although I often saw a newspaper. By contrast there was a bookcase in the children's room full of children's books. Tracy was very proud of this and pointed it out to me on the first observation.

Tracy considered herself to be 'English from an Irish background', and Norman told me that:

> ...Even though I was born in this country I don't think of myself as English. I've visited Jamaica several times, but I also don't think of myself as West Indian. (Obs 4)

There was a mixture of black and white cultural influences in the household. There seemed to be no conscious decision on the part of either parent to present the children with input from their own culture, although culture formed a backcloth to daily family life.

I realise that this description is written from a white, male, middle-class perspective, and therefore may misrepresent the true picture. I do know that I made some mistakes in my perceptions of the cultural environment, for example I wrote towards the beginning of the observations:

> ...they seem to be very integrated into the local community. Very often I have seen Tracy or Norman outside talking to the neighbours, and often there are people popping in and out of the flat... (Jul '86)

Much later Norman complained to me that he felt isolated in the estate because there were too few black people, and he did not get on with the neighbours (Obs 20). I presume there were more mistakes that were not subsequently corrected.

Although *culture* was not often explicitly mentioned in this family, *race* and *colour* were often alluded to and were a constant factor of the family dynamic.

Parental Conflict

In the sixth observation I witnessed an argument between the parents where the conflict was couched in terms of race. Norman had disciplined Roberta for some misdemeanour and Tracy told him to leave her alone. She turned to me and said that Norman was too strict with Roberta and he would not let her play with toys. He treated her like a woman not a child. Norman then exploded, saying to Roberta: 'You are a woman, aren't you?'

Turning to me he said:

> We have different ways of bringing up kids. I bring my children up like black parents, very strictly. If it was up to Tracy the kids would be running around doing what they want.

Tracy retorted: 'My daughter isn't black, she's half-caste.'

This interaction illustrates two of the ongoing themes within the family in which race became part of the dynamic:

First, conflict was often *racialised*. This argument could have occurred without reference to race being essentially about parenting style, but the parents saw the issue as a clash of cultures. Second, Tracy's ambivalence about her children's blackness. Here Tracy seemed to be denying that Roberta was black, but later we will see that there were times when she did acknowledge their blackness.

Mother's Preoccupation with Colour

In virtually all my observations in the first year there are references to Tracy discussing Cathy's colour. Cathy was apparently born with a very light skin, and Tracy told me that when Roberta first saw Cathy she had said that Cathy could not be her sister because she was too light. According to Tracy, who monitored it closely, Cathy's skin darkened. Tracey often asked me, 'Do you think she's darker this week?'

There was always an element of anxiety in these questions and clearly she hoped Cathy would remain light skinned. I thought Cathy was coffee-coloured and her colour remained constant, similar to Roberta's.

Racist Language

Tracy often made racist remarks to and about her children, usually expressed in a joking tone of voice and ranging from offhand comments like: 'She sure has a wide enough nose to pinch' (Obs 11), to calling Roberta a 'Black bitch!' when she was naughty (Obs 6).

Tracy's explanation for this behaviour was that the children would suffer racial abuse when they got to school and that she was preparing them for it. I was not convinced that this was Tracy's real motive, because these remarks were said spontaneously and were never followed up by explanations or warnings about racism. I suspect that she gave me the explanation because she felt self-conscious and needed to justify her remarks. This was my 'gut response' to Tracy's action, and it may be inaccurate – there may have been real concern in her actions.

Parents' Relationship

During the observations the marital relationship went through different stages. The parents rarely talked to me directly about their relationship, and I had to infer from their behaviour or conversation. There were, however, several occasions when they made critical remarks about each other to me in a half-serious or in a bantering tone of voice.

They seldom expressed any positive feelings towards each other. Instead conversation was couched in a constant 'cheeky' banter, often with sexual overtones. When they demonstrated closeness by hugging or kissing it was always in a playful rather than tender way. Generally their interactions were competitive.

In contrast to their awkwardness in expressing tenderness, they expressed anger very easily and often had arguments in my presence. The arguments were always short and equanimity was restored fairly quickly. Despite the air of competition and conflict the couple were committed to each other and expressed no regret about the relationship.

Norman's irresponsibility, however, caused constant difficulties in the relationship. He would disappear without warning, sometimes for several days; he did not keep the house clean. Tracy also suspected him of having affairs but he denied this to me (Obs 20). He acknowledged that he did go off with friends, but felt it was a man's right to do so.

Parental ability to work in partnership varied, and although Norman was willing to change nappies, bath the children, and so forth, I felt that he only carried out these tasks when he wanted to. Although she complained about him a great deal, Tracy seemed to be rather passive in the relationship and rarely challenged him openly about behaviour. The relationship operated on several different levels – orally they were usually very aggressive towards each other and seldom gave each other support. They tended to have a stereotyped image of the children (e.g. Cathy was invariably seen as Norman's favourite) and of each other, and they related to these stereotypes rather than to the real, changing person.

On another level, however, they worked quite well together. Norman's irresponsibility and absences gave Tracy the control over the children and the flat that she desired most of the time, for example she did not feel it necessary to tell him beforehand about my impending observations. Although Norman was the more powerful character, Tracy had more power in her own domain. The couple had been through many testing periods together, however, and their relationship was strong enough to survive.

Yet on another level it seemed to lack intimacy. It seemed they seldom discussed their feelings or their relationship, often keeping secrets from each other about important matters. They seemed to lead very different lives and, for both of them, their life-style suited their difficulties with closeness and commitment. Ironically their relationship deteriorated *after* they were married, eventually leading to Norman leaving the home. It may be that the commitment marriage symbolises was too much for them.

There was a volatile quality about the relationship which was exacerbated by external factors such as accommodation, financial worries and Tracy's depression. The relationship was complex and many facets were hidden from me but I felt that its vicissitudes played a key role in Cathy's identity development.

Cathy's Patterns of Development

I have already commented on Cathy, her behaviour during my first session and how many of the actions which were evident in that single observation became evidence of patterns which developed over time. By the time I started the observations Cathy had already developed some very distinctive ways of interacting. Some were to disappear but others became more complex as she grew older.

Cathy at Seven to Twelve Months

When I began observing Cathy (at seven months) she was just beginning to sit on her own, could move about on her tummy, but could not crawl properly.

Perhaps the most striking thing about Cathy's behaviour in the first months of the observations was her pattern of moving from a state of intense concentration to a state of distractedness when she seemed hardly to be aware of her surroundings. In the second observation (Cathy at eight months):

> Tracy stuck her tongue out at Cathy who first looked blankly and then made an attempt to mimic her, slightly and slowly protruding her tongue. Tracy carried on talking to her, making faces and putting out her tongue, but Cathy's attention drifted to me and she stared at me with a long squinty stare. Tracy commented that Cathy was fascinated by me.

> Cathy began to put her thumb, index finger and forefinger together and Tracy took this up, clicking her fingers. Cathy responded to this by hesitantly making a click-like motion with her right hand. She repeated the action again and again, each time approximating a click better. While doing this she brought her fingers closer to her mouth until they were almost inside it.

> Tracy then got up to make the coffee leaving Cathy propped up on the chair. Cathy looked around sleepily and began moving her arms around, spreading the fingers of her left hand and continuing to 'click' slowly with her right hand. She didn't focus on anything and she made no sound.

> Tracy gave Cathy a brief cuddle and then brought some paper which she gave to Cathy. She told me that Cathy loved to tear paper. Cathy grabbed the paper in a jerky movement and started to crumple it, still with a distracted look on her face. She made as if to tear it with short, sharp, pulling motions, but the paper didn't tear. She let the paper drop and Tracy gave it back. Cathy still didn't tear it, but dropped it and turned away. Tracy then gave her the rag doll and Cathy again fingered it, turning the doll around.

In this observation Cathy demonstrated her three most common 'states' of attention. showing:

- concentrated and exclusive focus on particular people or objects – e.g. me
- repetitive and 'ritualistic' behaviour seem almost in a trance – e.g. tearing the paper; and
- distractedness – seeming hardly aware of what was going on around her.

In all three 'states' there was an air of slow deliberateness about Cathy's demeanour. She rarely verbalised and when she did, she did not seem to be expressing any intense emotion. This lack of emotional intensity was another common pattern at this time. Although she responded to her mother and to me, she did not smile, frown or otherwise demonstrate emotion. Her emotional state was more *implicit* in the way she acted than explicitly shown.

In this observation Tracy showed that she could be responsive to Cathy. She both initiated interaction by sticking out her tongue and responded to Cathy's actions by imitating her clicking. On the other hand, her interaction with Cathy did have a stop-start quality about it and she did not follow through the interactions she started. Tracy and Cathy's habitual ways of interacting at this time were:

Tracy starts an interaction – sticks out her tongue

Cathy responds to her – imitates mother's action

Tracy responds again – repeats action with variations

Cathy loses interest – looks away from mother

Tracy loses interest – makes coffee;

and

Cathy starts an *action* – 'clicking' her fingers

Tracy imitates her

Cathy continues her action – looking at mother

Tracy responds again

Cathy loses interest

Tracy loses interest.

It is interesting that in this period (8–10 months) I could not find any record which shows Cathy actually initiating an interaction with her mother, nor of Tracy terminating the interaction. Cathy seemed to be able to tolerate only a certain amount of stimulation from her mother before reacting to her as if she were an *impingement* (see Winnicott, 1965). Cathy's demeanour at this stage had a quality about it which suggested *holding things together*. This quality is hard to extract from mere descriptions of her behaviour, but the following extract from Obs 5 (Cathy at nine months) provides an illustration:

Tracy gave Cathy a bottle of orange juice and put it on her chest saying 'You can hold it yourself'. Cathy sat with her fists clenched and looked at Tracy. She gave a short cry, screwing up her face, but relaxed almost immediately. Tracy went up to her and put the bottle in her mouth and Cathy sucked on it a few times but then let it drop. She again started making noises, going 'ah' and straining almost as if she were constipated. Tracy put the bottle in yet again, Cathy again took a few sips and let the bottle drop, going 'ah' as she did. Her arms were at her sides with her hands next to her head, her fists clenched. Her feet were held away from her body and she pointed her toes toward the ground. She tapped her right foot on the ground, softly at first then more loudly… (The sequence with the bottle was repeated a few more times)…

Tracy then said that Cathy was letting the bottle go because I was there and that she normally held it. Tracy stood back and took a daffodil from a vase while Cathy looked at her she waved it in front of Cathy. Cathy responded by following its path two or three times but soon stared in front of her without focusing.

This extract shows another typical interaction between mother and daughter – a graphic illustration of the passive resistance with which Cathy dealt with the impingements of the outside world. She did not fight against the bottle being repeatedly put in her mouth, nor did she succumb to her mother's insistence or cry or show her distress. Her way was to accept the bottle and after her mother had turned away, spit it out (or let it fall) showing little overt emotion. Only her body language suggested what was really happening. She clenched her fists, tapped her feet rhythmically and tightened her muscles. I felt that she was saying 'I won't let anything in!'.

Her controlled behaviour was in stark contrast to the chaotic nature of her environment, and may have been a way of resisting its effects. She would sometimes respond enthusiastically to Tracy's advances but her typical reaction was to resist passively.

Tracy interacted with Cathy in certain typical ways during this phase of development. She frequently tried to get Cathy to 'perform' for me but was usually disappointed. When this happened Tracy either lost interest or persisted until Cathy made some response. Thus in Obs 3 (Cathy at nine months):

Tracy told me that Cathy has a new trick – blowing raspberries. She blew a raspberry at Cathy, but there was no response and Cathy continued to hold her fists tightly clenched. Tracy said 'Come on stinky pops!', screwed up her face and stuck out her tongue at Cathy who responded by slightly protruding her tongue. Tracy then repeated the action, but this time there was no response from Cathy who looked away towards the fire. Tracy then made a 'brrr' sound and blew strongly on Cathy's neck. Cathy made a flapping movement with her arms and legs. Tracy said in a baby voice 'I don't want to play.' and then to me 'She plays all day, but when she needs to, she won't.'

As before Tracy was here showing her need for Cathy to 'perform'. In some ways this need gave an impetus to the relationship; these interactions were some of the most intense occurring at this stage of Cathy's development but often Tracy's style of relating did not take Cathy's needs into account. Tracy seldom took the cue from Cathy; it was usually she who decided when and how Cathy should behave and Cathy was expected to respond accordingly. It seemed that Tracy needed affirmation from Cathy to prove that she was a good mother, to produce a daughter who performed well.

Tracy's need may have stemmed from her own feelings of depression and low self-esteem. Perhaps her self-esteem was vicariously improved by having a child who was 'good'. When Cathy did not meet these needs Tracy may have felt that this was not a reflection on Cathy, but that Cathy was punishing her, making her feel even worse. On a more immediate level the 'performances' were clearly aimed at me. Tracy's anxiety during the first observations may have been fuelled by her belief that I was an expert in child development who had come to assess her parenting. I was also a white middle-class male representing the mainstream society from which they were so conspicuously excluded.

Her persistence in relating to Cathy in this way over a long time, and the frequency with which it occurred, made me feel that this was a deep-rooted response which probably occurred outside of the observations.

Tracy's use of the phrase 'Come on stinky pops!' was another typical pattern in her relationship with her children and she often used phrases which referred to Cathy as being smelly or dirty. (In contrast, references to Roberta were usually about her being naughty or nasty.) These references to the children hid a complex web of emotions. They were always said in a flippant tone of voice but they seemed to hide deeper aggressive feelings and there was often a note of exasperation about them. On the other hand, this was also Tracy's way of showing herself and her children that she could be endearing, but the joking manner protected her from having to reveal her true tenderness.

During these early observations Norman was present for at least some of the time. His interactions tended to be short, intense and playful. He tended to relate to Cathy in a far more overtly physical way than Tracy. He would pick her up with a 'whoop', turn her over and throw her into the air. He also had more eye contact with Cathy than Tracy did.

Cathy's responses were also different – she frequently smiled when she saw him, and often squirmed and giggled when he played with her. She hardly ever went to him when she was distressed and used Tracy to comfort her, but she obviously relaxed in his presence. This excerpt gives some indication of their relationship:

Norman sat on the sofa, still cradling Cathy who looked into his eyes and blew a raspberry at him. We all chuckled at this and Tracy remarked that we had been sitting for several minutes, but Cathy had done nothing.

Cathy became more active, holding onto Norman's dressing gown and then looking inside to see his chest. She made the 'clicking' motion again, and extended and clenched the fingers of her left hand. At the same time she blew one or two more raspberries and made an 'ahh' sound, and then repeated this... Norman said that he could understand her talking, and Tracy told of a program she had seen on TV in which a mentally handicapped child's voice had been slowed down on tape and could then be understood. (Obs 3, Cathy at nine months)

This vignette followed one of the episodes when Cathy did not hold her bottle as Tracy wished her to. It illustrates not only Cathy's different response to Norman, but how the parents' responses differed, with Tracy comparing Cathy to a handicapped child and saying she had done nothing, whereas Norman talked of understanding Cathy and cradling her in his arms.

The relationship between the siblings was also noteworthy. Cathy seemed to derive endless pleasure from watching her sister play and talk, even when Roberta totally ignored her. She was beginning to imitate some of Roberta's behaviour. When Roberta did interact with her Cathy's face would light up and she would grunt appreciatively. Roberta, however, seemed to resent Cathy's presence and often behaved angrily towards her. She would imitate many of the flippant remarks that Tracy made to Cathy, but with a much more aggressive tone. She often 'punished' her dolls when she was playing at looking after them. On the other hand she seemed to enjoy looking after Cathy and often fed her and helped Tracy care for her:

> Cathy and Roberta sat on the sofa. Cathy looked at Roberta and slowly put her hand onto the strap of Roberta's dress. Roberta angrily brushed her away, saying 'Leave me alone, you!' but then she happily gave Cathy a biscuit, putting it gently into her hand, but Cathy dropped it. Tracy put her head into the room and told her to put it into Cathy's mouth. Roberta did so, but said 'Ow!', pretending that Cathy had bitten her. (Obs 5, Cathy at nine months)

This short excerpt was part of a sequence of events in which Roberta changed rapidly from being almost motherly towards Cathy to being angry and resentful. She competed with Cathy for my attention and found it hard that I focused on Cathy. Sometimes she was protective of her sister.

Roberta's volatile relationship with Cathy contrasted with Tracy's somewhat inexpressive mode of relating. Roberta may have acted out for her mother many of the feelings towards Cathy which were suppressed and which she was unable to acknowledge herself. Thus both Tracy's intensely destructive and tender vulnerable sides were given expression by Roberta. Roberta herself was in a position where she sometimes competed with Tracy's mothering, but also with Cathy's babyhood.

In the second half of her first year Cathy had developed a unique way of responding to the world. At a basic level she had evolved many individual patterns and sequences in her actions. Among these were:

- 'clicking' with her fingers
- staring intently
- looking around vaguely
- clenching her fists
- tearing paper methodically

- ° closely following Roberta's movements
- ° a slow and deliberate way of moving
- ° dropping things or letting them slip; and
- ° avoiding eye contact while responding to physical contact.

Cathy had developed several well-defined *roles* within the family (e.g. 'daddy's favourite', 'well behaved'). They arose out of her distinctive ways of interacting with other family members and out of the labels she had been given by them. Some labels were assigned before she was born, (e.g. 'younger sibling', 'child from a difficult pregnancy') and some were given because of the way she presented herself (e.g. 'slow developer'). Yet others were assigned without much reference to how she actually behaved (e.g. 'naughty baby').

Some of these patterns, for example dropping things rather than fighting, seemed to demonstrate Cathy's *defences* against her mother's intrusiveness on the one hand, and lack of emotional involvement on the other. She also seemed to defend herself against the chaos of the household by methodically controlling her own movements.

Some patterns showed her increasing ability to perceive and manipulate elements of her environment, for instance her ability to look for biscuits she had dropped earlier. Cathy was moving into the *domain of interpersonal relatedness*, building the sense of interpersonal self – demonstrated by pointing at objects she wanted, or when she imitated Tracy or Roberta, as she was beginning to do during this period. The interaction of these higher order processes constituted the development of Cathy's identity. They combined in a unique and coherent way to form her embryonic sense of self and her place in society.

It would be a mistake to assume that Cathy's roles within the family were entrenched and inflexible. The relationships were dynamic and changing and Cathy's behaviour often differed from her typical patterns. In the following extract from Obs 10 (Cathy at ten months), for example, she shows an unusual degree of activity and emotion:

> Cathy was now rocking and rattling furiously; rocking herself in the bouncer and banging the rattle hard on it and onto her thigh. Her feet were banging in unison on the floor and she made a 'mmm' sound. She had a very intense, almost angry look on her face, frowning and pursing her lips.

Only when these individual interaction sequences are placed in the context of Cathy's overall patterns do they make sense. Some sequences, rare at this stage, developed into characteristic patterns later, illustrating the difficulty of establishing what is a pattern, a temporary sequence or a one-off action.

Cathy at 12 to 24 Months

In the first half of Cathy's second year, the family situation changed. In June, two weeks before Cathy's first birthday, Norman and Tracy were married. Temporarily this seemed relieve some of the pressure and Tracy's depression seemed to be less severe. There was still a great deal of upheaval and both Norman and Tracy held jobs for short periods of time.

Cathy's development remained very slow. She could only crawl properly at 14 months and she was still not walking by 18 months. Her speech development was also slow and she did not say any words other than 'mum' and 'da', although she seemed to understand most of what was said to her.

Of interest is the way some of the patterns, described in the previous section, developed during this phase. Some habitual patterns occurred less and less often and simply died out. A good example of this was her repeated finger 'clicking' which disappeared at about 17 months.

Her pattern of dropping things took a very different course. By 14 months Cathy was regularly throwing things on the ground as well as simply letting them slip:

Cathy looked at the spoon and I gave it to her. She took it in her left hand and looked at it, turning it around. Then she threw it on the ground, just as Tracy was coming into the room with a bottle of Coke for her. Cathy took the bottle, sucked once or twice from it, then seemed to lose interest in drinking and started playing with the bottle. She took it out of her mouth and looked at it, held it by the neck, waved it around, then brought it down quite forcibly on to the settee and spilled some Coke. (Obs 15, Cathy at 13 months)

The changes in this pattern showed that Cathy was beginning to engage much more with her environment and that her methods of controlling what was happening to her were becoming more active. The pattern itself continued to develop so that by 15 months Cathy was throwing things on the ground and retrieving them.

Cathy resumed sucking the chicken bone which she had found again. She put it in her mouth with her left hand and sucked powerfully. Then, smacking her lips loudly, she lifted her hand above her head and threw the bone on to the floor. She picked it up off the carpet and put it back in her mouth and continued to suck. Then she repeated the action and threw the bone with an 'uh' sound and made a sort of giggle. The dog picked up her bone and Cathy made a crying face, but no noise. Mother took the bone from the dog saying 'you dirty sod' and gave the bone back to Cathy, who sucked it again. (Obs 18, Cathy at 15 months)

Soon afterwards Cathy was not only throwing and retrieving things but also looking for things which had rolled under the furniture.

This pattern of throwing things was virtually continuous at this phase of development. Many of the observations around Cathy's fifteenth and sixteenth month record her doing little else. Tracy was concerned, but said that Roberta at this age had bitten people all the time and had grown out of it, as would Cathy. The pattern had many interesting variations which seemed to represent various states of mind, among them anger, attention seeking and gaining physical pleasure from the experience of using her body.

Cathy's relationships were also taking on a different dimension. By her first birthday she was beginning to imitate behaviour:

> Roberta then got down on the floor and put another 'fag' (sweet cigarette) into her mouth. Cathy crawled towards her and reached for the 'fag', trying to get it out of Roberta's mouth. Roberta moved about a foot and Cathy moved after her grabbing at the 'fag' again. Roberta giggled and moved again, and again Cathy crawled after her, smiling and reaching for the sweet. Finally Roberta gave Cathy one of the 'fags'. Cathy was now leaning on her elbows and had the sweet in her mouth sticking out in exactly the same posture and expression as Roberta. (Obs 13, Cathy at 11 months)

This was the first example of true imitation I witnessed. It also shows Cathy engaging with Roberta in a much more active way than before. Previously she had cried for or looked at something she wanted, now she was grabbing for things and pursuing Roberta to get them. Cathy was also beginning to play real games involving other people in which she took control of the situation. In her first year Cathy had only been able to play 'peek a boo'. At 15 months she had become much more sophisticated:

> Cathy was on the ground playing with a crumpled photograph. Mother said 'Oh, is that what you think of your dad?' She reached out to take the photo, saying 'Give that here!' Cathy reached out as if to give it to Mother, but at the last moment she pulled the photo away. Mother held out her hand and said 'ta' a bit more insistently. Cathy looked at her and kept still for a while and then again held the photo out in her left hand as if to give it to Mother. She again pulled away just as Mother was about to grab it. The next time Mother quickly grabbed the photo. Cathy tugged a bit, again without any expression, but Mother took it out of her hands. Cathy looked at her but didn't move. Mother said 'Got it'. Cathy flailed her arms around a bit and crawled towards me. (Obs 18, Cathy at 15 months)

Here Cathy had clearly taken the initiative in the interaction and for a while controlled the situation and her mother's response. Tracy was aware of the change and commented that Cathy moved around all the time, saying the change came about more or less when Cathy began to moving on her own, just before she was a year old.

Despite this qualitative change in Cathy's behaviour, she still had a core of passivity in her interactions, for example when she showed little excitement in her facial expression and failed to respond when Tracy finally took the photo away from her. In the same observation there is another example:

> The puppy licked Cathy's face, and Roberta admonished him, saying 'Leave my sister alone!' Cathy winced slightly, but otherwise didn't react. Then Roberta went out and while she was away the puppy ran up to Cathy and licked her face. Cathy grimaced but made no real effort to protect herself and I called the dog away.

Tracy's responses to Cathy showed a parallel change during this period. She continued to push Cathy to do things and became quite upset when Cathy did not perform. She also seemed to feel 'persecuted' when Cathy did not respond the way she intended. Several times between her thirteenth and sixteenth month Cathy said 'Da da da da da' to which Tracy responded 'No, it's ma ma ma ma!' When Cathy was eventually learning to walk, both parents tried desperately to get her to do so even when she seemed to be quite unhappy:

> Norman said he wanted me to see how well Cathy walked. He knelt on the ground, held her upright, and said 'Come on girl' and Cathy fell on her bottom at his feet. She started crying and he said gently 'Give us a good cry'. He picked her up again and Tracy also knelt on the ground. Cathy looked at Tracy, let out a large 'ah' sound and tottered over to her. Tracy caught her and said 'Good girl!' I looked at Roberta and she was also smiling at the proceedings. Only Cathy was not smiling, but looked rather dazed and bewildered. (Obs 20, Cathy at 17 months)

This way of interacting with Cathy had been a feature of their relationship since my observations started. Yet in the same observation Tracy displayed a new tenderness in her relationship:

> Cathy sat next to Tracy and put her arms around Tracy's neck. Tracy jiggled her up and down and said 'Ah, that's nice.' Cathy responded by kissing Tracy on the cheek and Tracy responded by saying 'What a sweet baby.'. . . Again she sat on Tracy's right side, this time laying her head on Tracy's shoulder, smiling at her all the time. Tracy turned around and kissed Cathy, who let out an appreciative 'ah' and again slipped down onto the ground.

This was unusual in that Tracy was able to show affection for Cathy without using irony or flippancy. Cathy was also showing her newly-acquired facility for initiating interaction with her mother. It would be wrong to infer a complete change in their relationship from this one observation, but the importance was in their *capacity* to relate in a new way. There were also some changes in Roberta's relationship to Cathy. Although the essential dynamics were similar to those previously, Roberta was now sometimes quite protective towards Cathy; she would fend the dog and other dangers away from her. She also continued to feed her, especially with sweets. Sometimes she interpreted Cathy's behaviour when Tracy could not grasp what Cathy wanted, such as getting out of her chair.

Cathy's relationship with me changed considerably. Whereas in the first few months she would stare at me intently, come to me and sit on my lap or even smile at me, she now became suspicious and refused to let me hold her. Often she would ignore me for a whole observation even if I tried to attract her attention. This attitude coincided with the general mistrust of strangers which often occurs around the 9 to 18 month period (Stern 1985), but I felt that there was something more to her actions than being timid, because she obviously knew who I was. Perhaps she was becoming aware that I was white and that differentiated me from other men in her circle or perhaps she was acting out her mother's unexpressed hostility towards me, just as Roberta may have done towards her previously.

Despite the qualitative changes that Cathy had made in her interactions with her family, she still needed to 'hold things together' as she had done in her first year. Her responses to people and events were still slow, and her facial expressions and actions were often muted. She was not easily aroused by things around her and seemed to be happiest just crawling around the room and putting things in her mouth or throwing them on the floor. When she was aroused she very easily went 'over the top' and her laughter would become 'hysterical' before turning to tears. This indicated that when she *did* express her emotions they could easily overwhelm her and therefore she did not do so very often.

It is clear that in the first half of her second year Cathy was beginning to develop two distinctive characteristic ways of interacting with the world around her:

- ° a passive, withdrawn and slow manner, which included repetitive, ritualistic actions; and
- ° a lively, spontaneous and engaging manner, which was characterised by close encounters with members of her family.

The period from 18 to 24 months was much more turbulent for Cathy than the previous 6 months had been. My observations were less frequent because the family were often out when I arrived. Towards the end the marital relationship seemed to deteriorate and I seldom saw Norman. This was when Tracy became pregnant but miscarried after 10 weeks, shortly before Cathy's second birthday. None of the family talked about this very much but it obviously affected them, especially Tracy. Although I did see the family after Cathy's second birthday, the observations effectively stopped when she was two.

She was still fairly slow in achieving her milestones and although she was walking by 18 months, her vocabulary was very small – I did not observe her saying more than 'mum' and 'dada' before her second birthday. Nevertheless, there were many significant developments in this time.

Perhaps the best way of illustrating them would be to continue following her pattern of throwing things on the ground. A good example of this is this from Obs 24 (Cathy at 19 months):

> ...the ball of socks became a weapon, mother and father playfully throwing it between themselves as part of the argument. In the meantime Cathy had picked up two batteries. She held them in each hand then lifted her right hand, ran a short distance, and with a loud 'ah' sound threw the battery on the floor. She then picked it up and with a broad smile on her face repeated the action. After that she faced me and threw the battery halfway between me and father on the settee. Having done this she then picked up a ball of socks and lifting her right hand high above her, threw it into my lap with a gleeful look on her face.

In this scene Cathy was continuing the pattern of throwing things on the floor and the sequence bore all the hallmarks of her previous actions: repetition, self-absorption and verbal ejaculation but she had developed in that:

- ° she was now able to seek actively for an object to throw

- ° she was able to pick the object up again after she had thrown it – the ritual was more elaborate, with each throw being slightly different; and

- ° she was able to relate her activity to events and people around her; throwing the battery on the settee was clearly an attempt to engage me and throwing the ball of socks seemed to have a connection with her parents who had just used it.

These additions conformed with the new, more active and interactive side of her personality. It was as if she was not only throwing off the bad feelings she could not contain, but was getting real pleasure from throwing and was seeking it out. At other times Cathy's throwing was more reminiscent of her early months and was done in a distracted and self-absorbed manner, rather than an excited one:

> ...Another game started, this time with a roll of masking tape. Cathy picked up the tape and threw it down in front of her, then she picked it up, ran a few steps and dropped it again. She passed the tape from hand to hand a few times and then ran along the floor into the bedroom. She lifted the tape above her head and with a loud 'uh' threw it on the ground in front of her with a distracted look on her face. This time she didn't retrieve it, and walked out of the bedroom smiling. (Obs 27, Cathy at 20 months)

Cathy developed many variations on this sort of game, not always involving throwing things, but always repeating variations of the same action several times. Most of these games now included linking into others around her:

> Cathy toddled over to the gas fire, took a mug off it and, holding it at arms length, gestured to me coming up and looking at me straight in the eyes with

an intense expression. I took it from her and held it out for her to take back. Cathy just stared at me, her hands at her sides and a slight frown on her face. I then put the mug on the armrest and she picked it up but immediately gave it back to me. I repeated the action and she took the mug and drank from it, slowly lifting it to her lips. Then she held it out for me again, this time with two hands. I said 'No thanks,' and shook my head, but she came up to me and held it out, so I took it. (Obs 23, Cathy at 19 months)

This vignette illustrates the development of a habit of offering things to people. Although she had occasionally done so before this period, she now incorporated handing over into many of her games and used this as a way of linking with people.

In contrast to the slow and deliberate demeanour she displayed during these 'handing over' games, Cathy was always animated when she played 'peek-a-boo'. At first these games were initiated by her parents, but she soon began to start them herself and they became an habitual part of the observations. Both these types of games were also associated with her developing physical skills. Her sense of balance and her motor skills in such areas as opening containers and manipulating toys were far in advance of her limited verbal ability. Perhaps this was her way of gaining control over her environment without losing her baby role in the family – where which there was enormous pressure for her to 'grow up'.

The events surrounding Tracy's pregnancy and miscarriage seemed to have a profound effect on the family, particularly on Tracy's relationship with Cathy. Until her twenty-first month Cathy continued to be much more linked into her father than her mother. After the miscarriage the relationship changed.

Tracy casually mentioned the pregnancy to me in a conversation about moving house and did not mention it again until she told me in a matter of fact way that she had miscarried. Her demeanour became even more flat and unexpressive than usual. In contrast, Norman kept up his happy-go-lucky facade, but spent more time outside the family. I recorded that Cathy seemed very fragile and broke down three times for no apparent reason. Tracy responded to her in an unusually tender manner, giving their interactions a very different feel:

Mother (who was holding Cathy) sat down on a chair next to Father and cooed at Cathy who was now looking at Father. Cathy's hands slowly rose and she moved them over Mother's body upwards over her side, her shoulders and then round her neck and let them drop to her side again. She whimpered and Mother said 'Dear dear!' and kissed the top of her head. Cathy was still looking at Father who ignored her and was watching TV. Mother said 'Do you want to go to dad?' and lifted her onto Father's lap. Father snapped at Mother 'Don't treat her like a baby.' Mother picked her up and put her next to me on the settee. (Obs 31, Cathy at 23 months)

Cathy seemed to become much more sensitive towards Tracy's emotional state and sometimes appeared to act out the emotions that Tracy could not express – a role

Roberta had previously played. These dynamics continued after Cathy's second birthday and were evidence of a qualitative improvement in the relationship.

In contrast her relationship with Norman grew more distant. He continued to provide stimulation and laughter, but his loss of instinctive knowledge of Cathy's needs that he had previously demonstrated was illustrated by his remark in the above scene. This attitude towards Cathy heralded a new phase in the family's life when he would move out of home and would see the children much less frequently. Roberta continued to express some of Tracy's feelings, but they tended to be the more maternal ones. Roberta was now much less competitive and acted in a more protective and motherly fashion:

> Cathy turned around and walked to Roberta, holding the pencil case in her hand. Roberta was lying on the floor drawing. 'Come on Cathy, do this.' said Roberta. She made a squiggle on the paper. Cathy looked, walked closer and looked again interestedly, but didn't draw. Roberta encouraged her further and eventually she squatted next to the paper and made a squiggle on it. (Obs 31, Cathy at 23 months)

Perhaps this was Roberta's reaction to the loss of the baby; unable to express her feelings of anger towards babies because these feelings were too overwhelming, she took on the role of the helpful older sister instead. This would also be in line with father's expectations, which were that she should not behave in a 'childish' manner.

Cathy's behaviour at this time indicated a change in her relationship with me. In the previous six months she had virtually ignored me and become anxious if she was alone with me; now she seemed to be trying to make a link and was making more eye contact, giving me food and objects, and even 'talking' to me. She also appeared to be making links between her mother and me by taking things from Tracy and giving them to me. In several of the observations between Cathy's seventeenth and twenty-second months, Cathy would take food from her mother (usually a chocolate or biscuit) and give it to me. Sometimes she would turn this into a game by taking it back and then handing it back again and at other times she would just look at me when I tried to hand it back. She seldom took things from me to her mother. She would still not let me touch her and she was still far more reserved towards me than Roberta.

Cathy at 24 to 28 Months

After Cathy's second birthday I only observed the family on four occasions and so do not have a coherent picture of Cathy's subsequent development.

These four months were traumatic for the family. Norman was accused of 'interfering' with Roberta and the family was referred to the social services. Norman was told to leave the family home and only to maintain telephone contact. He went to live with his mother. Tracy was told to attend a family centre with the children. In reality the couple seemed to have quite a lot of contact and Tracy only attended the centre for a few weeks. No statutory action was taken and Norman was back in the family after some three months. I had no way of verifying what the allegations were or whether they were substantiated.

For Cathy's development, this seemed to be a period of consolidation, although at my last visit she was still only saying 'mum' and 'dad', her dexterity had improved and she was able to manipulate quite fine objects and almost to catch things.

Her patterns of interaction continued to manifest themselves in two distinctive ways, one passive, and the other more robust. Generally she behaved in a more outgoing manner than she had previously done. She *still* liked to throw things on the ground while exclaiming 'uh'. She loved to play peek-a-boo, and her skill at this developed considerably. Her other favourite game was to hand things to others and then take them back. This was an aggressive side to her behaviour when she played with the kitten which the family acquired after her birthday. She would pull its tail and squeeze it until Tracy took it away from her.

Norman's absence from the family's life brought Cathy closer to her mother and Tracy made more comments about her being 'sweet' or 'lovely' (although still quite often calling her 'toe rag' or other names). Cathy in turn hugged Tracy and made more eye contact with her.

Tracy herself seemed to be more depressed than she had been in the early observations. She was seldom dressed and the flat was in perpetual half-darkness with the drawn curtains. Her demeanour was flat and she talked in a resigned offhand tone. She complained continuously about the flat and how desperate she was to move.

The relationship between the sisters continued to be competitive, although they now played together more often. In some respects the competition was keener because Cathy could now move and do most of the things Roberta could, albeit more slowly. Roberta now had to compete on other grounds. A remark she made during my last visit (Obs 38, Cathy at 28 months) was a telling comment on their relationship and on the racial aspects of the family:

Look at that horrible brown balloon – I'm going to change to white, but Cathy will stay brown.

No longer able to rely purely on her size and her ability to walk and talk, Roberta had to find something else about Cathy to deride and chose Cathy's supposedly darker colour, which she clearly understood to be a negative quality.

This was one of the very few remarks explicitly about colour that Roberta made but it illustrates her association of white with good and brown with ugly. If, as alleged, she had been abused by Norman she might have associated 'brown' with 'bad'. She could also have been responding to racist messages which she had picked up within the family and/or outside it.

Summary and Discussion

This chapter has described Cathy's development from the age of eight months to two years, with some additional remarks about the four months after her second birthday. By her eighth month Cathy had already developed some distinctive patterns of behaviour which were becoming part of her characteristic ways of interacting; she had already developed an embryonic identity. At this stage Cathy displayed a *self-contained* mode defined by her habit of being either distracted and seemingly unaware of her environment or of focusing exclusively on one aspect. The patterns which made up this stance continued throughout the time I observed her and many of them became very complex.

Soon after her first birthday Cathy began to develop a different set of characteristics which functioned alongside the self-contained mode – these made up the *robust* mode of interaction which involved a more outgoing and aggressive attitude combined with an ability to accept and receive affection from others. This mode slowly became more prominent so that by her second birthday she displayed both models almost equally. According to the theory of development proposed in Chapter 3, the course of Cathy's identity development should have been determined by three main interlocking factors:

   ° her psychological predispositions

   ° her physical and intellectual development; and

   ° her external environment, especially her relationship with her mother.

Although both of the modes of interaction were originally generated by Cathy's defences against hostile inner and outer *bad objects*, they both had potential for developing in either self-destructive or self-enhancing ways. Thus the robust mode, although it enabled Cathy to make relationships and compete with her sister, involved a degree of aggression and hostility to others. In the self-contained mode Cathy was able to survive without needing very much mothering and it enabled her to maintain a degree of equilibrium in chaotic surroundings. Conversely, when in this mode, her ability to relate to her mother was impaired and she became generally withdrawn from the outside world and passive in her social relationships.

This potential for different outcomes becomes an important consideration in the discussion about Cathy's identity development beyond her second year. It means that her future psychological make-up is very difficult to predict from observations of her first two years because, depending on *external* environmental factors, different defences would be mobilised.

The self-contained mode had many of the components of the *False Self* psychic organisation described by Winnicott (see Chapter 3), especially with regard to the passive and ritualistic defences which they share. Cathy may not have developed a fully blown false self-organisation (it is too early to tell at this stage) but certainly the potential for such a response was evident. Similarly, it seems that Cathy's position in her family and her response constituted a *primary role confusion* in Berger and Luckmann's terms. Again it is too early to tell, and it may be that the robust mode will develop sufficiently to allow Cathy to develop a truly integrated rather than fragmented identity. The signs are, though, that the chaotic nature of her family life did not provide a firm foundation for integrated identity development no matter what her constitutional disposition was.

Both of the basic components of Cathy's identity development had been well established by her second year. Future developments would build on the foundations laid down in this period.

It could be that Cathy was continuing to act out patterns which were established in the family before she was born, but which changed in the course of the family's life. In the A family, adversity seemed to follow adversity, for example, Roberta's birth was followed by homelessness, a new home was followed by miscarriage, marriage was followed by Norman having to leave. So the family went through successive periods of activity followed by withdrawal. Similarly, the boundaries between the family and the world were a combination of rigidity and diffuseness; the hole in the door was offset by the drawn curtains, Norman's going out with friends was balanced by Tracy's increasing withdrawal into the home. It is possible that Cathy's development of the 'selves' was an acting out of different aspects of the family myth, and not merely an individual response to the family's chaotic nature.

I have deliberately avoided explicitly discussing the racial component other than where it was overtly part of the interaction, because race was mainly an *implicit*, albeit ubiquitous, factor in the family's day-to-day life. Cathy's racial identity was an integral part of her global identity.

Cathy's racial identity was only one component in her overall identity, although a pervasive part of the family milieu and the interactions within it. Because so many aspects of the family's interactions had become *racialised*, she developed a potential for responding to racial situations that reflected the fundamental aspects of her identity differentiation.

Racialisation is used here to describe the dynamic within the family when conflicts or other interactions and behaviours are attributed to race rather than being personalised. Several instances of this have been described. Because race was such an emotionally charged issue it permeated many of the day-to-day interactions and feelings. Cathy was seen as darker than Roberta and therefore more like Norman.

I would like to suggest that Cathy's fundamental *psychological* modes of being could potentially become associated with the *racial* components of her make-up. Cathy had developed a potential for her self-contained self to be associated with her black aspects and the robust self to be associated with the white ones. Race in the A family was usually associated with conflict, and always highly emotionally charged. Cathy's different selves were a response to the different emotional situations she faced in the family. Thus it would be a small psychological step for her to begin to associate different ways of being with different racial environments. (Stonequist (1937), although he was describing the experiences of adults, identifies a similar dynamic.)

Cathy could grow to associate being black with being passive, threatened and possibly even disturbed. She would find it difficult to make positive identification with black people or black culture. Faced with situations where she was confronted with her blackness, she would have a low self-esteem.

Paradoxically, it was Cathy's spontaneously joyful relationship with her black father that initiated her robust mode of relating, but her relationship with her father changed, and this, combined with messages from within and outside the family about the negativity of blackness, may produce an association between blackness and her self-contained, passive self.

The rationale for this contention is that the defences which Cathy established to deal with psychologically damaging impingements from her internal and familial environments would be used later to defend her against social impingements. If the marginal and racial theorists are correct, her most important psychological threat will be racial, either taking the form of contradictory messages being given from different quarters (role confusion), or of direct racist threats because she is seen as being black. The observations indicated that race was often associated with conflict in this family and that Cathy's defences were developed in large measure to deal with this conflict.

It is interesting to note the different perspectives of the parents regarding race and culture. Tracy was mainly concerned about the children's physical appearance and developmental achievement. Norman was concerned with what he saw as cultural aspects and was more concerned than Tracy about racism. Cathy was therefore subject to more than one conception of race and racism. It is difficult to predict how she will integrate these different versions of race and culture when she grows up, especially because of the increasingly peripheral role Norman was playing in her care. Nevertheless, Roberta, who was much closer to Tracy, and who may have even been developing racist attitudes, was able to identify with many of the cultural factors which Norman introduced into the household. Cathy, who had been 'daddy's girl' may therefore make some positive identifications.

It is difficult to predict how Cathy's 'selves' will manifest themselves at a later date, because they would need to develop over time. According to both marginal and prevailing social work theory, the crisis for Cathy may come when she is a teenager and is rejected by white society, forcing her to acknowledge that she is black. This study cannot predict that such an event will actually occur, nor how Cathy would respond. What the observations have revealed are the kinds of defences Cathy has available to use in the future. They have also shown that she experienced racial conflict at a very young age and it is unlikely that there will be a single traumatic event in her life which will precipitate a crisis of identity.

Although race was associated with conflict at the intrapsychic and interpersonal levels in Cathy's early life, there was integration on the cultural level, where the milieu consisted of influences from both parents' cultures. There was little conflict about food, music or other cultural elements in the household. At this stage Cathy and Roberta had elements of both cultures available to them. This availability seemed less secure by the end of the observations but was still evident. Perhaps Cathy will be able to integrate positive identifications with her father, even if in a fantasised form. The important thing may be how she, herself, perceives the issues of race and culture, and whether she can hang onto the 'good bits' from both her parents, rather than simply the series of events which occur in her life.

CHAPTER SEVEN

The *B* Family

Introduction

This chapter contains observations of the B family, the second of the two families I observed in this study. This description is not detailed as that of the A family, because the observations took place over only one year, and because Dave was younger than Cathy, and therefore his identity was less developed than hers had been. There were 24 observations between September 1986, shortly after Dave's birth, and August 1987.

I was introduced to the B family by their health visitor who had asked the mother whether she would be amenable to the observations. The health visitor described her as 'a very nice lady' but other than that I knew nothing about her. The initial meeting took place six weeks after Dave's birth.

The B Family

| Mother (Rose) | age: 28 yrs |
| Subject (Dave) | age: 4 weeks |

Description

The family lived in a two-bedroomed flat in inner London. The area had been working-class, but was in the process of 'gentrification'. It still maintained a working-class atmosphere and there was also a substantial ethnic minority population.

The flat was on the first floor of a Victorian terraced house, recently converted into four flats. Rose had bought it about 18 months before Dave's birth because of the cosmopolitan area and its proximity to her work. She shared the flat with a lodger, who was away most of the time and had very little to do with Dave and her.

The flat was small, and well-furnished. Most of the observations took place in the living room. The room was always clean and neat and there were never toys or other objects scattered around. There were no visible signs of any African Caribbean cultural influences in the flat, and the decoration was suggestive of a white middle-class home.

Rose was a tall, softly spoken woman. Her general demeanour was relaxed and calm.

Dave was a large six-week-old – a light brown colour with wavy black hair, a flattish nose and a small mouth. He was active and very alert for his age and seemed content, only crying when he was hungry, cold, or needing a nappy change.

Observation Patterns

Rose was ambivalent about the observations from the beginning. It transpired that she suspected some hidden motive for them and my passivity and quietness during the sessions made her feel very uncomfortable. Nevertheless she was always very hospitable and divulged many intimate details about her life and her feelings. She also allowed me to observe details such as breast-feeding. She seemed to find the observations *very* intrusive *and* comforting, in that I was a non-judgmental and reliable presence, in contrast to most of her family and friends who did not offer consistent support.

History

Mother's Background

Rose was the youngest of three children. She came from a middle-class English family and both her brothers were several years older than her. Her parents were teachers who, although well-educated and culturally aware, had a very spartan life-style. They lived in a large cold house with no central heating. Art and music were very important. Rose described her parents as 'liberal minded people who were concerned with various social issues'.

Her relationship with her parents was close, especially with her father. Her mother was rather domineering but her father was much gentler. Her parents encouraged her to achieve academically and to pursue a career in music. Her mother had wanted this for herself, but had not had the opportunity.

As the 'baby' of the family (she was the youngest by eight years) Rose was indulged by her siblings, whom she adored, but was kept out of their games and activities:

> I was obsessed by my older brother 'J'. I idolised him, but he would never let me join in his games and he always teased me, so I got cross. I guess that since then I've always had a feeling of being excluded. (Interview)

Her adulation later turned to ambivalence, and as a teenager she struggled with her need to be like her brother and her need to express her anger with him.

Rose was a shy and awkward girl who found it hard to make friends and who grew up rather isolated. She went to the local grammar school and achieved good results. On leaving school she went to college and obtained an arts degree. She moved to London and after several temporary jobs started working in music and was still doing so when Dave was born.

Father's Background

Dave's father Paul was a Martiniquan living in France – the youngest of seven children. His own father left home when he was young and he was brought up by his mother. He came to France with his family at the age of eight. Rose met him while he was attending a language school in London. She had a short and stormy relationship with him before he returned to France. When she knew she was pregnant she telephoned him and when Dave was born she sent him a card, but there was no further contact.

The Pregnancy

Although the pregnancy was totally unplanned and Rose's initial response was shock and dismay, she soon came to terms with it. The pregnancy was normal and she did not suffer very much from morning sickness or other problems. She continued to work until three weeks before the due date. It was a time of great emotional volatility. On one hand she experienced feelings of intense pleasure and fulfilment at becoming pregnant, but on the other she felt panic about losing her career and, with it, her identity. She was also worried about being isolated and that she would not able to cope with a child on her own. While she was pregnant she decided that she was going to breast-feed the baby.

Before this time Rose had had little experience of pregnancy or children. She did not have a partner with whom she could talk intimately about her hopes and expectations. Possibly as a result of this she developed a number of intricate fantasies she held on to. The fantasies fell into the following categories:

Relationship with the Infant
WHAT SHE WAS GOING TO GIVE THE INFANT

These fantasies were mainly associated with things that she had not had as a child and which she associated with the deprivation of her childhood. They included such things as central heating and living in a 'friendly' area:

> I don't want him to have to go through the kinds of things I had as a little girl. I'm determined that he will be more comfortable! (Introductory meeting, Dave aged six weeks)

NURTURING THE INFANT AND INFLUENCING HIS DEVELOPMENT

Rose was desperate to have someone to love and she saw Dave as an object for these feelings. Sometimes her fantasies took on an almost an omnipotent character when she spoke as if her love could create the kind of child she intended to produce:

> When I was pregnant I loved to sit quietly and think about the kind of child I would have...he's turned out exactly as I had imagined. (Obs 1, Dave aged six weeks)

WHAT THE INFANT WOULD GIVE TO HER

Rose was also desperate to be loved and she saw the infant as the source of uncritical positive regard for her. She was staking her own self-esteem on the infant's responses to her.

BEING CONSUMED OR OVERWHELMED BY THE INFANT

Rose was terrified of the responsibility which looking after an infant would bring and the potential of destroying her life-style and her fragile identity. At times these fantasies became unbearable as if she feared literally being consumed by the demands of motherhood:

> I was afraid that by having a baby I would lose my profession, and that I would be nothing. I rely on my job and it makes me feel like I have an identity – it's not about money; I suppose its about status or something. (Obs 1, Dave at six weeks)

About race her fantasies were:

Race

MAKING UP FOR HER OWN DEFICIENCIES AND STILTEDNESS

Rose had a very deep belief in the differences between black people and white people. She saw whites as being intellectually orientated with little ability for emotional expression or sensuality. In contrast she saw black people as being sensuous, spontaneous and passionate. She saw herself as being typically white and despised her own lack of spontaneity. By having a black child she felt that she could enter the sensuous world of black people which otherwise would be denied to her:

> When I walk down the high road black people often stop me and look at Dave. I feel close to them...I sometimes wish that I had been black, black people seem to appreciate life so much more than whites. The ones (whites) I meet in the music business are all so straight-laced. I don't want Dave to grow up like that...I play soul music on the radio to him. (Obs 2, Dave at seven weeks)

Rose was very aware of the racial component of her relationship with Dave and she 'racialised' some of Dave's characteristics in a way similar to that of Tracy (See Chapter 6). When Dave responded to music by 'dancing' she attributed this to his black genes despite her own interest in music.

BEING ACCEPTED BY A GROUP OF PEOPLE

Rose had always been marginalised, first within her family and later by choosing friends outside her peer group. As a teenager she had chosen friends much older than herself and later she had chosen gay men. Her lovers had all been black. None of these groups fully accepted her and she felt that by having a black child she would be welcomed into the black culture and would no longer have to be peripheral.

PROVING HER CREDENTIALS AS A 'LIBERAL'

Having a mixed-race child drew Rose closer to her family because they saw her acting out in a concrete way their moral and political beliefs about the equality of humanity. Many of the ideas she held about black people were apparently shared by her parents.

CONFIRMING HER SENSE OF ALIENATION AND LOW SELF-WORTH

Despite bringing her closer to her family and the black community, the paradox for Rose in having a mixed-race baby was that she became more alienated from her peer group and white society generally, and saw herself even more as a loner.

Rose's fantasies expressed the ambivalent and contradictory aspects of her racial attitudes, as well as the tendency to idealise the unobtainable, part of her character since she was very young.

For Rose the birth of a mixed-race child confirmed contradictory aspects of her life story. On one hand she had always seen herself as 'different' from her family and her peer group, and had actively sought out different friends. Nevertheless, she also had a strong need for continuity with her family, as evidenced in her choice of occupation. Dave's birth continued both these themes, confirming her separation from the mainstream of society, but strengthened her links with her mother, who was very supportive around the time of the birth. These themes of continuity and difference were to become important in the way she parented Dave, and in the way he responded.

Dave from Birth to Six Months

Dave was a happy and contented baby from birth, soon developing a fairly regular sleeping pattern and only crying when he needed a nappy change, a feed or when he felt cold. Rose was amazed at how quickly he learned to focus – he began smiling at about five weeks.

Patterns

The interactions between Dave and Rose soon developed into observable patterns as follows:

FEEDING

When the observations began Rose was breast-feeding Dave four times during the day and once or twice at night. She was very committed to breast-feeding and it became a central part of her relationship with Dave.

From the first few weeks Dave responded to the breast by becoming acquiescent and relaxed. Even seeing the nipple was often enough to pacify him when he was distressed. But he found feeding difficult at first and often became distressed during the process. Rose seemed to be able to take this in her stride:

> Dave seemed unhappy, making 'uh' noises... Mother said in a concerned way, 'Oh! Maybe you're hungry'. She quickly pulled back her blouse, exposing her left breast, and laid Dave across her lap, placing his head next to the breast. Dave immediately found the nipple and started sucking powerfully. His whole body relaxed and he seemed to 'melt' into Rose's shape. Even his hand, which up to now had been clenched, relaxed and unclenched. He slowly stroked the breast and then held onto the blouse with his thumb and forefinger.

> Dave's breathing became more and more laboured and he suddenly started spluttering. He pulled his mouth away from the breast, kicking his feet simultaneously...he began sucking again almost immediately, but only sucked once more before he pulled away again. He repeated the sequence, moving upwards and she gently pulled him back to the breast. 'Poor Dave, it is difficult.' she said, as she stroked his head. She moved him to the other breast, but again after three or four sucks he became fitful and spluttery.' (Obs 4, Dave at ten weeks)

This illustrates how Dave immediately relaxed when offered the breast, but became disturbed after a few sucks. This was a common pattern during the first few months of life – he seemed to find it difficult to gain comfort from the breast for very long.

At other times Dave became relaxed and sleepy when offered the breast. He used feeding time as an opportunity to develop his sensual experiences and he always explored Rose's breasts and clothes with his hands while feeding. Feeding for Dave was generally an *active* process of taking things in. Whether he was pulling away or feeding hungrily, he did not seem to accept the breast passively from Rose, and I felt that there was always part of him which needed to control the feeding experience.

Rose was able to contain Dave during these feeding experiences. Despite the difficulty he had at first, she persisted with breast-feeding. Although she found it very difficult when he 'rejected' her by not feeding well or by bringing up his feed she did not usually take this personally and would try different feeding positions, in contrast with her response to other parenting problems where she often interpreted his behaviour as a personal rebuff.

Feeding seemed to provide her with the reassurance that she was needed by Dave, and also with a degree of closeness which she found both exhilarating and frightening. She admitted:

> I am sometimes scared that he will become too close to me because I am breast-feeding him, and because I'm a single parent and he hasn't really got another adult to relate to. (Obs 3, Dave at two months)

This feeling that there was someone who depended on her was an important factor in her enthusiasm for motherhood and was underlined by her ambivalent reaction to Dave eating solid food. Although she was proud of his development (he was adept at picking up food with his hands), she found the mess very difficult to cope with and often seemed wistful when talking about his rapid development which was making him more independent of her:

> 'Look at how he's trying to feed himself! He's growing so quickly that I feel I need to remember every moment of when he is a small baby.' (Obs 10, Dave at six months)

AROUSAL

Dave was generally responsive and often focused his attention on objects in his environment, chatting to flowers, pictures, and so on. There were two specific triggers which habitually stimulated him to become very aroused – looking in the mirror and having his nappy changed.

Whenever he saw his reflection in the mirror he produced a barrage of lively 'conversation' and became physically very animated:

> As soon as he saw himself in the mirror his eyes suddenly sprang wide open and he stared with a look of complete amazement at the reflection. He smiled broadly and started making a chattering noise. He stuck his tongue out, pulled it back and stuck it out again. He moved his arms in an animated way, jerking his hands up and down. Rose said 'Oh there's your little friend, Dave'. Dave continued his fascinated stare at the reflection and chatted away at it. As soon as he lost sight of the reflection he calmed down and became almost silent. Rose commented that he was more fascinated by his own reflection than by other people. (Obs 5, Dave at three months)

Rose was very proud of Dave's liveliness as it confirmed that he was contented and therefore that she was a good parent. It also confirmed her conviction that the black element in Dave's nature made him physically demonstrative.

Nappy changing elicited a similar response from Dave.

> While she was changing him, Dave's expression changed. At first he still looked tetchy…but as soon as his nappy was off his expression relaxed. He looked around to face me and then focused on the light. The jerky movements of his arms and legs became less noticeable and smoother and his hands moved randomly in a sort of circle. His fists were still clenched and he kicked

vigorously, opening and closing his mouth. He let out a long 'ah' sound and smiled brightly at me. He then looked at Rose and gurgled. Rose said 'That's better, Dave' as she put on the new nappy. She picked him up and held him. He was still smiling and gurgling... (Obs 8, Dave at five months)

It was also a time when he was able to see his body and move it around freely and when he had eye and body contact with his mother. Possibly he was reacting to her delight at being able to do something for him and his faeces may have been perceived as a 'gift' to her. For her part, Rose certainly seemed to feel that changing Dave's nappy brought him much closer to her. She once told me:

'I now feel that my needs are the same as his. Getting up at night to change his nappy is just like getting up to make myself a cup of coffee.' (Obs 3, Dave at two months)

This statement dramatically highlighted Rose's response to Dave during his first few weeks. It showed how completely she had identified herself with him after his birth. She seemed to revel in this inter-dependence, having moved from being highly ambivalent about motherhood during her pregnancy, to being completely absorbed by it after the birth. The daily routine of mothering a baby completely submerged her concerns about career, finances and relationships but presaged later problems.

Dave's patterns were manifestations of a characteristic trait which began when he was very young, perhaps even pre-natally, and continued to develop throughout the year of the observations. He seemed to be developing into a child who was normally self-contained, even-tempered and calm; was not normally a particularly sensual infant. On occasion, however, something would trigger an outburst of animated and sensual action lasting for some minutes and fading as the stimulus was removed.

ECZEMA

Dave's eczema appeared during his first month. It was never very severe, but it did not go away. It worsened when he was ill or otherwise under stress, for example when he had his vaccinations. Rose was most concerned and tried to control it by dieting methods, but often had to resort to steroid creams. On one level the eczema was merely a minor skin complaint. However, it may have had a more significant symbolic meaning for both Rose and Dave, relating to his temperament and their relationship.

RESPONSE TO CHILD MINDER

Rose considered Dave to be an easy baby to look after; from an early age he developed regular patterns of sleeping and feeding. These habits evolved and changed over time and were interrupted by illness or being away, when it took some time for regular patterns to resume. They spent a week with Rose's parents over Easter, when Dave was seven months old. He would not go to sleep at his usual time for several weeks afterwards and Rose reported that she was exhausted.

Initially the daily routine was determined mainly by Dave's own rhythms – so that he was allowed to feed and sleep on demand but changed as external pressures began to impinge. The major external pressure was financial. Rose had a large mortgage and the expense of having a child was far greater than she had anticipated. She had to return to work sooner than she would have liked and Dave had to go to a child-minder.

The decision to return to work was complicated. Before Dave was born Rose had decided that she would return to work after three months and she was determined that the baby would not affect her career. After the birth her priorities changed and she invested far more in being Dave's mother than in her career. She was therefore extremely reluctant to return to work but slowly other factors began to encroach – her financial situation became acute; she began to feel guilty about colleagues who were covering for her; and her anxiety about her career began to re-emerge.

When Dave was four months old she decided to return to work part-time and Dave went to a childminder. This meant that Dave had to change many of his regular patterns. He had to learn to drink from a bottle, change his sleeping and eating patterns and to be in a new environment without his mother. Initially Rose reported that Dave could not settle, but soon he did and Rose said that he was responding well because he could relate to the older children there.

Dave's response at home to these changes was subtle rather than dramatic. For three or four weeks his sleep patterns were disrupted. He went to sleep at eight rather than six pm. Both felt very tired and Dave would often cry before going to bed. Otherwise he seemed to adjust well to his new circumstances.

Rose was also affected. She was relieved to return to work and to find that she retained her skills, but she felt guilty about leaving Dave. She was suspicious of the childminder whom she suspected of giving Dave forbidden foods, not changing him often enough, and other minor misdemeanours. She was jealous that the childminder had Dave's attention when he was most alert and she felt threatened that Dave could trust another adult. Later, when Dave was eight months old, she returned to work full-time. By this time her anxieties had diminished and her only real problem was the amount of 'quality time' she could spend with him.

This sequence demonstrates how Dave's characteristic patterns and habits changed over time as a response to Rose's need to return to work, and her feelings about this. The responses were not only his, though; Rose was able to come to terms with her guilt and loss on returning to work partly because Dave seemed to settle down well with the childminder. He may have picked up Rose's more relaxed attitude when he went to the child-minder for a full day and he was able to trust her enough not to feel abandoned by her. Rose therefore was able to move away from her initial position of total preoccupation with Dave and finding it difficult to separate her needs from his. By the end of the year she was clearly able to identify her own needs and take responsibility for them, although she remained ambivalent about returning to work.

Changes in Rose's Responses

Rose's feelings about being a parent, and especially about being the single parent of a black child, changed and developed throughout this period. This was particularly evident in the way she linked her feelings and ideas about Dave with the *fantasy* baby of her pregnancy. Her responses to him became more attuned to the 'real' infant rather than the idealised one. This process bears strongly on the question of Dave's racial identity development because many of Rose's fantasies were about having a black child. Although the racial element was therefore inextricably bound up with her feelings about parenthood generally, it is sensible to try and disentangle them for the purposes of this study.

As a new parent Rose spent a great deal of energy during the first six months of Dave's life in separating the fantasised from the real child. Often it was painful for her to let go of the idealised infant and she held on to her picture of Dave as a spontaneous, easy-going and relaxed infant, despite evidence to the contrary. As mentioned earlier she also tended to 'racialise' some of Dave's behaviour, another example of her need to experience Dave as an extension of herself.

Dave seldom expressed intense emotion, perhaps because the process of separation from Rose was painfully being achieved at some cost to him, and his pain had to be expressed somatically. Nevertheless their relationship was healthy enough for both to negotiate these difficulties reasonably successfully and for Dave's development apparently not to be jeopardised.

Dave at Six Months to Twelve Months

Dave's second six months were dominated by the process, begun when he was four months old, of separating from his mother during the day. The major event during this period occurred when he was eight months old when Dave and Rose visited his paternal grandmother in France. This event proved to be significant, although they did not see Dave's father. Rose was very impressed by Dave's grandmother who was very warm towards her and accepting of Dave. Dave apparently responded very well to her and loved the attention of all his aunts and cousins. His grandmother warned Rose not to have anything to do with Paul, his father, but after the visit Rose sent him a picture of Dave and herself. Some of her fantasies about Paul's family were allayed and she became much less frightened that Paul would come and snatch Dave from her, believing that his mother would stop him from doing so.

Some of the patterns which were very apparent in the first six months seemed to diminish in importance during this time, the two most marked being Dave's response to mirrors, which declined, and his eating patterns, which became much less fraught and difficult. New patterns also emerged.

Milestones

Dave continued to reach his milestones early. By eight months he was crawling, and he had begun to walk at twelve. He could say 'mum, mum'. He was relatively dextrous and was able to do rudimentary shape sorting, with help, by his first birthday (Obs 20, Dave at 11 months). He did not excel in any particular skill or ability, nor did any one ability lag significantly behind the others. His weight and length remained at about the 97th percentile, and he was a good eater. Rose's continued to gain satisfaction from his progress, but she was concerned that he would become a fat child. When he started walking he lost weight and Rose relaxed.

Response to Strangers

At around eight or nine months Dave's responses to me changed, becoming more diffident. He shied away from touching me at first for several sessions. Rose said that he was responding differently to black strangers than to white ones, especially men. He was apparently much more interested in black men than white men and was more willing to be picked up by them. It is difficult to assess the strength of this preference and I did not observe it personally. Part of the explanation for his response to me may have been that there had been a three-week break in the observations, so I was less familiar to him than I had been. Nevertheless, one cannot discount the possibility that my colour played a part in his response – perhaps he was unconsciously picking up a message from his mother. Another factor probably affecting his behaviour was his full-time attendance at the childminder's, which might have made him anxious about strangers.

Play

In his second six months Dave developed distinctive patterns of playing which became increasingly prominent. The most distinctive were:

ABILITY TO PLAY ON HIS OWN

Dave had only a small number of toys – blocks, a trolley, a caterpillar to pull, a wooden snake, and so forth (no battery toys) and a confined space in which to play. For several sessions he spent most of the time playing on his own on the floor, only occasionally going to his mother to show her something. His favourite activities were building towers and sorting shapes. He liked pulling the books off the bookshelves but apart from this he did not play with furniture or equipment in the flat.

TIDINESS

Dave's toys were kept in a toy box stored under the settee. He habitually put his toys back into the box after taking them out. He also gathered them together whenever they were spread out over the floor. Rose commented several times on his tidiness. My impressions confirmed this – he made less mess than any other child his age I have seen and hardly ever became dirty or grubby in the course of his play.

LACK OF AGGRESSIVE PLAY

Although he often babbled happily to himself or Rose while playing and occasionally chuckled with delight, he seldom showed intense emotion. His play typically consisted of putting things into containers and removing them, and he did not seem to show any destructive or aggressive aspects. He did not throw things which many children of his age do, nor did he deliberately knock things over or tear pages out of books.

> Dave takes out a pink bear from the box and says 'ng'. He takes out a red bus and puts the pink bear back inside... Then he takes a small plastic man from the box and turns it over in the fingers of his right hand, concentrating on his hand. He then picks up the box and throws it on the floor with an almost gentle movement. He picks up the man and puts him into a red plastic cylinder. He takes the man out, puts the cylinder on the floor and tries again, but this time he can't do it. He tries three or four times and then, frustrated, puts the cylinder down again. His face slowly crumples and tears begin to well up in his eyes. He starts crying quietly. Rose picks him up and puts him to the breast, he lies across her and sucks, and his body relaxes quickly. (Obs 13, Dave at seven months)

Generally Dave's play had a strange, self-controlled flavour. Although he seemed to be happy and relaxed most of the time, cooing to himself while playing, his body movements were generally somewhat stiff and deliberate. He often held his fists tightly and seldom moved quickly from one place to another as infants of this age often do. He confined himself to a small area in which he felt secure.

Although the patterns described above were fully apparent after six months, they emerged much earlier in Dave's life. Dave was always a rather self-contained child and as he grew older the patterns became more elaborate. Dave always demonstrated contradictory sides of his identity and the more sophisticated the patterns became, the more contradictory they seemed. On one hand he was an outgoing, friendly and relaxed child who developed relationships easily and was interested in the world around him, but he could be restrained in his movements, wary of strangers, and lacking in spontaneity.

Running through these observations, therefore, was the unfolding of two distinctive modes of interacting with the world – the development of two 'selves'.

The 'Defined' Self

The defined self arose out of Dave's need to control his environment. By carefully defining his actions and ensuring that his environment was under control Dave could maintain a degree of equanimity. This pattern was evident from a very early age when Dave began to show definite preferences. The first instance was his preference for the right breast and continued in his definite likes and dislikes for different foods. He also demonstrated a need to define a certain area in which to play and he was careful to put his toys in the 'right' place. Later this pattern emerged in the social domain when he showed a preference for black rather than white strangers. All this points to a developing characteristic of Dave's which showed a need to categorise and control aspects of his world. The development of his play also points to an increasing ability to suppress the angry and destructive elements of his personality. He was able to establish good relationships with others and in many ways seemed relaxed socially if not physically. He was also able to adapt to new situations and routines, if sometimes with difficulty. Certainly he was not a disturbed infant in any common sense of the word so his need to control did not lead to a rigid and inflexible response or an intolerance of new stimuli as in some of the infants described by Stern (1985).

The 'Fused' Self

The controlled or 'defined' mode of interaction did not prevail in all Dave's social intercourse. One of his characteristic patterns was when his self-controlled demeanour broke down and he became very excited or distressed for short periods of time. He showed a reluctance to fall asleep on his own and needed to be cuddled. He became very clingy to Rose, especially when his routine was disturbed.

It is very possible that Dave's eczema was a somatic manifestation of this characteristic. Eczema is known to be related to psychological stress (Leach, 1979). Bick (1968) discusses the significance of skin as a *psychic container* and its importance in early psychological development. Very young infants use their skin (the *physical* barrier between themselves and the world and also the 'container' of their physical bodies) as a *psychological* container for their powerful emotions. This enables them to develop a *psychological skin* which protects them from threatening projections and introjections, and contains their powerful impulses.

Sometimes the emotions are too strong to be contained and break through the psychological skin. This shows itself in various forms of behavioural outbursts or disturbances. At other times the psychological skin remains intact, but the outbreak is symbolically manifested by the physical skin, for example eczema. Thus the infant will seem to be relatively placid and contained, but will actually be subject to almost uncontainable projections and introjections.

Dave fitted this pattern very well. The tension between separateness and psychological union was apparent in his relationship with Rose. In some ways their relationship was contained and the psychological barriers between them strong; for example, their daily routine was fairly regular without being rigid. In other ways, however, there was psychological fusion.

Dave's eczema might have been a physical manifestation of an internal psychological conflict in which he was struggling with his sense of separateness.

The eczema, a breach of the physical barrier between him and the world, represented a psychological breach between the *me* and the *not me* (Winnicott, 1988). This hypothesis, although tenuous, is supported by some of Rose's statements such as the one quoted above regarding nappy changing, in which she clearly points out her own difficulty in psychologically separating from Dave. Her response to changing the nappy was very typical of Winnicott's *primary maternal preoccupation* and she certainly experienced their relationship as one of psychological fusion.

A further symbolic role for the eczema lies in the possibility that Dave was able to perceive the difference in colour between his own skin and that of his mother. The eruption on his skin therefore represented an attempt to break through this barrier. This is an even more tenuous hypothesis, but throws an interesting light on how an infant's perception of colour differences may develop. Possibly the difference in skin colour is recognised by the infant (see Dave's response to the mirror above) and is unconsciously experienced, even at this early pre-verbal age, as a barrier between himself and his mother. Depending on the infant's temperament he may feel frightened, angry, or rejected, or may by contrast even see it as a source of comfort. His response would also be determined to some extent by his mother's own feelings about his skin colour.

Dave's mother was certainly preoccupied by his skin colour and he could have been aware of some of this anxiety. This, and his constitutional propensity to 'erupt' psychologically, could have combined with a natural susceptibility to cause his eczema.

A similar dynamic may have been operating when Dave responded so dramatically to his image in the mirror. He was much too young to recognise himself in his reflection (Piaget, 1951) but something about his reflection continuously triggered his interest. Could it be that he recognised a person of the same *colour* as himself or, at least, different from his mother? It is an interesting, if tentative, hypothesis that some embryonic awareness of colour was present even at this early age and so his response may have contained an element of reaching out to that part of himself which was individual and different. Dave differed from Rose not only in race but also gender. The same response to his image when his nappy was on as well as off makes it unlikely that this hypothesis could also apply to the development of his sexual identity.

Why did Dave develop these different selves? In some ways he was very like the child Rose expected to produce. It would seem plausible that his patterns of behaviour were at least partly moulded by his mother's needs and expectations but he was reticent and wary of people and needed to control his environment. This reticence, and the way he carried himself physically, reflected her own characteristics rather than her expectations to display the kinds of traits she lacked.

These traits may have developed because of Dave's constitutional predispositions, but there must be a question regarding how much he was acting out his mother's fantasies about him. There are three hypotheses which may explain this apparent contradiction in Dave's characteristic traits:

Dave acted out Rose's conscious fantasies but unconsciously separated from her

In this hypothesis the 'relaxed' aspects of Dave's personality were superficial attempts to conform with his mother's expectations. His need to control the external environment, however, was an outward manifestation of a deeper need to control the inner psychological environment in which the boundaries between him and his mother were blurred. To do so he had to control the powerful internal and external forces impinging on his psychological 'skin'. His controlling and controlled behaviour is then seen as an unconscious attempt to separate from his mother. He seemed to be acting out in a concrete way his need to create a separate and distinct identity for himself, a dynamic also manifested somatically in his eczema.

Dave acted out Rose's fantasies at both the conscious and unconscious level, but Rose's fantasies themselves were contradictory and ambivalent

Rose's stereotyped ideas about children and black people may have represented only one aspect of the picture. Rose saw herself as a stilted and unspontaneous white person. She had a low self-esteem and seemed unable to acknowledge the side of Dave's character which mirrored her own; preferring to see him as a spontaneous, relaxed, and sensual representative of black people, she may also have resented and envied this attribute. Dave's obvious physical difference from her also made her feel less able to 'own' him than she would have liked and she sometimes said that she felt that he did not rightfully belong to her but to the black community. Unconsciously, therefore, she may have needed Dave to be like her, to improve her self-esteem and to allow her to feel that she had a right to him.

Dave's personality developed independently from his relationship to Rose

It may have been that Dave's development was constitutionally rather than environmentally determined and he just happened to be an infant who demonstrated both a defined and a fused mode of interacting with his environment.

These three hypotheses are not mutually exclusive and elements of all these processes possibly operated in the formation of Dave's identity, but because of the complex nature it is difficult to establish how they intermeshed and which were the most powerful. Also, Dave was only one year old by the end of my observations and these patterns and characteristics were still in an embryonic stage of development. One cannot say whether the 'relaxed' or the 'controlled' aspects of his identity were more fundamental. Both were present very early on in his life, if not at birth, so they were either genetically determined or he developed his characteristic defences very early in his life.

Perhaps the most plausible explanation is that Dave was endowed with the *potential* for responding to the world in both a defined and a fused manner. His early development would then have been driven by the realisation of these potentialities as he confronted the world outside, principally through interacting with his mother. He was also born physically robust.

Rose's response was evident on several different psychological levels. The healthy, adult part of her was able to nurture and care for him and to contain his frightening projections. Another part of her felt threatened and overwhelmed by him and could only respond to the idealised infant of her prenatal fantasies. Dave, in turn, had quickly to develop defences against the uncontained aspects of his mother, while at the same time being able to relate to her healthy side in an undefended manner. He had to develop both a relaxed way of interacting, corresponding Rose's healthy side, and a controlled way, corresponding to her uncontained side.

Rose's Responses

For Rose, the major task of this period was to re-establish her identity and to allow Dave to establish his own. She became increasingly more able to see him as separate, and to acknowledge his individual needs and characteristics – see above for examples regarding feeding, play and leaving him with other carers. Although Dave's fundamental modes of interaction with the world were already set by the first year, the emotional conditions under which they were determined had already changed considerably.

Nevertheless this is not the whole picture as there were many areas in which little change occurred, for example the ability to express anger. Rose was never confident enough in her relationship to be able to express irritation or conflict with Dave without feeling that she would destroy him, or at least irreparably damage their relationship. Dave also showed very little overt aggression, either directly towards Rose or in his play.

Future Identity Development

Although the observations were undertaken when Dave was very young, one can to make some hypotheses about the possible future of his racial identity development.

The environment in which Dave grows up is likely to have a profound effect. He had quite a lot of contact with black people in the area and had some contact with his father's family. Rose tried to introduce an element of black culture into the household by playing black music and buying books with black people in them. She also sought out black friends for Dave and chose the childminder partly because there was another black child being minded by her. Dave's immediate family and social life were, however, essentially white. The attempts by Rose to introduce black culture into the household were somewhat forced and self-conscious and it did not form an integral part of Dave's life as it had for the A family in the previous observation.

When Dave becomes old enough he will be encouraged to choose black friends and this may give him a more immediate experience of black culture than he had during the observation. If this does not happen then Dave's experience of black culture is likely to remain second-hand.

BOUNDARY ISSUES

Dave's tendency towards maintaining well-defined boundaries will probably continue as he grows up. It would not be a great psychological step for him to begin to discriminate between individuals and groups of people on the basis of those aspects of his identity they represent, and to project on to them some of the feelings associated with those internal constructs. This process could extend to his relationships with members of different racial groups who could come to represent the more controlled or more relaxed part of himself. Thus black people may come to represent the relaxed aspect of himself, and whites the controlled aspect, and he would then choose to associate largely with black people. At ten months Dave apparently showed a preference for black rather than white strangers, illustrating that this process may have begun.

The above is only one of a number of possible outcomes for Dave, even given the fact that his basic social environment remains the same. The evolution of Dave's tendency to create clear boundaries does not necessarily imply that he will continue to favour black people, nor that he will identify himself as a black person. His particular identifications will arise out of his experiences at school and in the community, as well as those at home.

This suggests that although it is not possible to predict whether he will see himself as primarily a black, white or mixed-race person, he is unlikely to be able to tolerate having a blurred identity and will strongly identify with one or another group. Other aspects of his identity will be suppressed, only becoming overt when he is under stress.

Like Cathy in the A family, Dave's responses were typified by two distinct modes of social interaction, one of which could develop into a superficial or *false self* and the other a *true self*. In Dave's case it is more difficult to predict how these 'selves' will turn out, because Dave was much younger at the end of the observations and his identity was less developed. Second, the two modes of interaction arose at the same time, whereas Cathy's robust mode was only evident in her second year. Because neither of Dave's characteristics chronologically preceded the other, neither was intrinsically more fundamental. Third, Dave's relationship with his mother was more fluid than Cathy's with hers, and Rose showed more ability to adapt to her child's needs. This means that she may eventually develop the capacity to acknowledge and contain Dave's pain and accept his need for separation. Perhaps both these 'selves' and indeed others which may develop, will coexist as part of Dave's personality.

At the time of the observations, Dave's preferences and categorisations were unselfconscious and spontaneous. As he becomes more self conscious it is likely that he will evolve intellectual justifications and defences for these emotional reactions. They will become part of his own self-concept and thus integral to his identity.

These observations provide some indication of the ways that Dave's identity was developing, and the major internal and external factors which influenced that development. Briefly these were:

- ° Dave's constitutional attributes, especially his large size, his skin colour, his tendency to reach his milestones quickly, and possibly his tendency towards self-containment and towards somatising his internal psychological conflicts

- ° the particular circumstances in which he was born, being the first born child of a white single middle-class woman

- ° the way these interacted with Rose's preconceptions, fantasies and personality, especially her view of herself as 'different' and her idealisation of black people and culture

- ° the influence of the factors on Rose's attitudes and behaviour towards Dave

- ° the mother–infant relationship, and Dave's struggle to separate psychologically from Rose

- ° Dave's development of two complementary *selves*, the defined and the fused, as ways of defending himself.

CHAPTER EIGHT

The First Set of Interviews

Introduction

The previous two chapters have considered racial identity development through the close observation of two children. This chapter considers the interviews which were carried out with the mothers of the two children and with three other mothers. The information gathered from the interviews supplemented the observations and provided more information about the background of the mothers and their current circumstances, and how these impacted on their children's identity development.

For each family I will give a brief sketch of the mother's and father's background and the current family situation and will then describe some of similarities and differences of the mothers' backgrounds and relationships.

The interviews were conducted with mothers alone in their own homes. They lasted for approximately two hours and were tape recorded. Before the interview I explained that I was researching the development of racial identity and that I would like to spend some time asking them about themselves and their families. I asked whether they would object to the interview being recorded and explained that information would be kept confidential and anonymity would be maintained in the writing. I assured them that they were free not to answer any of the questions and could stop the interview at any time. At the end of the interview they were invited to feed back about the experience.

The mothers seemed to relax as the interview progressed and often returned to previous topics to elaborate on them. This enabled them to cover more sensitive material when they were more relaxed and confident.

Issues Raised in the Interviews

The attitude of the mothers varied considerably, but they were generally accepting of the process. Despite the fact that very personal questions were being asked, they soon relaxed and were willing to answer all the questions. There was far less resistance to the interviews than had been shown in the initial stages of the observations. Of the two mothers who had been observed, Rose said that it had been a relief to talk openly about her condition and feelings. It was also an opportunity for her to check out the fantasies she had about what I was really looking for. Although I had outlined the purpose of the observations to her before they started, she had 'forgotten' and assumed that I was checking out her adequacy as a mother. Tracy also used the interview to ask me what I was *really* looking for and questioned me about what I had found. The feedback given at the end of the interviews was uniformly positive, although three mothers queried why they had to be seen alone.

The role of the interviewer was much more active than that of the observer. The structured nature of the interview made it easier for the mothers to talk about themselves than had been possible during the unstructured observations. However, in the more active role of interviewer I was less able to pick up nuances of meaning than I was able to do as observer.

Despite their less sensitive nature these interviews were all highly emotionally charged for both the mothers and myself. Each interview took on its own nature, part of which was reflected in a tacit collusion between myself and the subject. Only after the interview, while listening to the recordings, was I able to discover some of these collusive patterns. Examples included the interview with Rose, which took on the nature of a mutual confession. It began with me 'coming clean' about the true nature of the thesis. At this point I needed Rose to see that I was a bona fide researcher and not simply a nosy and intrusive person. She responded by revealing intimate details about her life in a manner which suggested a need to 'reveal all' in trying to uncover the hidden reasons for her attraction to men.

In contrast, the interview with Lucy was more like an interrogation. Although she was overtly pleasant and hospitable, she spent the whole interview denying in various ways that race was an issue for her. My questions became unconsciously more and more aggressive as I tried to establish some link between what she was saying and my expectations.

Although transference and counter-transference are powerful forces, it must be recognised that there were many other factors which may have biased the answers, including:

° questions may have been phrased in a way that led to irrelevant or distorted answers

° there was no independent corroboration of the answers, especially in the case of the three mothers whose infants were not observed

° mothers consciously avoided questions because they were uncomfortable or difficult to answer

° my own political or other biases

° the fact that I am a white male.

Many of these overt biases interacted with the more covert transferential influences, and so the picture is very complex. For example, my race and gender may have biased the answers by making the mothers feel more ill at ease and defensive than they might otherwise have done and these factors may have made me less sensitive to some of the cultural nuances. White maleness could unconsciously represent to the mother those elements of the family of origin that she had rejected by choosing a black man as a partner, the partner she may have had if she had not chosen a black man, or a group of people from whom she felt rejected.

Despite these concerns I believe that the interviews provided much valuable information about the mothers and children.

The Interviews

In this section I will try to identify the salient features of the five interviews I conducted. I will concentrate more on the three mothers whose children I did not observe because I have already given fairly detailed descriptions of the two observed mothers. However, to spare the reader from having to page backwards and forwards I will repeat some essential details.

The A Family

Family Structure

Mother	(Tracy) age at interview:	27 yrs
Father	(Norman) age at interview:	28 yrs
Sister	(Roberta) age at interview:	5 yrs
Subject	(Cathy) age at interview:	30 mths

Background

MOTHER

Tracey came from a white English/Irish working-class family which lived on a council estate. Her friends and neighbours were mostly white. She came from a close family, but was closer to mother than father. She was a happy, outgoing child. She has no educational qualifications. Her friends were mostly white, she had a couple of black boyfriends before Norman, but Norman was her only serious relationship with a black man. Her family were not very happy about the relationship but came to accept it and now the couple are closer to them than Norman's family.

FATHER

Norman was born into a working-class family in Jamaica. His parents worked for London Transport. He came to England aged seven, and his childhood milieu was mostly African Caribbean. He left school aged 16, and had no regular occupation, working in the building trade, cleaning, hotels, etc. Music is his major interest.

This is his first relationship with a white woman, all others being with African Caribbean women.

Present Circumstances

The family live in a small council flat in an inner city multi-racial area. Norman is nominally separated from family, but spends most of his time in the home. Tracy and Norman work intermittently. The family are desperate to be rehoused, and Tracy is depressed, blaming her depression on the flat.

There is intense sibling rivalry between the sisters. The milestones of both children were late. Cathy was especially late at talking. Norman was suspected of sexually abusing Roberta but no legal action was taken.

The B Family

Family Structure

Mother	(Rose) age at interview:	34 yrs
Father	(Paul) age at interview:	25 yrs (lived abroad)
Subject	(Dave) age at interview:	15 months

Background

MOTHER

Rose is the youngest child of a teaching family. Because her brothers were much older she grew up as an only child and was given a lot of attention. Her father was a gentle man, her mother was rather domineering. The family were very liberal. She had few friends as a child. Her parents always wanted her to take up a career in music so after school she moved to London to read music. In London she became more gregarious and had a few relationships. At this time she was friendly with a group of gay men, then had several black lovers. She met Dave's father while he was on holiday in the UK, when she conceived Dave. She has had no contact with him since the holiday other than a postcard.

FATHER

Paul is a European of African Caribbean origin. His family came to Europe before he was born. He comes from a large, matriarchal family and is the youngest of seven siblings. He is reported to be described by his mother as the 'black sheep' of the family, and as 'happy go lucky' by Rose. Seems to take little interest in Rose or Dave now and what contact he has maintained is through pressure from his mother.

Present Circumstances

Rose and Dave live in a small flat in an inner London area. Rose works full-time and Dave attends a childminder near her work. She is not involved with anyone at present. She keeps contact with her parents, but is fairly isolated. She and Dave have visited Paul's family for a few days, but did not see Paul. She is generally content to be a single mother.

The C Family
Family Structure

Mother	(Ruth)	age 39 yrs
Father	(Jai)	age 36 yrs
Infant	(Seree)	age 1 yr

Background

MOTHER

Ruth was born and spent the first seven years of her life in central London. The family then moved out to north London where she spent the rest of her childhood and adolescence, and where she now lives. At that time the area was predominantly a middle-class Jewish area, but more and more Asian families were moving in. Now it is fairly cosmopolitan, but still with a strong Jewish and Asian presence.

Both Ruth's parents were born in Europe and came to the UK several years before her birth. Ruth's father was an artisan and the family struggled financially through most of Ruth's early life. Throughout this time there were lodgers living with the family. Ruth's mother insisted on having black lodgers because they found it so difficult to get lodgings in London.

Ruth is the elder of two sisters and she describes the family life as 'very close and intense'. Her parents were concerned with the children's education and introduced arts and music into the home. Ruth was closest to her father. Ruth's family are Jewish and, although there was very little religious input into the family, she was taught to be proud of her Jewishness. In most ways her upbringing and environment were very similar to the mainstream, yet she always felt different from the other children around her:

> I never felt completely English; there is a lot of continental stuff in my background.

Politics played a very important role in the family. Ruth's parents were committed socialists and they instilled in the children a strong sense of fairness, justice and support for the underdog. Political discussion was very much part of family life:

> There were always books and newspapers and people having arguments.

Ruth's parents were also a lot freer and more open than those of her friends. They treated the children as responsible people. Ruth felt different from her contemporaries because she was Jewish and culturally different from the 'English' children around her. She was less well off than many of her schoolmates, and her political beliefs were different from those of her contemporaries.

These feelings of being different, and her father's socialist ideology, were to become driving forces in her life. Unlike Ruth, her younger sister became a conventional middle-class Jewish woman.

After leaving home Ruth went to college and studied social sciences. She spent some time in France during the student uprising of 1968 which she found very exciting. Her experiences there confirmed her political beliefs and she began to be more outgoing and to mix with people from all over the world. She returned to England, completed her studies and pursued a successful professional career.

She met Jai while they were both students at the university. They mixed in the same circle of friends and knew each other for several years before eventually becoming lovers.

FATHER

Jai was born in India and moved to London with his family when he was seven years old. He is the elder of two children. His family are middle-class and lived very near to Ruth's family, although they only met as adults. Jai's family are Bengali Hindus. They spoke Bengali at home and mixed with a community of Indian people locally. They were not very religious and Jai grew up absorbing both Indian and English culture. He always had a wide range of friends from different cultures. Both he and his sister chose white partners.

After leaving school Jai went to college and has pursued a career in the arts.

The D Family

Family Structure

Mother   (Jenny)   age 35 yrs
Father   (Tony)   age 36 yrs
Daughter (Maddie) age 2 yrs

Background

MOTHER

Jenny is the eldest of five children. She comes from a professional family and was brought up in a small town in the north of England. Jenny describes her childhood as being reasonably happy. The family were very close and although the siblings 'fought like cat and dog', they were very fond of one another and still remain close. Jenny was close to both parents, but she feared her father who had an explosive temper. Although the family were well known in the community her parents did not have any close friends and the family relied mostly on one another for social contact.

The family situation was very supportive and secure for Jenny, but she also found life to be very restrictive. The family's values were very middle-class and rather conformist. In retrospect she feels that she led a rather cloistered life until she left home. As the eldest child she had extra responsibilities in the home and this further restricted her contact with the outside world.

When she was 18 Jenny left home and spent a year in London working in a school for severely handicapped children prior to going on to college. This year was very significant for her. It was the first time that she had been exposed to people who were different from her own background, with different ideas and perspectives. Jenny feels that this experience enabled her to cope with college life because she was used to looking after herself, coping with her emotions, and relating to a wide range of people. She also became more gregarious and for the first time mixed with a group of fellow students. She met Tony in the first term of college and soon started going out with him. They married after they qualified. Tony went on to do a further degree and she has just completed a Masters degree.

FATHER

Tony was born in Jamaica and came to London with his parents at the age of four. He is an only child, but is part of a fairly large extended family. Tony's father worked for London Transport and his mother was a nurse. Like many African Caribbeans of their generation they were concerned that their son should be well educated and 'have a better chance in life than they had' and they pushed him hard to achieve. They were a close family but Tony became culturally more and more distant from his parents and now, according to Jenny:

He has more in common with my parents than with his own.

Nevertheless, he remains emotionally close to them. Tony's parents returned to Jamaica in the early 1980s after they retired. The family have gone to see them once and intend to return soon.

Tony grew up in a multi-racial area and at school had a number of friends from different backgrounds. After leaving he lost contact with his school friends and now his friends are largely from college and work, and are all white. After leaving college Tony went on to work for a bank and has reached a managerial position. He is virtually the only black person in the higher ranks of the organisation.

The E Family
Family Structure

Mother	(Lucy)	age 39 yrs
Father	(George)	age 40 yrs
Daughter	(Pippa)	age 7 yrs
Son	(Gary)	age 18 mths

Background

MOTHER

Lucy described her background as 'very English'. She was born and brought up in a middle-class family in a town in the Home Counties. She is the younger of two sisters and her parents are both professionals. Family life for Lucy was very happy and she can remember no major crises in her youth. The family were very close to one another, having no close relatives and few family friends.

Despite this warm and supportive background, Lucy was an anxious child and had very little self-confidence. She was quiet and shy and, although she had many acquaintances, she had few close friends. As a teenager she never had a close boyfriend. By the time she was a teenager Lucy also found her family situation restrictive and her parents over-protective. They gave her very little freedom and would not allow her to leave home. She carried on living at home until she was 25, when she left to do a degree.

For Lucy, leaving home was a liberating experience. She became more gregarious and began to enjoy life. She met George during the first month of college and they had a wide circle of friends, mainly white. After college she and George married. She worked until their first child was born.

FATHER

George was born to a wealthy family in Singapore. His mother was Chinese and his father Indian; he has two natural siblings. When he was very young he was adopted by an Indian woman. He moved to England with his adoptive family when he was seven and has lived in England ever since. George went to a good school and college. He was a successful student and is successful in his career. He is an outgoing person who makes friends very easily.

George's family had become anglicised and he grew up speaking English and eating a mixture of English and Indian food. The family did not practice any religion although they retained elements of Singaporian culture. George has a large extended family which is racially very mixed. His adoptive mother's sister married a white man and his adoptive siblings have also intermarried.

Discussion of Interviews

This discussion will consider how the information collected in the interviews relates to the data gathered during the observations. The intention is not to draw general conclusions from the data; the sample of mothers interviewed is far too small and unrepresentative for any generalisations to be valid.

Background

Tracy came from a working-class family. The others all came from middle-class homes which were stable, two-parent, nuclear families. None of the families was overtly 'abnormal' and all the mothers and their siblings grew up without experiencing major social problems. All had reasonably happy childhoods, and although there were various degrees of closeness in their families, they all maintained ties with their families into adulthood. Rose, Jenny and Lucy came from small towns and their parents were professionals. All described their childhoods as being happy but found their parents very restrictive during adolescence. They experienced leaving home and coming to London as an exciting and liberating time in their lives. All the middle class mothers had obtained degrees and had done well professionally before having children.

The apparent similarity of the families disappears when considering the roles taken on by the mothers in their own childhood. Their attitudes towards their families, and their parents' responses to them also differed in many important respects. An example of this is the difference between Rose and Jenny's relationships with their siblings. Jenny was the eldest and she took some responsibility for looking after her siblings when her parents were busy. Her first job when she left home was caring for severely handicapped people. She seemed to enjoy the role of eldest sister and as an adult her siblings still came to her for advice. Her relationship with her siblings was close and relatively uncomplicated both as a child and an adult. She also had a relaxed attitude towards bringing up her own child, possibly because she was happy in the nurturing role. Rose, on the other hand, was by far the youngest member of the family and always felt excluded by her siblings. Although rather indulged by her parents she always felt deprived. As an adult Rose continued to feel left out. She struggled with her own sense of identity and had a much more difficult task as a parent.

These differences were probably influenced by several factors including temperamental differences (Rose may have been born with an anxious disposition), their adult circumstances (Rose was a single parent), their early experiences and the subtle dynamics within their families.

These interviews only provide a hint about how these forces have operated. To find out more one would have to have a much more in-depth knowledge of how they were parented themselves, especially about their early relationship with their own mothers and also some of the other influences on their early lives. The interviews do show that seemingly similar families can produce very different mothers.

Racial Contacts

None of the mothers had any close social contact with black people when they were children. Ruth had some contact with adult black lodgers but not black school friends. Only Ruth and Tracy, who were brought up in London, had any black peers as teenagers. It was only after leaving home that any of them began to mix socially with black people. In the case of Jenny and Lucy it was only through their partners that they made other black social contacts.

These apparent similarities again hid great differences. Both Ruth and Rose felt that there was an element of inevitability in their forming relationships with black men and that as teenagers they knew that they would never have a white or English partner. Tracy said that she was physically attracted to black men, but didn't like black culture. Jenny and Lucy, while acknowledging that their partners' colour added to their attractiveness, maintained that it was pure chance which led them to having a black partner.

It is interesting to relate the mothers' relationships with black people to their families' attitudes. Both Jenny and Lucy declared that in their family of origin race was never discussed. These families were also apolitical and were mainly concerned with internal family matters. In Ruth and Rose's families, social issues were often discussed and race often came up in family discussions. In both families black people were seen as victims of racism, but black culture also represented an exotic alternative to the dull reality of English life. Tracy's family had contact with black people and occasionally made racist comments. For these women the choice of a black partner contained an element of the family culture.

Race was a significant factor in all these partnerships because of its key social and emotional significance in our society. It must be emphasised, however, that the partners' racial backgrounds were not the only important attributes in the choice. Their personalities, physical appearance, socio-economic status, intelligence, and so forth, were also very important factors, and each would merit as minute an analysis as race.

Identities of Mothers

All the mothers in this study considered themselves to be essentially English, although there were varying degrees of commitment to their Englishness. Lucy considered it to be very important that her family felt English. Ruth only grudgingly conceded her Englishness, preferring to be identified as Jewish, although she did not mix in a Jewish milieu. Rose was ambivalent about English culture, seeing it as restrictive, but also living a very English life-style. Tracy considered herself English, but valued her Irish roots. Jenny enjoyed having some access to another culture, but was essentially English.

Despite their English identities, the mothers, with the exception of Ruth, had a much more cosmopolitan life-style than their family of origin. For the three mothers who came from small towns (Rose, Lucy and Jenny) their move to London was a conscious decision to break away from the restrictions of their families and the limited cultural diversity offered by small towns. The decision preceded their involvement with black people and they had therefore consciously decided to broaden their horizons before they met their black partners. It may also be that, having taken one risk in leaving home, they were prepared to take another risk in forming a relationship with a black man. Forming a relationship with a black man was part of a larger pattern in their lives and not a random event.

The mothers' class backgrounds formed a major part of their identity. Each of these women chose a partner of a different race but the same class, even Rose, who only had a short relationship with Paul. Jenny and Lucy explicitly stated that they could not have chosen a partner from a different class. This consistency shows that in a multi-racial environment, class may be a far greater factor in choosing partners than race. In some cases class may also be as fundamental as race in identity development.

In summary, the mothers had different views about their own cultural identities and these views were brought into their respective relationships with their partners and their children. Their own identities were formed though a process which started when they were young children and developed over the years until adulthood. Cultural issues interacted with other influences such as gender, self-esteem, political beliefs and class to form their identities. As mothers of mixed-race children, part of whose culture they did not share, they faced a more complex parenting task than their own parents.

Despite the wide variation in how they saw themselves, the influences on their choice of partner, and the way they mothered their children, the mothers in this study did not represent the range of identities which mothers of mixed-race children could display.

Choice of Partner

Four points have already been made about the mothers' choice of partner:

- ° race was a factor in all their choices, but it varied in importance among other factors such as, education, culture and class
- ° their choices were to some extent a response to and determined by their family of origin
- ° they all made a decision to widen their social horizons; and
- ° the fathers' blackness was attractive to them either physically or because it represented something to them.

Thus black partners were chosen *because* they were black or their colour was irrelevant, rather than *despite* it, but that their blackness was not the only factor in their choice.

The two extremes of the continuum of attitudes in this sample were represented by Rose, who said that she could not have sexual relations with a white man, and Lucy, who said that race was not very important in her choice.

Relating this variation in the women's choices to the reasons given in Chapter 3 for inter-racial partnerships it is clear that none of the women fit neatly into any of those categories. In all cases their choices were far more complex than this simple typology allows for. This confirms that those categories do not explain the choices made by individuals, but are ideal types. Similarly all the women received parenting which would be low on Adorno's Authoritarian Scale, yet only Rose and Ruth came from households which positively viewed people from other races and cultures. Their choices are in line with Adorno's theory but one could not have used the theory to predict their choices.

There was no convincing evidence that there are any specific precipitating factors which influence women to choose black partners, nor that women who make such choices fall into definite types. This may be because:

- ° the methods employed in the study were too 'blunt' to measure the subtle influences of their early childhood
- ° the sample employed was too small to identify any patterns; or
- ° there are no such patterns because choice of partner is dependent on so many factors that no single attribute such as race is predictable.

The following sections will concentrate on what the interviews revealed about them as mothers, and about their children.

Pregnancy

The interviews did not reveal very much about the mothers' preconceptions prior to the children's birth. Most of the information obtained from Rose and Tracy about their pregnancy was given during the observations rather than the interviews, and has already been discussed. The others limited their comments to what they expected the children to look like rather than personality or identity. They revealed little about their feelings during pregnancy.

Ruth, Lucy and Jenny said that they had expected their children to be dark, to have curly black hair, and to look like the fathers rather than themselves. All the pregnancies and births were normal and there were no major traumas during this time, although Cathy's birth was very difficult.

Physical Appearance

The physical appearance of the fathers was an important factor in their being chosen as partners. How did the mothers' responses to colour translate to the children?

All the mothers were to a greater or lesser extent preoccupied by the physical appearance of their children, especially their colour. They all commented on how much lighter their children were at birth than they had expected and how they darkened later on (except Seree, who stayed very light). Several of the mothers also commented that their children's skin was not the coffee colour one would expect of a mixed-race child, but was 'honey' (Maddie) 'light' (Seree) 'oriental' (Dave). They seemed slightly surprised and delighted that their children looked as much like them as like the father.

Jenny, Lucy and Rose described their children as being exceptionally attractive. These statements seemed to indicate more than a natural tendency to see their children as beautiful and may have suggested that physical attractiveness 'made up' for a dark skin.

The preoccupation with the colour of their children tended to be greater when the children were very young, and was part of the process of integrating the new arrival into the family. Their responses may indicate that they needed to deny their children's darkness at some level, but I would not like to make too much of this because virtually every parent wants their children to look like themselves; it could be argued that if they did not want this then it would demonstrate a degree of pathology. Having said this, it is interesting that in Cathy's case it was her father who put oil on her skin and hair, accentuating her dark colour, and her mother who said that this was messy and a waste of time.

Culture and Class in the Home

All the mothers had made some effort to bring an element of the father's culture into the home. All the homes were very 'English' in their decoration and apart from a few pictures they did not have the feel of the fathers' home cultures. The home that had most evidence of 'ethnic' influences was Cathy's family. In this home Reggae music was often played, maps and pictures of Jamaica were on the wall, and black people were often in or around the flat. In this family, though, these influences all came from Norman, and Tracy made very little effort to encourage them. In all the other families the mothers made a conscious effort to bring father's culture into the house, encouraging their children to eat different foods, watch black programmes on television, and so forth.

Despite this obvious commitment, all the mothers felt distant from the father's culture. They related to the minority culture with interest and sympathy rather than feeling strong identification with the culture itself. This feeling of distance was a fundamental element in the dynamics which determined how children's identities were formed within the family.

The mothers felt to varying degrees that their own, as opposed to the father's attempts were self conscious rather than being a spontaneous part of their parenting. This in turn meant that the mothers had to make a special effort to introduce these cultural elements into the home and this was not always a very high priority. The mothers' (sometimes unconscious) ambivalence towards black culture may have also been picked up by the children, hampering their own attempts towards identification.

The fathers also had varying degrees of commitment to their cultures of origin. In some cases fathers were quite conscientious in this respect, for example, Jai, who kept close contact with his extended family. Others like Tony and George confined their activity to occasionally cooking 'ethnic' meals.

Mothers tended to hold the major responsibility in the home for matters such as diet and so forth. This area of family life is a traditional area of responsibility for mothers and in this respect the families were merely following western convention. The families also conformed to English models on the more subtle level of family structure and family dynamics. For example, the role of the father in all the families was more like that of the host culture than of their culture of origin. All the mothers felt that their partners were engaged in day-to-day child care to a much greater extent than their counterparts in their original cultures. This may have been partly because of the fathers' own socialisation into mainstream English culture, but was also a response to the mothers' expectations of a father's role. The families were all nuclear, reproducing the mothers' rather than the fathers' culture.

None of this implies that the mothers were unable to introduce black culture into the home, nor that the children were bound to reject their fathers' cultures of origin, still less that they would be unable to see themselves positively as black or mixed-race people. What it does signify is that the task of mothering black children required thought and planning.

It is illustrative to contrast how the dynamics concerning race and culture in these families differed from those of class. The importance of class in the choice of partner and in the mothers' own identities has been discussed above. Class was also crucial in the parenting of the children.

In every family the physical environment of the home reflected the educational and class background of the parents. The books, records, furniture etc were all part of the 'natural environment'. The mothers did not have to ask themselves 'How am I going to make this house into a typical middle or working class home?' – their taste and their budgets ensured that this happened.

The social environment of the children invariably reflected the class make-up of their family. Thus Cathy's parents lived on a council estate and their friends and neighbours all came from working-class backgrounds. The others said that most of their friends came from backgrounds like their own. Not *all* the social contacts in the families had the same class background, and class was not a rigid and uncrossable boundary – Tony, for example came from a working-class background, but through education had achieved a middle-class life-style.

The patterns of parenting also reflected the class of the parents in terms of the family structure, the parental roles and their attitude to child care. For both parents, rearing their children to be members of the same class as themselves was an unselfconscious process which was part of their daily existence. For the mothers, parenting children to be a different race was a deliberate process in which conscious and sometimes difficult choices had to be made.

Childrens' Identity

The mothers felt similarly about their children's racial identity. All of the mothers said that their child should have a positive mixed-race identity. All agreed that the children should be subjected to both white and black cultural influences and that they should be encouraged to mix with both white and black people. None of them considered the children to be either black or white.

Despite this consensus they had quite different ways of perceiving their children's identity and dealing with identity issues in child care.

At one extreme, Lucy saw her children as essentially 'English', but with dark skins and an interesting background. She introduced eastern culture to her children as interesting and important, but not necessarily 'owned' by them.

At the other extreme, Rose saw Dave more as a black person, on whom she had only a partial claim, than as white.

Tracy also had mixed feelings about her children's identity. She considered them to be 'half-cast', not black or white. Their home showed many African Caribbean cultural influences, and she herself had a number of black friends, yet she often teased them about their flat noses and called them 'silly black cow' and other names.

There was a clear relationship between the mothers' perceptions of their children's identity and their views about the possible effects of racism. Tracy was the only mother in the first set of interviews who believed that racism would be a daily factor in her children's lives. It is no coincidence that her family was the only one which experienced racism to any degree as part of their day-to-day existence. This family also racialised many of the marital and parent–child conflicts. However, Tracy's way of dealing with the potential of racist attacks was to tease her children with racial jibes. This was a counter-productive tactic in that Roberta began to mimic Tracy and abuse Cathy in a similar fashion. In addition, Tracy's justification for these actions may have hidden the fact that she was expressing her own racial prejudice while pretending to joke. This would be a similar process to the way she expressed other aggressive feelings. Thus, although Tracy recognised the potential for racism and took steps to help her children, the steps she took did not seem to be appropriate measures for combating its effects.

The other mothers, however showed different attitudes and tactics regarding racism. Essentially they argued:

> If I give my children a positive view of themselves by giving them the advantages of a loving home with good education, a high standard of living and a positive view of their father's culture of origin, then they will develop into stable people who will be able to resist racism. I will also bring them up in an environment where racism is less likely to occur.

None saw racism as a real threat to their children and none of them, or their partners, experienced racism as part of their everyday lives. It is difficult to evaluate the effectiveness of this strategy. The middle-class mothers, all of whom had been socialised into an environment where education, high self-esteem and achievement were paths to successful class identity, extended these beliefs into the domain of race.

In summary, the mothers all saw their children as needing to develop a positive mixed-race identity, although their views of this identity differed considerably. All of them consciously worked out strategies to ensure that their children would see themselves positively. The mothers' views of their children, and the strategies they used, were influenced by their own upbringing. The strategies fell into two main categories which seem to have been determined by class. No wider generalisations can be made from this small study, but the influence of class on racial identity should be studied further.

It is difficult to draw conclusions from the statements of the mothers about the children's responses to black and white people as these were second-hand accounts. Gender rather than race seems to have been the most important factor in the children's responses to strange adults. Yet there are some interesting issues arising from the mothers' reports.

The only mother who definitely believed that her child expressed a racial preference was Rose, who also felt insecure about Dave 'belonging' to black people rather than to herself, and who was the only mother who acknowledged race as an emotionally charged issue in her relationship with her child. The other mothers felt that their children expressed no preference.

What is really extraordinary about the difference between Dave and the others is that Dave was the only child whose father was not part of the household and who had little or no intimate contact with black people. Unless he had an innate ability to identify with black people it is difficult to see how he could have had enough contact to form strong identifications. There may be alternative explanations; either Dave was acting out subtle messages from Rose who unconsciously encouraged him to respond differently to black men (Rose acknowledged that she saw black men as less threatening than white men) or Dave did not respond differently at all, but Rose experienced him as responding differently because of her own feelings about his identity. Both these explanations take into account that the child's responses seem to be a function of the *mother's* feelings about race.

These reservations about Rose's explanations of Dave's behaviour and the fact that I never observed his responses myself, mean that it cannot be safely concluded that Dave provides a clear example of racial preference beginning in the first year.

Despite the lack of evidence it does seem plausible that pre-verbal children have some awareness of race. Jenny's description of Maddie mistaking other black men for her father clearly indicates that she had some notion of blackness, and provides much stronger evidence than the much vaguer descriptions of Dave's preferences. Roberta's remarks about Cathy, although made when Roberta was three years old, indicate that well-entrenched attitudes have emerged soon after she developed verbal skills.

It is probably safe to assume that some children do develop an awareness of racial differences at a pre-verbal (sensori-motor) stage. This development is possibly analogous to the way infants develop different responses to people of different sexes, although sex is a much more emotionally charged issue for infants. Race, especially the racialisation of emotional conflict, can also be a potent factor in family life and there is some evidence here that infants may become aware of race at an earlier stage in situations where race is a powerful conscious or unconscious factor in the family.

This conclusion would support the findings of the doll studies which found that black children became racially aware earlier than whites because race was a more salient factor in their lives (Milner, 1983; Wilson, 1987), although it would push the age of initial awareness from the fourth to the second or even the first year.

Unfortunately, interviews are not a sensitive enough research tool to get really to grips with this issue. For example, it could be argued that those infants who did not show any overt racial awareness or preferences, were relating equally to both black people and white people and developing the positive mixed-race identity that their mothers were hoping for. These issues will have to await further research in a setting outside the family.

In summary, the conclusions about the children's own sense of identity are very tentative. Nevertheless, some interesting hypotheses can be drawn:

- an embryonic sense of racial identity may begin in the first year

- racial preference may also manifest itself in the first year but may recede later when the infant learns to relate to individuals rather than classes of people; and

- the degree of racial awareness and preference is related to the emotional significance of race and the degree of racialisation within the family.

Conclusions

The interviews provided a great deal of evidence that the mothers' backgrounds had some effect on their parenting patterns. In itself this is not surprising and would be predicted by the theories discussed earlier. The interviews added substance to this finding, showing how mothers entered into the relationship with their new-born child with a host of feelings, ideas and fantasies which were generated by their responses to past experiences and their own personalities.

The interviews did not indicate any specific relationships between past experience and partner selection or mothering styles. They do not provide any basis for making predictions or generalisations about what factors in a woman's past are likely to engender particular types of parenting or racial attitudes. Rather they trace an individual pattern of development in each mother, in which early experiences, later chance events and current circumstances all played a significant role. It is interesting for example that the interviews seemed to show a closer relationship between attitudes and gross social indicators, such as class, than to more personal factors such as their relationships with their fathers.

All the mothers adapted to their children after the birth and began to relate to the 'real' rather than the 'fantasised' infant. This process depended on many factors, especially the role of the father, the marital relationship and class issues. In general it seemed that the women who saw race as a more superficial issue were able to relate more easily to the individual child rather than the child's race. On the other hand they were less able to acknowledge the possible significance of racism for their children, and were less emotionally involved in the issues surrounding race.

Each one of the mothers brought race into the interactions in her own way, and none considered herself to be racist. On the other hand they all had a degree of ambivalence about having mixed-race children. They faced difficult choices in bringing up their children, and all were aware of the potential conflicts for children of mixed parentage.

There were no correct solutions to these dilemmas. The choices were made in response to the mothers' own circumstances and their mothering style, and there was a price to pay for every choice. For example, the mothers generally felt that if they over-emphasised the threat of racism, then their children would feel vulnerable and threatened and would develop a negative view of their 'blackness'. If they did not acknowledge racism the children would have no resources to counteract the threat.

The mothers were constantly being given feedback from the infants, their partners and other black and white adults. This meant that their attitudes and behaviour were flexible rather than rigid, and were capable of shifting in response to events. Their basic attitudes and feelings were mediated by the meaning they gave to current events, so it was not possible to establish a causal link between past experiences and mother's parenting styles – the links were complex and dynamic rather than linear.

Because of the emotive nature of race, their sensitivity to racial issues was greater than to other issues concerned with their parenting. Race was a very different issue from class and gender in that our society has many role models for parenting children of particular class or gender. Black families deal with the issue of racism as part of the parenting process in the same relatively unconscious way as class and gender are dealt with in white families (Peters, 1988). Yet all of the mothers in this study (and perhaps many other white mothers of black children) had few role models of white mothers with black children. None had more than one friend or relative in the same situation as themselves. Most had not confronted the issue of racism until adulthood, and their early experiences gave them little guidance about how to bring up children of a different race. In addition, there are very few references to their situation in the media. The few references to inter-racial families are usually around trans-racial or inter-country adoption. They are often hostile and always present the situation as a problem. It is not surprising that with the lack of role models the mothers often adopted the attitude that they would take things as they came, because they had little indication of the real possibilities for them and their children. The parenting of the mothers was also perhaps more fluid and less rigid because their role was less well defined.

The uncertainty of the role of white mothers in inter-racial families highlights the question of the similarity between gender and racial identities as consequences of the mother–infant relationship. Some feminist psychoanalytic writers such as Chodorow (1978); Oakley (1981); Eichenbaum and Orbach (1983); and Boyd (1989), have considered the mother's role in passing on the accepted submissive feminine role to her daughters. According to these theorists, daughters learn how to be women by identifying with their mothers. Mothers unconsciously pass on messages to their daughters to be the same as themselves, that is to act out the nurturing, caring and submissive role expected of women in patriarchal societies. Mothers also teach their daughters to mother their own daughters like themselves.

In contrast the messages mothers give to their sons are different; to be active, assertive, and to expect to be cared for. So mothers mother their daughters for sameness and their sons for difference. The daughters' struggle to separate psychologically from their mothers is the major task in their process of maturation towards adulthood.

The crux of this argument is that early mothering experiences are a fundamentally important factor in the development of gender identity. This is a reiteration of the views expressed by Winnicott and the Object Relations theorists, but includes a new dimension, claiming that mothers affect an area of identity which is commonly held to be largely genetically determined. If mothers are able to affect their children's gender identity profoundly, are they also able to affect their racial identity? In discussing mothering for gender identity they differentiate between mothering for sameness and mothering for difference and between mothering for power and mothering for submission.

The question is whether mothers keep to this formula when mothering children of the same and different *race*, and the interaction between race and gender. This study has not provided answers to this question. Some mothers (e.g. Ruth) were as concerned that their daughter did not develop a submissive gender identity as they were that they should develop pride in their racial identity. Others were less explicit, or tacitly accepted the traditional gender differences (e.g. Jenny). This illustrates that racial identity development cannot legitimately be conceived or analysed as a separate entity. Race must be seen in the context of difference and how the issues around difference have been dealt with in these families.

Another issue regarding the role of the mother is whether early mothering determines the future course of development as the feminist psychoanalysts, along with Attachment and the Object Relations theorists believe. Others believe that mother's own parenting is mediated by later events and interpretations. Brazelton and Cramer (1991) assert that it is impossible to predict an individual's identity development because of the importance of later events and experiences on early structures and the subjectivity of meaning. Early experiences are reinterpreted later in the light of intervening events, and current events are interpreted in relation to early experience. Similarly it may be possible to construct a chain of meaning from the present to the past through such techniques as psychoanalysis, but the past will always be interpreted in the light of the present.

This discussion points to some of the methodological and conceptual gaps which informed the original hypothesising for the thesis, and determined the methodology used. The original theory posited a movement from primary to secondary socialisation which depended on the infant's relationship with her mother. This in turn was seen as determined by mother's early experiences. Thus the model was basically cumulative in nature, and depended on a series of cause–effect relationships. Neither the observations nor the interviews were able to uncover these set relationships, nor could they point to any real generalisations which could lead to a general theory of racial identity development in mixed-race children. Perhaps this is because there are no general rules, and, as post-modern theory states, identity and its development are contingent and contextual, rather than essential characteristics of individuals.

Another problem is that the fathers' perspectives are lacking from these accounts. The focus on the mother–infant relationship was aimed at establishing linear connections between past events, mothering and identity, albeit that these relationships were mediated by mothers' subjective interpretations. But fathers themselves may have interpretations, which may influence mothers'. It seems clear that the analytical gap here is to examine how families make sense of issues around sameness and difference, and how the parents' responses to these issues affect their children's concepts of themselves.

CHAPTER NINE

Second Set of Interviews

Introduction

The second set of interviews were intended to gather more material and to address some of the theoretical and methodological problems raised in the previous fieldwork. This entailed the use of a new method which considerably changed the nature of the interviews.

This phase involved interviewing the parents in nine inter-racial families. It must be remembered that these interviews were the only part of the study which were carried out with the explicit intention of testing out post-modern theory, and that the first two phases took place before this theory was available to me.

The Biographical Approach

The interviews conducted during this third part of the study differed in several respects from the interviews which constituted the second phase of the study. In the second phase a semi-structured interview approach was taken, in which the interview questions were based on the theoretical underpinning of the thesis. This phase adopted a 'life history' or 'biographical' approach.

The life history approach is not a rigid method for gathering information from subjects. Rather it is a constellation of methods aimed at obtaining a narrative or life story from the subject (Bertaux, 1981). Some life histories focus on one individual and try to obtain very detailed accounts of that person's life. Others involve more limited accounts from larger numbers of people (Bertaux, 1981; Denzin, 1983; Plummer, 1983).

The purpose for obtaining narratives of people's lives is to make sense of the ways in which people view themselves in relation to their culture or society. It can be seen as allied with the infant observation techniques used in the first part of the study because it is based on subjectivity. Another similarity is that the information is gathered in as unstructured and a-theoretical a way possible, but is then subjected to rigorous scrutiny to identify patterns and themes, both those consciously recognised by the interviewees and also less conscious ones.

These methods aim to obtain an account which is closest to the subjects' own views of the world rather than fit their accounts into a pre-existing theoretical stance. In this study the method used was the unstructured interview in which the interviewer prompted and probed but did not use predetermined questions. The pace, style and content of the interview were determined as far as possible by the subjects.

People's accounts of their lives are not seen as the 'true story'. Each account is provided by a person talking about past and present 'selves' to another person at a particular point in their life and in a particular context. All these factors are very important in understanding and analysing the story.

It is particularly important to note that the life history approach views the account or narrative as being separate from the narrator. The autobiography is seen as a 'text' which is open to study and interpretation by others as well as the narrator. Thus the narrative is seen as *an* account of the individual's life rather than the objective account. The narrative also serves a function for the narrator, that is, to make sense of his or her life. This approach assumes that life is contradictory, discontinuous, conflictual and problematic. Narrative provides continuity, justification, explanation and legitimation. In the process of narration the narrator is making a 'text' of his or her life. In this formulation it is not only the individual's life that makes the text. In many ways the text also makes the life:

> We assume that life produces the autobiography as an act produces its consequences, but can we not suggest, with equal justice, that the autobiographical project may itself produce and determine the life, and that whatever the writer does is in fact governed by the technical demand of self-portraiture and thus determined, in all its aspects, by the resources of its medium. (de Man, 1984, p.69)

Narratives can be compared between narrators either by comparing the *content*, the *structure* or the *function* of the story. For example in this study many of the respondents discussed what happened to them when they first arrived in England. One could consider the content of the story; that is, how they came to the country, why they came, what happened after they arrived and how they felt about it. It is also possible to look at the structure of the narrative; was it a long or short story, was it told in a continuous way or in 'bits and pieces', were there things left out, or irrelevant things put in and how did the story relate to other stories which the person told, for example about their childhood. Finally the function of the story can be considered in terms of:

° Why is this person telling me this at this time?

° Who is the audience for the story?

° What purpose does this story serve in building up a picture of the person? etc.

   ◦ What are the social, personal and cultural contexts in which the story is being told? (see Denzin, 1989)

The biographical approach is not confined only to analysing stories which people tell. This approach can use a further level of analysis; the 'meta-narrative'. The meta-narrative refers to the way the individual 'totalises' his or her life story so that it makes sense as a coherent whole. The meta narrative also 'legitimates' the narrative by justifying how and why he or she has that particular story. Meta-narratives can apply to individual life stories or to his-stories of nations, cultures or societies. In all cases they:

> ...are second order narratives which seek to narratively articulate and legitimate some concrete first order practices or narratives. Typically a grand (i.e. meta-) narrative will make reference to some ultimate telos; it will seek to place existing practices in a position of progress towards or regress from the originating principle or ultimate end. (Bernstein, 1991, p.102)

According to Plummer (1983), stories are always given a teleological colouring by the narrator. The researcher's task is to try to look for acknowledged and unacknowledged continuities and patterns, and to try to uncover the underlying discontinuities and conflicts which the narrative addresses.

Another dimension of narrative study is the interview itself. The subject remembers events, feelings, people, opinions, scenes and so forth which are strung together as a narrative. In the interview the researcher is presented with fragments of these fragments and, like the subject, must make sense out of them. The book itself presents fragments of the fragment of the fragment. Each time the story is told it is mediated by the narrator and adapted to the audience.

Mishler (1986) points out that mainstream social science attempts to standardise interview techniques and so undermines the narrative nature of interviews with the consequent loss of richness and depth of data. He proposes a form of narrative interview similar to Bertaux and Denzin and further proposes that the interview itself can be seen as a story with narrative qualities. Mishler's account of a narrative method of interviewing claims that this method allows people to speak in 'their own voice' and is also a method for empowering the respondent and breaking down the traditional hierarchy between the research interview and the subject. Thus there are ethical as well as methodological advantages in the biographical approach.

In this study I was not only concerned with individual narratives of parents. It was also important to obtain a view of the family narrative, with questions such as:

   ◦ How much do the partners share the narrative?

   ◦ How different are the two narratives from each other?

- ° How do narratives reflect the power relationships within the family, and between the family and the wider community?

- ° What stories do the parents tell about the identity development of their children?

- ° What differences are there in the narratives of different types of respondents? Are there typical male stories, female stories, black stories, white stories etc?

In the light of the methodological concerns mentioned above, the interviews were adapted for this phase of the research:

The interviews were extended to include both mothers and fathers

In the original study, interviews were confined to mothers because of the psychoanalytic theory base which maintained that the infant's primary attachment is with the mother and therefore the mother is the primary determinant of socialisation and identity development in early years. However, from the mothers' accounts it was clear that the fathers, even those who were not present in the household, were important in the children's development and in the mother's perception of herself as a parent and a woman.

The second reason for not interviewing fathers had been my reluctance to research black people because of the hostility of some social work academics (e.g. Small 1986) towards white people researching black people. However, the result of this was to deny them a voice with respect to their children's identity and also meant that I could only comment on their perspective at third hand.

The interviews did not follow any predetermined pattern

No interview schedule was used, but some prompts were provided to begin the discussion. Typically the interview would start off with a question such as 'How does being a parent remind you of how you were parented?'. This then led to discussion of their own childhoods and began their account of their life story. The interviews reviewed the lives of both parents and then went on to talk about their lives together, their children and how they saw the future. As far as possible they were encouraged to tell stories about various phases of their lives or things that happened to them.

At the end of the interview I asked for feedback from the parents about how they felt, and also whether they had any questions for me. The interviews lasted between three to six hours. They were normally held in two sessions of two to three hours. Where I was interviewing only one parent the interviews were shorter, lasting about three hours. After one difficult interview in which children were present, I tried to arrange the times of the interviews so that children would not be present.

The Sample

The nine families discussed here were all located by personal contacts. The parents knew the broad outline of the research before I visited, but none had any real idea of the study. The interviews were conducted in 1993.

The full sample for this study is therefore fourteen families. These families were selected because of their willingness to participate in the research. They are not a representative sample of inter-racial families in London today. Nevertheless, they represent a wide range of cultures and backgrounds and it is their diversity rather than their homogeneity which is striking. It is unclear what a representative sample of inter-racial families would consist of. No statistics exist as to the racial make-up of inter-racial families, nor is it apparent what the class, cultural or ethnic makeup of a representative sample would be. Within this sample there are obvious gaps, mainly in the under-representation of white fathers and black mothers. In addition, none of the black parents interviewed was born in Britain and three of the white parents are also not British. This may have been pure chance or may represent a genuine factor in the population of inter-racial families as a whole.

Presentation of Data

In the previous phase accounts of each interview were provided (see Chapter 7). However, in this phase I will summarise the information obtained about each family and briefly describe the interview. The bulk of this section will be devoted to drawing out themes from individual narratives and drawing comparisons with other narratives.

Because of the volume of material it is obviously very difficult to choose the most important themes. Even when 'irrelevant' material is excluded, there is an almost inexhaustible amount which could be analysed in various different ways. Inevitably, therefore, the choice of material is determined by my own interests and concerns (see Denzin (1989) on this point).

The Families

The F Family

Mother:	Linda, 38
Father:	Ezekiel, 36
Children:	Angela, 3 years 6 months, Max, 18 months

MOTHER'S STORY

Linda was born to a secular Jewish family in North London, and has lived virtually all her life in the same area. Her childhood was relatively happy and she was close to her whole family, especially her father. She was brought up in a fair degree of physical comfort and did reasonably well at school. As an adolescent she was quiet and retiring and not very gregarious. She began having relationships with boys at 16 years old. After studying she went on a long overseas trip with a friend and this was a watershed in her life. She began to take risks in relationships with other people and became much more assertive and outgoing.

Linda met Ezekiel when she was working in a summer job at London Zoo and he was working there as well. She had some relationships, but no long term relationships previously. Linda had always known that she would not marry a Jewish man. She was immediately attracted to Ezekiel and pursued him. Their relationship was initially quite difficult but after an overseas trip she came back and decided that she would settle down with him. She worked as a social worker and since having the children has returned to work part-time. She is still in very close contact with her own family whom she sees daily.

FATHER'S STORY

Ezekiel comes from a large, reasonably well-off family in Ghana. He is the youngest child of his father's senior wife (His father had four wives and he has nine half siblings). Although Ezekiel was indulged by his parents and had a good relationship with both of them, he did not feel very close to his siblings and there was some rivalry between them.

Ezekiel was a natural leader at school and did reasonably well academically. After school he went into banking in Accra and stayed with a relative of the family. Later he decided to come to London to study banking. At first Ezekiel found London very difficult to manage. He was lonely and had few friends. He stayed with relatives but he only had two cousins in London. He later gave up banking and obtained a well-paid job in industry. Despite some racism at work he was promoted to a senior post. However, he had a serious injury at work and was off sick for several months, and later he was made redundant. He is now trying to set up a business. If it succeeds the family will move to Ghana.

The G Family

Mother:	Joan, 36
Father:	Hari, 35
Children:	Ravinder, four years 6 months, Jabeer 18 months

MOTHER' STORY

Joan was born to a lower middle class family in a small town in the north of England. The family were very well established in the town. Joan was an only child until she was ten when her sister was born. Although she had a reasonably happy childhood she describes her mother as rather cold and distant and she was closer to her father. At age 17 Joan began to become politically aware and started taking part in political activity such as CND and so forth. This distanced her from her family and she felt very restricted by life in the town. As soon as she obtained her A Levels Joan went to live in Rome for a time. This period was very important for her development. She became independent, assertive, and more able to relate to people from different cultures and backgrounds. She returned to England and studied psychology, later becoming a psychotherapist. Joan had several boyfriends and was involved in a long term relationship before she decided to split up with her partner and have a relationship with Hari.

FATHER'S STORY

Hari was born into a Sikh family in India. His childhood was generally happy and he was very close to his mother. At age ten Hari came to England with his mother and sister. His father had preceded them. They moved to a small town where his father had acquired a job. Hari was the only child in his school who was not white. He had a difficult time as a teenager, suffering racist abuse at school and also having conflicts in the home because he wanted to become 'westernised' and this was strongly resisted by his parents. When he was 18 Hari's mother was killed in a motor accident and a year later he left home. His relationship with his family was very poor and he saw very little of them. He became an academic. He is involved in anti racist work.

Both sets of parents were resistant to their relationship. Since having the children both Hari and Joan have become closer to their own families but this has been and continues to be a difficult process.

The H Family

Mother:	Theresa, 33
Father:	Sanjay, 37
Children:	Matthew Suchdev, 6, Carly Amrit three years 6 months, Mia Sunita 11 months.

MOTHER'S STORY

Theresa comes from a working class family in a small village in the North of England. She is the eldest of four children and the only girl. The family are strict Catholics. Theresa's mother was the dominant person in the family and the family generally were very close when she was a child. Theresa left home after obtaining A Levels, feeling that life in the village was very restrictive. She went travelling and worked in Wales for a time. She then went to university to study social science. Theresa found leaving home very liberating and she began to make friends with people from very different backgrounds. She met Sanjay at university. They were friends for some time and then became closer and closer. Both her and Sanjay's parents were very opposed to the relationship and when they got married it was in secret without either of the parents being present. They moved to London because Sanjay couldn't find a job in the north. Theresa is now employed as a social worker working with under eights.

FATHER'S STORY

Sanjay comes from a half Punjabi, half Hindu family. His father was a self-made man who made and then lost a great deal of money. Sanjay has two sisters and a brother and he is the oldest son. His childhood was quite happy and he was part of a fairly large extended family. Sanjay came to England at 21 to study engineering, intending to return to India and get married in a traditional arranged marriage. In Britain, however, his ideas began to change, and he began socialising with people from different cultures. After he met Theresa they both resisted developing their relationship but then realised their love for each other was too strong and they decided to marry. His family were originally very hostile but later became more accepting of the situation. Sanjay got a job as a computer programmer but has recently taken voluntary redundancy and is now working as a freelance programmer. The family live in a very Asian area and most of their immediate neighbours are Asian. The children also have a number of Asian friends, although they attend the local Catholic school where most of the pupils are white. They eat a mixture of English and Indian food and the children attend church and occasionally Hindu temples. Sanjay has a sister living in east London and the children are close to their cousins.

The I Family

Mother:	Michelle, 39
Father:	Salman, 36
Children:	Farida 7, Abel 5, Phillip 1

MOTHER'S STORY

Michelle comes from a farming family in Australia. The family was a happy normal family and she has very fond memories of her life on the farm. She was always a shy, intellectual person who did not enjoy parties but preferred her studies and did well at school. After school Michelle travelled for some time and came to England to work as many young Australian people do. She worked in a dentist's office where she met Salman. She had not had any long term relationships before and she and Salman became more and more friendly. Since they have been married Michelle has become more involved with Salman's culture and has now converted to Islam. There was no adverse response from her family to the relationship and she still keeps closely in touch with her family and visits Australia every two years.

FATHER'S STORY

Salman comes from a Moslem Asian family. He came to the United Kingdom when he was three and has no memories of life in South Africa. He has never returned there. Salman had a happy family life and his mother is an outgoing and gregarious person. For most of his life he has lived in the same area of west London. At school Salman was the only child who was not English but he never experienced racism and had a wide range of friends. He was very sports orientated, and played for the school cricket team. As a teenager Salman noticed the area becoming more multi-racial and white people being racist to other children but he himself did not experience this. Salman's family were liberal Moslems, and although they never drank alcohol or ate non-halal meat they were not very religious. Salman became a nurse and has continued to work in that profession.

CURRENT SITUATION

The family live in the same part of London where Salman grew up. His mother lives nearby and they have a lot of contact with her and his siblings. The area is now more multi-racial and the children have friends from different cultures. The family observes Moslem custom and the children go to Islamic school at the weekend. However they are not regular mosque attenders, and other than in their religion the family have an English middle class life-style.

The J Family

Mother:	Agneta, 32
Father:	Tom, 38 (Not living with Agneta)
Child:	Otis, 3

MOTHER'S STORY

Agneta was born in Norway, the youngest of three children. She had a difficult childhood and her parents split up when she was a child. She lived with her mother who remarried and then divorced again after having another daughter when Agneta was a teenager. At age 15 Agneta's father died in an accident. She had been very close to him and was very traumatised by this event. Agneta was always a shy girl and her father's death caused a great deal of difficulty for her at school and for her health. Her relationship with her mother deteriorated and she eventually moved out of home while still at school. Later Agneta studied Law but dropped out because of her health. She managed a flower shop which she inherited from her father and then travelled to Spain where she had a relationship with an older man. She then came to England and worked first as a singer and then as a waitress. She was briefly married to a musician but this lasted only a year. She then met Tom at work. They had a short courtship and then lived together for some time before Otis was born. After the birth Tom left home but still has regular contact with her and Otis whom he sees several times a week when he is in town. Tom wants to marry Agneta and settle down, but she feels that this isn't realistic at present.

FATHER'S STORY

Tom was born in Manchester of a Welsh mother and an African American father. He was adopted as a baby into a white family and grew up in a white area. Most of his friends are white, but he has some interest in black culture, especially soul music. Tom works as a martial arts instructor. His relationship with Agneta deteriorated after Otis' birth because he was away so often but also because there were personal difficulties, and he moved out. He was not interviewed for this study.

CURRENT SITUATION

Agneta now lives in a rented flat with Otis. She is not currently working. The area they live in is multi-racial and she has friends from different cultures and is establishing a network of Scandinavian people. She has some contact with her own family but does not feel particularly close to any of them.

The K Family

Mother:	Flo, 33, Artist
Father:	Derek, 36, Artist
Children:	Peter and Ben (twins), 3

MOTHER'S STORY

Flo was born in England but spent a lot of her childhood in the Middle East, returning to England as an adolescent. As a teenager she was quite rebellious but achieved well at school. She then went to art school where she met Derek who was also an art student. Derek obtained a scholarship and they lived in America for several years before returning to Britain. Since having the twins Flo now works part-time as an artist and Derek works as an artist and art lecturer.

FATHER'S STORY

Derek was born in Jamaica and came to England at age seven. His mother died when he was young and he grew up in Liverpool. He was a good artist and went to art school in London. He continues to have contact with his father and brother but this is sporadic as they live in Liverpool and his relationship with his father is not very good. Derek is involved in anti-racist politics. He was not interviewed as part of this study because he was unavailable when the interview took place.

CURRENT SITUATION

The family in their own house in a multi-racial part of north London. They have a wide range of friends including other inter-racial families, and within the family there are African Caribbean and English cultural influences.

They have contact with both extended families but much more so with Flo's family. The boys are aware of their colour and have discussed it with Flo.

The L Family

Mother:	Shirley, 30
Father:	Dick, 50
Children:	Angie, 5 and Josie, 18 months

MOTHER'S STORY

Shirley was born in Guyana. When she was a young child her father came to the United Kingdom leaving her mother with the children. Later when Shirley was six her mother followed leaving her sister and brother with her grandmother and aunt. Shirley was very close to her siblings but distant from her parents. Shirley later joined her parents in England but her father then got a job in West Africa and the children went to boarding school. Although she was the only black child in the school she was outgoing and generally happy but did feel different, and she encountered some racism. She went to university and studied languages then changed to psychology and went on to become a psychotherapist.

Shirley originally met Dick when she was an undergraduate and they became very friendly. However, she married someone else, but because her husband refused to have children the marriage broke up. She went back to Dick with whom she had continued to retain contact. Her husband was very bitter and caused problems for her, and her parents were at first ambivalent but later supportive of the relationship.

FATHER'S STORY

Dick was born in a small city in the USA. He is the only child from a 'patrician southern family'. He described his mother as a difficult, neurotic and manipulative person and his father was more easy-going. Dick did very well at school and obtained a scholarship to go to Harvard where he studied philosophy. He found it very liberating to be away from his restrictive family situation. He married very young and came to England to pursue his studies. Dick had two girls by his first marriage. After his marriage broke up he became involved with Shirley, and later he had a long-term relationship with another woman which lasted several years. Eventually that relationship broke up when he decided that his relationship with Shirley was the more important.

Dick's parents, especially his mother, had a very adverse response to their relationship including being hospitalised and disinheriting him.

CURRENT SITUATION

Their relationship has now improved to some extent, but there is still difficulty between Dick's parents and Shirley. His parents adore the children but there is still a racial edge to their relationship. Shirley's parents still live in Africa but visit from time to time. They too were also slightly resistant to the relationship but get on very well with both the children and with Dick.

The family live in a predominantly white area of north London. Angie attends a school where most of the children are white. Shirley and Dick are a gregarious couple who have a large number of friends, mostly white.

The M Family

Mother:	Harriet, 32
Father:	Pargat, 37
Children:	Shanti, 6 and Nusrat, 3

MOTHER'S STORY

Harriet came from a lower middle class family in the West Midlands. She is the younger of two girls and had, what she referred to as a very conventional upbringing. Her mother was a teacher and rather strict. Her father was less strict but the family was not very close and she did not confide in other members. After leaving school Harriet went to university. She became involved, first, with volunteer work and then more politically in anti-racist work. It was at university that she met Pargat, who was also involved. Although their relationship was intense Pargat returned to his home country and Harriet eventually followed for a holiday. Later Pargat came back and they were married. They lived abroad for three years where Shanti was born and then returned to London. Harriet worked as a probation officer but has now given this up and is working for Pargat's company writing reports on foreign countries.

FATHER'S STORY

Pargat was born to a Punjabi family in Malaysia. The family was quite religious and traditional, and he had a fairly large extended family. Pargat went to school originally in Malaysia and then in India. He intended to study medicine in India but then came to England to study, intending to return to Malaysia. When he came here he began to be involved in politics, never having being 'political' before. He became particularly involved in anti-racist politics. After he finished his under-graduate degree he returned to Malaysia. He had already started his relationship with Harriet but made the decision to return home. Harriet followed 'as his friend' but then returned to England. Subsequently Pargat also came back and they were married. When he completed his MBA they eventually moved to London where Pargat was offered a job in housing. Later they left England and lived in Malaysia for some time but found it difficult to get on with the extended family. They then moved to Hong Kong before returning to London. Pargat's family were very opposed to the relationship at first and put enormous pressure on him to marry another Punjabi. However they have now come to terms with the situation and relationships are better. Anne's family were also resistant, but again relationships have now been restored to a certain extent. Pargat now has a senior position in a multi-national company and spends a lot of time travelling around the world.

CURRENT SITUATION

The family live in a multi-racial part of east London. They are both still actively involved in anti-racist politics and are very involved with the local community. The children's friends are mainly Asian, but they have a wide range of contacts. Shanti did attend a state school but the education was considered to be very poor and she is now in a Church of England School which has a large number of Asian pupils. The family are considering moving to Malaysia at some point in the future.

The N Family

Mother:	Sally 28
Father:	Victor 29
Child:	Nora 9 months.

MOTHER'S STORY

Sally was born and brought up in Accra in Ghana. She has one younger sister and two half-sisters and a brother. When she was young Sally's mother and father split up. Her mother was from a poor family but her father from one which was well-off. Sally stayed with her father who then had three other wives in turn who looked after her as step mothers. She had very little contact with her mother until she was a teenager and even then her contact has been sporadic. Sally attended boarding school for both primary and high school education eventually obtaining her GCE 'O' Levels. She intended to study to become a bi-lingual secretary and after leaving school and spending two years in Ghana she came to England to further her studies. She qualified as a secretary and has worked in London every since. She had one long term relationship with a Ghanaian man but soon after this broke up she met Victor. After a year she became pregnant and just before Nora was born Victor moved in and they are now living together.

FATHER'S STORY

Victor was born and brought up in north London. He was the youngest of three children. His family life was fairly happy although he described his mother as a difficult person and he was much closer to his father who shares his interest in sport. After obtaining his 'A' Levels, Victor worked in various jobs in the civil service and spent some time in America. He eventually returned and began working for social services and he continues to work as a residential social worker. Sally is Victor's first long-term relationship but he has always been attracted to black women. Sally and he met through a friend of a friend. Victor's mother initially disapproved of his liking of black women but apart from some 'digs' has not shown a lot of resistance to the current relationship. Sally's family were not resistant to the relationship at all.

CURRENT SITUATION

The family currently live in a small flat in west London and intend to move soon. Sally maintains contact with a large number of Ghanaians as well as other people. Victor's friends are mainly white.

Summary

These short sketches, which are inevitably selective, show the diversity of family types and structures from which the parents originated and the different situations in which they now find themselves. They all live in more or less cosmopolitan areas of London and all maintain a fairly wide range of social and professional contacts. In the next section I will draw out some themes from some of the stories to examine, in more detail, the issues confronting individuals involved in inter-racial families. Subsequently I will sketch out in more detail some aspects of the accounts which were provided in the interviews in order to consider the similarities and differences of identity and family life within the families. In some instances I will look in more detail at the accounts themselves to see what can be learnt from them.

The F Family

A notable factor in this interview was that for the first three quarters of an hour, I spoke to Linda alone. During this time she talked about her own background, and mentioned issues such as her own sexual experiences and some of the difficult feelings she had about her relationship with Ezekiel:

LINDA: I remember having a boyfriend who went to school with my brother.

IK: Right

LINDA: Not anything in particular or specific event except he used to like put me on a pedestal and I felt really uncomfortable about it, so I was really nervous about boys.

IK: Do you remember anything...

LINDA: ...well it was like...

IK: about what you did together?

LINDA: He lived in Birmingham and he was down in London and we went to a party and I just like got up and left I think and left him there. I remember doing that to him. I treated him really badly. I think I was dead scared about getting into some clinch with him. I don't know how old I must have been, 14 to 15 I think.

          ...

IK: OK, if you bring it then further, I mean you've talked about sort of 15 to 16 to after school. Is there anything around that time which you think was important to you.

LINDA: After, I suppose my first, after school, when I left school my first sexual experience, that sort of thing, I remember, I remember that I think. I remembered something like, I had this boyfriend, I must have been about 19 or something and then we both got into bed and I kept all my clothes on. Things like that I remember, sort of with my jumper on and feeling like really really hot. I remember that sort of thing.

IK: Were there things about that you remember, was there a particular event or something that actually happened that was important for you as a person?

LINDA: Well, I think, you know, my first, when I first had sex with him, when I first had intercourse, I mean that was quite significant. I remember thinking, feeling quite different, because I think I was really very scared of having any sexual relationship then, so yeh that was quite something.

IK: Do you remember that sort of quite vividly still?

LINDA: I think, I think just how I felt afterwards, because I think he was at university and I think I was travelling home and I actually felt as if I looked quite different. I remember feeling that...I don't remember the actual happening actually.

IK: In what ways did you feel different?

LINDA: I think in terms of having been through an...you know, its like, how did I feel different, I think maybe feeling grown up more, sort of more mature and knowing I had this knowledge now or I'd had this experience so I knew more than other people. I think maybe I felt a bit more confident, I think it must have been a really big thing for me, that it actually happened. I felt much more relaxed.

I wonder whether these issues would have been disclosed in the same way if Ezekiel had been present? Certainly when he came it took some time for the interview to return to the personal and intense level which it had developed during this first period.

One notable issue in this interview was that the stories Linda told about herself contained two fairly consistent themes; power and transition. For example, the story Linda told when I asked her to talk about an experience in her childhood, was an account of leaving her brother at boarding school and returning home and feeling sorry. The story she told about being an adolescent was about having her first boyfriend, and then ending the relationship. He was very upset by this and she felt guilty but free. The third story was about a trip to the Far East when she was a young adult. Linda described how for the first time she spontaneously went up to a stranger and started chatting to him and then ending the relationship without having any sexual experience.

The themes of these three stories were complex but seemed to relate to Linda feeling increasingly powerful in relation to men, exercising that power and (in the first two cases) feeling guilty about this. In the third case she did not feel guilty but prevented the relationship from reaching a point where ending it would have any consequences.

Linda described herself as being very shy and lacking in confidence as a child and as an adolescent, but gaining confidence as an adult. She now sees herself as quite gregarious and outgoing in contrast to her childhood. The trip overseas which she described was the watershed in her life and seems to have engendered a major shift in the way she viewed herself and her relationship with others. It was seen by her as a moment of 'transition' in which she saw herself as powerful and in control. It also enabled her to engage with difference, especially people from other backgrounds and cultures. It was this 'new' Linda who met Ezekiel when they were working together on a temporary basis. Linda took the initiative in arranging a meeting and it was she who initiated the relationship. Later she felt ambivalent about it and went on an overseas trip. When she returned Ezekiel took the initiative and they then decided to live together and get married. Within their relationship Linda also sees herself as being the dominant partner in the sense that she makes most decisions about their lives and the children and so on. At the moment Ezekiel is unemployed and she is working part-time but she still takes the major responsibility for the children and arranges for their day care and so forth.

Ezekiel's stories show a complete contrast to Linda's. Although he describes himself as fairly quiet as a child, he saw himself as a 'leader' and his stories about childhood referred to him leading other children to do things at home and at school. Ezekiel talked very happily about his own childhood and showed none of Linda's insecurity. For Ezekiel the watershed came when he arrived in Britain. He found London very cold and uninviting and at first struggled to survive here. He had come to further his studies in banking but decided to change course when he arrived and eventually became a printer. This was a lucrative job and he did well, being promoted despite experiencing racism at work. However, he was severely injured and then made redundant when the company restructured. He is now attempting to change course again and become a businessman. Thus, for Ezekiel, a smooth and relatively easy lifestyle was interrupted by coming to England and his career, which had been very promising, was (it is to be hoped temporarily) in a state of hiatus when he was interviewed.

After meeting and marrying Linda, Ezekiel broke off most of his ties with other Ghanaians in London and has become isolated from his own 'roots'. An important issue for this couple was the way that difference and sameness were managed in the relationship. For example Linda first found Ezekiel attractive because he was so different from the English men that she know. She told me that she always knew that she would never marry a Jewish man and that what she immediately liked about Ezekiel was his unselfconsciousness and easy-going attitude towards life. However, aspects of this attitude became frustrating for her. The couple talked about the Ghanaian trait of being very casual about arrangements, a particular example being that Ezekiel's cousin came very late to their wedding and disrupted proceedings. Several such examples were given by both of them to illustrate the difference in the way Ghanaians view punctuality.

Linda's attitude during the recounting of these stories was one of resignation mixed with anger, while Ezekiel was in turn amused and defensive. Linda now finds Ezekiel's lack of introspection and his fatalistic attitude towards his life difficult to cope with at times and she sometimes resents having to take all the responsibility for the children and the home.

It was Linda who pointed out to me that Ezekiel's career had been affected by racism. He himself insisted that racism had never bothered him and downplayed the significance of the racism at work. From his point of view the difficulties are purely cultural and have nothing to do with colour or race at all. On the other hand Ezekiel was concerned about racism in the media. He talked about having to protect the children from seeing black people either as victims or criminals on television and also looking for positive images of Ghana for them. Thus, although he did not acknowledge the effect of racism on him personally he was concerned about the effects on the children.

Linda was concerned about her own racism. She described to me her responses now that the family are under a great deal of stress and how she often shouts at the children and at Ezekiel.

LINDA: Yeh, I think so. I suppose, there's also, I'm trying to think, there are things, I mean I roar at him, I really shriek, I didn't used to, I think with my kids around I do. I'm much more uptight. And I sometimes, you know, I get concerned, God, would I shout at somebody English. He tends to let it bounce off him and sometimes God I don't know. If it was somebody else would he let me roar, you know, like I do it?... I don't know what I've done to him that sort of thing I think and the other thing is that he is very much at home with us, he spends a lot of time at home, he's actually had an accident to his hand which has made it, that is a different dynamic to the whole thing and so I felt gosh he's dependent on this family, particularly me, and here I am treating him like he has to jump up when I, God you know. Why don't I just let him relax. So those, and that is, I think, that is sometimes a cultural issue I think.

IK: In what way do you think that particular, let's take that particular example...

LINDA: Well it's really difficult I sort of sometimes think well is he subservient? I don't think he is or do I assert myself because I'm a white person, treat him like shit, because he is black, you know, that often goes through my head and is it just, or I would be like this with anybody. Maybe I would, I don't know.

Linda had not previously shared these feelings with Ezekiel and later in the interview when she talked about it, he completely denied any racial element in the relationship. He said that Linda was shouting because she was under so much stress, and that he just accepted that this was the way she is. He sometimes feels angry towards her but has never attributed either his or her feelings to a difference in race.

The interesting thing about this account of conflict within the relationship is that the themes, that is, Linda being powerful over another man and feeling guilty about it, are similar to the stories she told about herself as a child and adolescent. They show her feelings of power and ambivalence towards men. However, in those cases the account was not racialised in the way it had been with Ezekiel. In addition, from my own experience of other Jewish women, her behaviour and feelings are similar to other Jewish women who are married to both Jewish and non-Jewish men. Thus the question emerges whether Linda's choice of stories for me was unconsciously coloured by her current relationships and experiences. This may have also been, in part, her response to the interview situation, in which she was telling her story to a white Jewish (but not English) man. In some ways I represented the type of man she had explicitly rejected as a potential partner, but who, in fantasy she saw as possessing the strength to respond to her anger.

Linda's ambivalence may lead to the enacting of a pattern with Ezekiel which is part of her life from an early age. However, in this case she is attributing her actions to a racial difference when, in fact, it is something about herself. The point about this account is that it is very difficult to extricate what are issues of personal identity and ways of being in the world for Linda and Ezekiel, what are 'cultural influences' on their relationship, and where race or racism enter into it. Is Ezekiel denying race as a way of coping with painful relationships, or as a way of maintaining his male power? Is Linda using her guilt about racism as a way of avoiding personal responsibility for her actions or is her guilt preventing her from asserting her power as a woman?

This dynamic can also be seen as a gender rather than a race issue. Linda has been forced to take the initiative in many areas of family life which are outside her conventional role as a mother. Ezekiel, despite being unemployed has not taken responsibility for the children and other domestic activities. Linda's anger, and her guilt about expressing it may have been in response to this situation, which she sees partly as a clash of cultures rather than a gender issue.

I do not believe that any of these questions can be answered directly and some of the themes mentioned above will re-emerge in the accounts of other families. This family intends to go to live in Ghana. If they do it will be interesting to see how the relationships and dynamics change and how the couple reconstruct their own life histories in the light of their experiences.

Interestingly, Ezekiel found Linda's extended family very congenial. It provided an experience which was familiar to him and he felt very comfortable in that sort of family situation. Linda's family has become almost a substitute for his own.

> EZEKIEL: And that has actually, I think that side has made, I think, made our marriage quite easy for me, because you see your family quite a lot, and if I were not to be used to that sort of family life, I think I would have found it difficult. I think if you were to marry an English man, I think now, well, it [your family] would be a sticking point you know.

The current life-style of the family is completely 'British' in the sense that their family structure is basically nuclear, the food they eat and so forth, and all other cultural influences are British. Ezekiel has made very little attempt to bring Ghanaian influences into the home but they do have some pictures, and occasionally relatives bring Ghanaian food.

Ezekiel said, however, that families in Ghana itself are also changing. His contemporaries also have less contact with their own families and certainly do not practice polygamy. His experience of a polygamous situation was not very positive and although he and his full siblings got on well, his half-siblings were viewed with hostility. Ezekiel is now the head of the family and has some contact with them through letters in which they ask his advice. When he returns to Ghana he will have to take on this role more actively. There was a hint in Ezekiel's account of a big difference between his 'Ghanaian self' which is active, responsible and so forth, and his 'English self' which is passive, fatalistic and accepting.

The G Family

I have chosen this family to study in some detail because they provide another example of personal and racial conflict which emerged in a very different way from Linda and Ezekiel. They also provide another interesting insight in how the story of the interview itself becomes part of the process.

This interview with Joan and Hari was one which was done over two sessions, two weeks apart. The nature of the discussion was radically different in the two interviews.

In the first interview I was presented with a picture of a couple who were actively exploring the ideas of sameness and difference in a warm and tolerant facilitating environment which was being menaced continually by outside racist forces which threatened to disrupt it. I was struck by the fact that, although, Hari and Joan come from very different backgrounds, there were parallels in their life stories which provided them with a sense of symmetry and sharing. Hari said of Joan:

> In many ways she's like my mum. She's very warm and she loves Jabeer the way mum loved me.

Joan however saw her relationship with her daughter as a contrast to her own mothering:

> My mum doesn't express her feelings at all easily, and can't cope with loss, and just gets on edge when there's any depth of emotion. I remember when Ravinder asked about some disaster on the news she was given the brush off.

HARI: She told her not to bother.

JOAN: Yes, but in an offhand way that made Ravinder feel she was angry.

> I can remember the disaster at Aberfan, and being upset about the news, and not being given any space to talk about it.

HARI: It was the archetypal 'Mummy do you love me?' 'Yes I do'. 'Don't I buy you nice dresses sort of thing.'

This was contrasted to Joan's relationship with Ravinder, which was seen as very open and expressive. Both Joan and Hari described their families as avoiding emotion:

JOAN: They were typical of a kind of Northern English 'get on with it, don't think about it in any depth as long as you're all right' sort of family.

HARI: That's very similar to my family in some ways; you do things, you do it thoroughly and you get on with it. It's interesting in the sense that we assume cultural things when they're universal, and universal things when they're cultural.

In this interview the couple saw their family as capturing the good elements of both families, especially Hari's, but providing a contrast to both families' inability to express emotion.

They pointed out that they both came from backgrounds in which childhood was very happy but adolescence was extremely traumatic. Both fathers were cold and uninvolved with them, but very concerned about their academic progress. They both 'escaped' from their families in their late teens, and rejected their families' values. When they met they both had little contact with their families.

Hari's story about his teenage years was very significant. After moving to a small town, he felt very isolated:

HARI: We were different not only because we were the only black family but because we were the only Sikh family. And I decided when I was sixteen or so after a lot of trauma that I was going to get my hair cut, and the sense of belonging and unbelonging was very powerful. So I needed to make a detachment from one aspect of my life in order to belong to another. So I wanted to play rugby and go swimming, you know. For a few months before my sixteenth birthday communication broke down completely so that we communicated by letter. The letters consisted of 'I am going to do it.' 'No you're not, if you do we'll disown you.' Until with my sister's help I had it cut, at the barber who did it roughly. I remember vividly my mum coming in, my sister catching her and saying 'He's done it.', My mum running wailing upstairs, my dad coming in and staring, completely speechless, and not knowing what to do...where to hide, and feeling that this wasn't viable. Didn't know what to do.

IK: What were your feelings?

HARI: Suicidal... The people who were attacking me weren't immediately inviting, understandably, but the family who were protecting me now rejected me.

The second interview provided a very different picture of this family. The narrative themes of two people who had both experiences symmetrical experiences in childhood and painful adolescence was replaced by a narrative which was asymmetrical, antagonistic and conflictual, in which the family, rather than being seen as a safe haven in which difference could be celebrated, was portrayed as a forum of painful exploration of difficult conflicts, some of them irresolvable. Despite these conflicts, though, the couple always portrayed the family as a coherent and continuing unit.

Early in their relationship the couple were able to explore their cultural differences in a safe relationship. They went to India where Joan met many of Hari's family. This trip was a watershed for both of them. For Hari it produced very ambivalent feelings:

HARI: It felt very strange you know, on the one hand it felt very familiar, the smells, the sights. Everything looked familiar and yet very strange. It seemed much smaller than I remembered, I suppose because my memories were as a child. But I also felt like a foreigner. I was aware that my command of the language was pretty basic. I was overwhelmed by the friendliness of the family...

JOAN: It was a very important experience and...for the first time I felt like Hari must feel, except of course there weren't the same, you know,

power relationships. I was the only white person, I remember
looking in the mirror and getting a shock, seeing how different,
white I looked.

The interview started, therefore with a narrative which described a shared
experience. But the painful aspects of their relationship became apparent when I
asked:

IK: How does being from different races affect your relationship?

HARI: It's terribly hard, you know, sometimes I feel that it's intolerable,
           and I just want to flee. I think to myself that as an anti-racist, why
           am I married to a white person? Is it because I feel badly about
           myself, low self-esteem. Is there no way out of the dilemma, and I
           wonder what it's going to be like for the children, I wonder if it
           will be much harder for them than it is for us.

JOAN (*rather desperately*):   It's very difficult, but we both know that whatever
           happens, we will both be there for the children, and in some way
           for each other.

HARI: At first we thought that we could resolve these issues, that it would
           be OK in the end, but now we just have to live with the
           uncertainty. Sometimes it's better, and other times it's worse.

IK: And for you, Joan, what is it like being in this family?

JOAN: I don't have any difficulty being in a family – being in this family
           when it's just the four of us. That feels very positive, I love the
           kind of things we do and the things we eat and the way we think
           about India... What I experience as difficult...is to do with your
           feelings about it. It makes me feel quite helpless that I sort of feel
           what can I do to make this experience feel more, feel easier for
           you. I don't feel I've made the wrong decision. When I go outside
           the family when I go to my family up north then it is hard to mix,
           that when my parents come here they don't eat the food we eat
           and they do make awful comments. That makes me feel quite
           despairing.

           Dealing with Hari's family is gratifying and energising. Dealing
           with half of the family anyway. I don't get on very well with his
           father and stepmother.

Hari agonised over his motives and felt torn between his love for Joan as a person
and what this represented in terms of his own identity as a black person and as
an anti-racist. Joan on the other hand felt completely powerless and impotent in
this situation. While Hari was talking her expression became more and more
distressed, expressing both sadness and frustration. Her attempt to mollify Hari

and replace some certainty into the relationship was rebuffed, and she then sat in silence. Hari's interpretation was that as a victim of racism, he had to deal with painful feelings for himself and the marital relationship was being used to explore these feelings. They both said that they felt the constant raw exposure of feelings was positive, and constituted a working through of difficulties, although Hari saw no ultimate resolution to the problems.

We just have to live with the undecidability.

Joan however, hoped for something more resolved.

Another interpretation of this narrative was that of a man who was exercising enormous power over a woman. By implicating Joan as a white person, Hari effectively prevented her from taking any active part in this exchange. He was no longer talking about his relationship with Joan as a person but was dealing with an inner conflict in which Joan became a symbol of white racism and was held to account for this. Thus, although Hari was portraying himself as a victim, in fact, within this exchange he was very powerful. Hari could be seen to be acting out the patriarchal relationship in which the man places the woman in the position of 'the other', where she is unable to challenge or play an active part in the exchange. Her role in this context is a container for Hari's inner conflict – a maternal figure who was expected to nurture him by containing his denigration.

But why did Hari do this? Why could he not assert himself directly as a man and as a black person, preferring to use his victim status as a source of strength? Perhaps this *was* because of the racism which he had previously experienced. Racism may have affected Hari differently from that which he acknowledged, forcing him to use his victimisation as a source of power in relation to white women. It may have been easier for Hari to acknowledge his own low self-esteem, caused by racism and family pressure than to acknowledge his need for power and control. It is interesting to contrast this exchange with Hari's story of his own childhood. His memory was of himself of going to school and waving goodbye to his mother:

> I felt so close to her that I had to do something bad so that she would be cross, and then I would leave in a huff, but underneath we both knew that we loved each other.

In some ways this exchange acted out the same themes of abandonment, ambivalence and power. Hari also talked of language, saying that his experience of racism had made him want to master the English language, to become articulate and powerful. It is possible that language was not the only arena in which he acted out his desire for power.

It was clear that Joan also saw herself as a victim. She felt unable to help Hari because it was not her as a person that he was responding to, but her as a white woman. On the other hand Joan was disappointed that her initial expectation of celebrating difference within the relationship had been undermined. Joan's life story was presented as a move from stifling 'sameness' to liberating 'difference' but in Hari's life story difference was always seen as a threat. It could be that Joan was able to value difference and diversity so much *because* she is white and living in a white society and was not threatened by difference.

This exchange illustrates how complex the association can be between personal feelings, gender, and ethnic differences, and how they are acted out within relationships. Some of this was acknowledged but most of it was not. It is also important to note that although their relationship was characterised by conflict and difficulty, most of what they said about it was also positive: the conflict itself was seen as ultimately a liberating force for them. This exchange was the most concrete expression of conflict I encountered in all the interviews. Most of the couples, while acknowledging similar external difficulties, especially the racism of the extended family, described their relationship in much more positive terms.

Another interesting point was that the difficulties were presented in racial rather than cultural terms. There was no conflict of values or ideas about the family or each other such as between Linda and Ezekiel; it was not a cultural conflict in which different conceptions of family life were being explored. Rather the difficulties were presented purely in terms of what each partner represented for each other as a member of a different race. It is perhaps because of this that Hari saw the problem as irresolvable and perpetual. Contrast this with Theresa's account of conflicts with Sanjay.

THERESA: Yes we do have conflicts. Sanjay is much too concerned with his own family and this comes from his Indian culture; for example, we were about to redecorate our house – you can see what a state it is in now – when Sanjay's brother got into trouble and he felt that we should give our money to him.

SANJAY: Yes if you don't help your family then who is going to help you. I think it is very important to help your siblings.

THERESA: Yes but at the expense of your own home?

SANJAY: Well the house is not so bad is it.

This was a conflict which, although severe, was seen by Theresa and Sanjay as resolvable and not threatening to their relationship. The difference between these two accounts is clear. Theresa and Sanjay saw their conflict as a difference of opinion between two people in which a compromise could be reached. Joan and Hari's conflict was not negotiable in the same way. It is what they represented to each other not what they did that mattered. Another difference was that, in general, Theresa expressed very positive feelings about Indian culture and Indian people, so that this conflict did not symbolise a global personality or culture conflict. Theresa and Sanjay were typical of most of the couples, who said they had little conflict at all over race or culture, but faced racism from the extended family and society as a whole.

There were other aspects of the interview with this family which were interesting. One of them was the way Hari viewed his own identity. During the interview I noticed that Hari had described himself in different contexts as Punjabi, Sikh, Indian and black and asked I him how he viewed himself. He said:

> It depends – when I'm with other Indian people I see myself as Punjabi. I like mixing with other Punjabi people and enjoy their company, even though I don't speak the language very well. 'Indian' is a kind of shorthand for other people in Britain so in this country I usually describe myself as 'Indian'. I see myself as black in terms of a political anti-racist struggle and feel that I share a history of colonialism and racism with other black people in this country.

So for Hari, Punjabi and, to a lesser extent, Indian was the identity which he felt had the most content, that is, was associated with a language, certain cultural practices and with people and places with whom he felt comfortable. 'Indian' was a shorthand and black was used in a specific context in relation to white society and was an expression of solidarity rather than identity as such. 'Asian' was a term that he never used to describe himself and he did not refer to it.

Another interesting issue was Hari's description of an incident with Ravinder. One day he had gone upstairs to call Ravinder down for supper:

HARI: She's upstairs the other night, and she's going to bed, I was cooking downstairs, and I came upstairs and she said 'Papa is that Indian food?' and I said 'yes', and the way that she said it was, 'well it smells funny'. She noted how I responded to her behaviour and she said, 'Yum yum', I ought to eat some.

You see what I mean, she's extremely sensitive. I'm not saying its a very good thing, sometimes she's a bit of a sponge the way she's able to pick up the nuances of behaviour, but for her, there was something she didn't like, saw my behaviour and tried to make me feel better. I think the capacity is brilliant, as long as it's not overdone.

IK: The messages that she picks up about being Indian are very subtle.

JOAN: She has had some exposure to the notion that black is worse than white...

HARI: She asked 'Is Sharon racist?' We try not to tell her overtly that racism is bad or that black people are wonderful.

JOAN: A year ago she got racism and sexism confused, and we realised that we were pushing it too hard.

HARI: She knows about where people are from, but she has no value to it.

JOAN: She has got an idea of Englishness in Northam and Englishness in London.

Hari used this example to show the subtlety of cultural influences on the family and how the children received subtle messages from him which changed their responses. A closer look at this exchange shows that Ravinder was using the word 'Indian' to describe the food (she was similarly reported by Joan to describe herself as half-Indian) Ravinder was using the shorthand or public expression which Hari used to describe himself rather than the more private 'Punjabi'. It may be therefore that 'Indianness' has also become a kind of icon in the family, representing for them a whole series of emotions to do with conflict and control.

Joan's whole account of her childhood and adolescence was peppered with phrases like 'I felt different' or 'I was a loner'. She portrayed her life as a journey from 'sameness' to 'difference', seeing sameness as equivalent to restriction, conformity and oppression, whereas difference represents to her power, individuality and rebellion. For Hari the picture was in some ways reversed. His stories were about how different he was forced to feel. Thus difference for Hari is portrayed as threatening, overwhelmingly and painful. Hari's myth therefore is one of trying to be the same as the society he found himself in, being almost successful to the extent of marrying and having children with a white person (who herself came from a very integrated family) but then finding that complete integration was impossible and part of him therefore withdrawing and trying to be the same as his 'roots'. Is Ravinder in the 'immersion–emersion' stage of racial identity development described by Maximé (1993)? Maximé's phases are, however, supposed to refer to identity development in young children!

Hari's inner turmoil can be seen as a conflict between his need to integrate into white culture and the need for sameness with his own origins, which he yearns for, but is unable to recapture. Both his family of origin and his current family are seen as safe havens from outside pressures, but also as antagonistic and threatening. His position in both families is as a victim of family norms, but a victim who constantly threatens to fragment the family by putting his own needs before theirs. Is he unconsciously playing out the universal role of minority communities through the ages?

But for both Hari and Joan the question must remain whether their accounts of these developments are reconstructions of past events in the light of their current situation or whether these events truly 'caused' them to be the kind of people they are and be involved in the kind of relationship they now have. Another notable pattern in these accounts are the minor but perhaps important inconsistencies. For example Joan described herself as a 'loner' in adolescence, but soon after she had left home: 'within a week made three friends when she went to Paris'. This portrays either a radical discontinuity or an inconsistency in her account.

Another example; Hari and Joan had complained about Joan's parents providing conditional love, both for Joan as a child and also for Ravinder. Both sets of grandparents were seen to be providing subtle but unacknowledged clues to their disapproval of the relationship by such remarks as the 'Delhi belly' occasion and excluding Joan from photographs. This was contrasted with their own relationship with the children which was portrayed as direct, unconditional and open. However, Hari's account of Ravinder's response in the 'Indian food incident' shows that at least some of their interactions were different, reproducing the unacknowledged and conditional nature of their own parenting. There is another clue to this. Hari's story about his own childhood in which he saw himself leaving to go to school was that he and his mother had to become angry with each other in order to tolerate him leaving the home because of the intensity of their attachment for each other. Hari portrayed this as an indication of how close he was to his mother, but this incident too contained an element of unacknowledged and collusive feeling between his mother and himself. It also has reverberations in his own relationship with Joan in which intense attachment is combined with a need to argue things out and acknowledge anger in order to maintain separateness. The point here is that Hari and Joan's family replicated their own families of origin but in ways that they did not acknowledge (at least in the interview) as well as ways which they were conscious about. Their family myth or meta-narrative contains both conscious and unconscious elements.

I have shown some of the conflicts, tensions and difficulties within this family, and am aware that this does not represent the whole story. Both parents felt that the family is a stable unit and that the children are growing up in a positive and nurturing environment, despite the conflicts and difficulties which have been presented. They feel that it is important to deal openly with the difficulties rather than hide them and pretend they do not exist. Their account of mixed-race relationship is similar to that of Eleana Thomas Gifford and Tony Gifford as presented by Alibhai-Brown and Montague (1992). For example Eleana is quoted as saying:

> ...in a black/white relationship, despite whatever deep feelings bond the two together, the relationship is being tested almost on a daily basis... Tony's and my relationship could not survive and will not survive unless we are totally honest with each other on all the really fundamental things. (p.57)

Other Stories

But are all black–white relationships like this? Harriet and Pargat whose backgrounds are in some ways similar to that of Hari and Joan have a very different situation. Like Hari, Pargat is a Punjabi although he grew up in Malaysia, not in India or England. He did spend some time in the Punjab itself at secondary school and later came to England to study. In some ways his family was quite similar to Hari's, in that his father was obsessed with the idea of education and he was close to his mother who was much more expressive. Both families were fairly traditional in their religious beliefs and Pargat, like Hari, became a fairly rebellious teenager.

Pargat also wore a turban and was also teased for it by his school mates in Malaysia. Both men have become active anti-racists as adults. When Pargat came to England, aged 18, he stopped wearing the turban and cut his hair, in a similar gesture to that of Hari. However, the meaning of the gesture as he described it now was totally different. Describing how he felt at the time he said:

PARGAT: I felt good…I wanted to be like the rest of the people and I knew I would come to England and cut my hair. It wasn't something really important.

HARRIET: Probably a teenage thing.

PARGAT: Yes I guess so.

For both Hari and Pargat cutting their hair was a symbol of rejecting their restrictive family demands and an expression of individuality. For Hari this gesture was fraught with feelings of guilt, betrayal and self-doubt, whereas for Pargat it was a step along the way to a more self-confident and assertive identity. Paradoxically, Pargat is much more culturally bound by his 'roots', in that he speaks Malaysian and Punjabi, knows more about the religion, and is closer to his family, even though they live in Malaysia. Perhaps it was *because* he basically felt secure in his identity that Pargat was able to cut his hair with so little ambivalence. In terms of the narrative of his life story this event had little salience for Pargat, and coming to study in England was much more important. In the interview it was I who pushed him to talk about it because of its similarity to Hari's story. Phoenix (1987) and Dominelli (1988) make the point that the so called 'gender gap' in Asian families – in which Asian girls are supposedly torn between western notions of partner choice and arranged marriage – is a pathologisation of the Asian family, and that these conflicts are 'normal' teenage rebellion. These stories show that neither is the case. The degree of pathology depends on the *meaning* attached to the act, not the act itself.

The precursor to the cutting of the hair also offers a contrast. Although both Hari and Pargat had been teased about wearing a turban Pargat dismissed this lightly as:

…it was just something you expected from the children. I didn't take it very seriously.

Hari however saw the teasing as a severe form of racism which threatened his own identity and his family stability. This may have been, in part, because Pargat was part of a minority community in Malaysia, whereas Hari was the only Asian at his school.

After completing his course at university Pargat returned to Malaysia, and then came back to England to be with Harriet. Harriet also initially went to Malaysia but could not find work and returned to England. Like Joan and Hari they both spent a period of time early in their relationship where they went to the man's country of origin. In Pargat and Harriet's case they later returned to Malaysia as a couple but again left, this time because Harriet found the extended family situation too difficult to cope with. They then lived in Hong Kong for some time and later returned to England because they felt much more involved in the community in London. They are now very active anti-racists. Their friends and contacts are mainly in the Asian community, and although Nusrat attends a Church of England School, they often go to the local Sikh temple and they eat mainly Malaysian food in the home. They describe their relationship as very positive and secure. Pargat talked about how many of the black anti-racists with whom they work are very surprised that he can have a good relationship with a white woman, and some are openly hostile.

Harriet and Pargat faced very strong hostility from both sets of parents towards their relationship. Pargat's mother had 'gone on hunger strike' when she found out about it and his parents had insisted that he return to Malaysia. He was put under incredible pressure to stay in Malaysia and almost had to escape from the family in order to return to England to be with Harriet. Harriet's family, although less overt, were equally opposed and her mother had made various remarks about 'those Indians'. Despite this there was not the same 'siege mentality' from this couple as there was from Joan and Hari and they now maintain equable relationships with both sets of parents. In fact, they intend to return to Malaysia or somewhere else in the far east at some point in the future. Interestingly, although Pargat is ethnically Punjabi he sees himself much more as a Malaysian despite the fact that Malaysia is a strongly Moslem state. In many ways Pargat's story is also similar to that of Sanjay's. Both came over at a similar age as students from their home countries, both experienced great hostility to their relationship with a white woman and both stayed on in this country despite that hostility. They both maintained close relationships with the extended family and both their children are growing up in a predominantly Asian environment while going to a Christian school. For both these families the extended family is a reality with positive and negative aspects.

Another interesting contrast is between Theresa and Sanjay and Joan and Hari in terms of their accents. Theresa and Joan come from adjacent areas of North England and left home at a similar age. Although Theresa is from a slightly lower social status they both come from lower/middle class families, yet Joan now speaks in a 'posh' southern accent whereas Theresa has a pronounced Northern accent.

Similarly Hari speaks with a southern middle class accent whereas Sanjay speaks with a distinct Indian accent. Hari attributed his change of accent to the racism which he experienced. He felt that the had to develop the linguistic ability to counter racism and this has made him articulate and English in his speech.

I would like to now turn to more general themes which came out of the interviews. Some issues were repeated in many of the interviews and became recurring themes.

For many of the parents, coming together with a black or white partner was described as the culmination of a process which had begun in adolescence. The common theme seemed to be that the individual had a restrictive, idyllic childhood, often in a small town or an extended family. As soon as they could, they left the home and experienced a new environment; often coming to London or leaving the country of origin. Once in London they were able to explore a large number of different cultures and people and revelled in the idea of exploring difference. This ultimately led to a relationship with a person of a different race. Once the children were born, however, the story changed again and they began to reestablish links with their family and/or cultures of origin and needed to provide the children with an experience of the positive aspects of their life. Parenting was seen by many of these parents especially the mothers as a contrast to their own parenting and very many of them described their own mothers as 'cold', 'withdrawn' or 'distant'. The exceptions were Salman and Hari, whose mothers were warm and affectionate, Dick whose mother was neurotic and manipulative and Pargat whose mother was loving but shouted a lot. Thus virtually all the woman saw their mothers as distant whereas many of the men saw their mothers as close and involved with them and some commented that they had chosen their partners because of similar qualities.

Family Myths and Narratives

But what do these stories mean? Are they an indication of the kinds of people who are likely to become involved in inter-racial relationships, or are they reconstructions of the past which make their current situation understandable to them? Possibly there is an element of both; that is, that individuals first have to develop ways of handling difference before they engage in a long-term relationship with someone from a different race. Many of the parents, both white and black, said spontaneously that if they had stayed in their original situation they would never have had the relationship with the person they did. Most of these families had experienced enormous hostility from parents to their marriage or partnership and this was seen as a way of testing their relationship. In most situations it had cemented their own relationship and provided an element of solidarity against adversity within the family. These accounts of life-stories fed into the 'family myth' which had both diachronic and synchronic elements to it in every case.

The diachronic refers to the myth of how the family got to where it is now. This element of the family myth involves an 'archaeology' – a view of the family in terms of its origins and the origins of family members and how they came to be the way they are. It also has a 'teleology' – a view of how the family and its members will be in the future. The synchronic element of the myth involves an explanation of why we are like we are now and refers to current relationships within the family and relationships between the family, the extended family and the outside world as a whole. Both synchronic and diachronic elements contain both conscious components which are acknowledged and discussed, and unconscious components.

In this study there was a remarkable similarity between many of the accounts given by parents in terms of their diachronic structure. Interestingly the similarities cut through both gender and racial divide. Many of the accounts had the following elements.

The families of origin of many of the parents were themselves 'mixed' but not racially. Sally, Dick, Theresa and Harriet all came from families in which there were class differences between the parents which had been seen as problematic by their grandparents, and in some cases still caused difficulty. Sanjay's parents came from different communal backgrounds within India as well as having class differences. Agneta's and Sally's parents split up when they were young. Thus the idea of difference was already part of the family culture for many parents. Most of the parents described their own childhood as 'happy' or 'idyllic' albeit with elements and events which were unhappy. Most were also conventional teenagers, but felt different from their families and others around them. They then left home and became exposed to outside influences and differences. These differences were either seen as a natural progression or as a radical discontinuity; for example when they came to London or had some other watershed experience. Meeting a person from a different race and especially having children was a confirmation of this difference and of their liberation from restrictive families. The relationship with a black person or white person was often treated with hostility and anger by their own parents and was seen by these respondents as a period where their relationship and commitment to each other was put to the test. Having passed this test they then had children which paradoxically brought them closer to their own parents, in some cases resolving some of the original difficulties which they had experienced as teenagers. Despite this the majority were committed to providing a style of parenting which contrasted with the parenting they had received. It was remarkable how many of these parents, especially the mother, described their own mothers as 'cool', 'distant' or 'withdrawn'. Fathers were seen as more open and honest than mothers, but also as rather distant and uninvolved. Both mothers and fathers in this study were invariably committed to providing parenting which was warm, involved, unrestrictive and honest.

The teleological element of the diachronic family myth involves the children growing up with an experience of both parents and cultures, and of being able to choose their own identity at some future date. The strategy that the parents were using to achieve this differed from family to family, as did the amount of influence from the different cultures. For Shirley and Dick, for example, the Caribbean culture was only represented by contact with members of Shirley's family. Harriet and Pargat on the other hand were committed to providing a high level of cultural input, specifically Punjabi/Malaysian but also Asian in general. Harriet said:

We think that the English culture is so dominant that we don't have to worry about them (the children) getting it; we are much more concerned about them being able to integrate the Asian aspect of their background.

Another teleological factor was the wish of some families to emigrate to a more tolerant or prosperous country.

The synchronic aspects of the family myth refer to how the family view themselves now in terms of the racial/cultural aspect. It refers to how they are currently integrating two cultures or races, how they relate to their families and the community. Relationships to religion and nationality are also included. In contrast to the similarities in the diachronic elements of the myths, the synchronic elements were very different between families. Some of the families saw themselves as being like fortresses against the hostile racism of both black and white extended families and society as a whole. Others saw themselves as fully integrated into their own families and into the local community and as part of a rich local cultural diversity, for example, Salman and Michelle, and Theresa and Sanjay. Still others, for example Shirley and Dick, and Joan and Hari, saw themselves as victims of white but not black racism.

Another difference was the relationship between race, culture, religion and nationality and how these were viewed by the families. The common sense view of family relationships which is replicated in many social work texts is of an individual surrounded by social systems; an extended family, culture, race and so forth (Thompson, 1993). However, these families did not view themselves in this concentric circle fashion. For Salman and Michelle, the most important element was religion. Culture in terms of food, music, or language was much less important and they saw themselves as being an ordinary British family. However, the children attend Moslem religious school and the family attend mosque from time to time. Salman and Michelle see themselves as 'liberal' Moslems and feel very different culturally from other Moslems at the mosque who are mainly Pakistani or Indian and form cliques of their own. Similarly Salman and Michelle do not regard race as an issue either within the family or for the children generally. Their main concern in the future is that the children will marry other Moslems who are similarly liberal minded and not 'fundamentalist'.

Significantly, Michelle is the only one in this sample who has changed religion. In the book *The Colour of Love* (Alibhai-Brown and Montague 1992), the only accounts of a change of religion were of people who were partners of Moslems. I was given second hand accounts by Theresa and Harriet of friends of theirs who were partners of Moslems and who had converted to Islam.

A similar point applies to colour. It was interesting that Sally, Shirley, Tracy and Rose in the first study all commented on the colour of their children. These were all women who were themselves either African or African Caribbean. None of the 'Asians' or their partners commented on skin colour. Similarly Dennis,

Shirley and Sally all described themselves spontaneously as black and Shirley later qualified this by saying: 'When I say black I mean West Indian'.

The Asians did not describe themselves as black, except in the restricted context of 'not white', in other words as a political fact in the British context, but the term black was used by them as a selfconscious expression of solidarity with oppressed people in Britain rather than as a term which described themselves or how they are (see Modood, 1988). It had a similar force to describing themselves as 'conservative' or 'feminist'.

It is interesting to look at the nature of the 'choice' that these parents are providing for their children in the future. All the parents said that they would like their children to be able to choose an identity in the future. However, on closer examination the nature of this choice is not quite as open-ended as it may seem. For example, the choice is not about values. Each family was committed to a set of liberal values and each set of parents fully expected their children to continue with those values. Similarly, they were all committed to a style of parenting which was designed to engender self-esteem in their children and this included a commitment to education, achievement and personal autonomy. Each family belonged to a particular class (most of these families were professional middle class families) and the language, values, and practices of this class were not offered as matters of choice for the children. The children's gender identity was seen as fixed and permanent and again not a matter for choice. What was offered for choice were cultural practices of the minority culture such as food, music, celebrating particular festivals, clothes, stories and so on.

There was an interesting teleology in the operation of these choices. The grandparents were seen as bound by the cultural choices of their own indigenous cultures. For them, these foods, music and so forth were part of a cultural system of signification in which they had meaning way beyond simply being one of many different foods or tunes. They signified the totality of that culture, which included values, religious beliefs and so on as well as cultural practices. The parents themselves had mostly rejected these values and many of the other cultural signifiers, often making very painful choices in order to do so. They retained those elements of the culture which did not clash with their new, that is, western value system. They were offering their children the opportunity to make the same choices they had done, but without the pain which they had experienced.

However, there seemed to be an unconscious element in this. The choices they were offering their children often mirrored their own ambivalence about their culture of origin. The image of their child choosing their own culture of origin sometimes seemed to involve a fantasy which they harboured of returning to their own roots, but which they themselves could not do because of the life choices they had made or their disruptive experience of migration. Similarly, a choice to embrace the mainstream British culture represented both a rejection of themselves and their culture. It fulfilled, however, their own need to become part of the mainstream, something they had been prevented from doing either because of their situation or because of emotional ties which they felt unable to break. Another diachronic element of this myth was that the culture itself was changing even in the country of origin. This point was made by several of the parents and shows that a return to cultural 'roots' was actually an illusion. The roots themselves have changed and evolved over time. What their culture offered was a sense of belonging, and also a sense of continuity to the parent, who could not bear to see his or her culture completely diluted by British mainstream culture.

This picture did have exceptions. Salman and Michelle were providing more cultural input than Salman's parents had done:

SALMAN: I never went to religious school. My father used to take me to the Mosque, but I just recited the Koran parrot fashion. Now I resent the fact that I never learned Arabic.

IK: How did you feel when he took you?

SALMAN: I was angry and bored... But I'm determined that my children will get the education I didn't get...I can understand why my parents never sent me, but sometimes I think they should have forced me.

Another interesting factor in these descriptions of the families' current position was the different accounts of racism. One factor was that the black partner was almost invariably more aware of racism than the white partner and often surprised the latter with their remarks. Every white partner acknowledge racism and many had experienced it themselves because of their association with a black person. However, the black partner often gave much more significance to particular events than the white partner. For example Shirley said:

I never go on the tube, I can see them looking at me because I'm a black woman, and often people will move away from me when they have had to sit next to me.

Then Dick said:

Oh I thought you didn't go on the tube because you were claustrophobic.

Shirley said

Yes that too.

Thus there was a potential in these relationships for remarks which the white person considered to be casual comments or jokes, to be construed as racist by the black person and be seen as dangerous and threatening. This applied especially to remarks made by grandparents.

SALLY: His mother came to the hospital and said. 'You're not going run away and take him back to Ghana are you?' I was really angry and upset.

VICTOR: I think she was just trying to wind you up.

SALLY: I know, but it really pissed me off.

Victor saw this as a nasty off-the-cuff remark and a joke but Sally saw it as semi-serious and a real threat.

Another interesting factor about racism was provided by those parents who had emigrated to England as adults. Two accounts were particularly interesting. Pargat described the racism of Malays towards Indians in Malaysia in a much less threatening way than white British racism towards black people. When I asked him about this he could not give an explanation but simply said:

> It just feels different. Its not that threatening, even though Malaysia is a Moslem country and quite repressive it doesn't feel racist to me.

Sally gave different and sometimes conflicting accounts of race in her own country. At different times in the interview she said:

> ...my parents had no problem with Victor, there is no animosity towards white people there and everybody is treated equally.

> We Ghanaians don't like the Lebanese. A quarter of the population is Lebanese and my parents would definitely not like me to go out with a Lebanese person.

> I don't think we could bring her up in Ghana – half-caste girls are seen as loose women there, and I wouldn't want that for my little girl.

In these three statements Sally was first not acknowledging racism, second claiming racism was less severe in Ghana but third claiming it was more severe, especially for mixed-race children.

Three of the Asian respondents told me that in Asia there is a definite hierarchy of acceptable partners, so that for their parents their marrying a white person was better than if they had married a black person, which in turn was better than marrying a Moslem. Pargat's brother had married a Moslem, Sanjay's married an African, and both these marriages had been more traumatic for their parents than their own.

Those families who intended to emigrate, for example Linda and Ezekiel and Pargat and Harriet, saw British racial categorisation and racism as a transient phase in their lives rather than the only reality. In a similar way their children's racial identity was seen as located in current time and current place. All the families who had discussed leaving the country believed that their children would grow up very differently in terms of their cultural and racial identity from the way that they would grow up in England. The temporary nature of identity was dramatically highlighted to me in a different context by an acquaintance of mine who is a refugee from Bosnia. He has a Moslem father and Croat mother and said 'Last year I was Yugoslavian and very proud of it. My identity was Yugoslavian, now I'm told that I'm a Bosnian and there is no such thing as a Yugoslavian.'

For these families racism and racial identity were both contingent rather than being an essential 'reality' with no alternatives. Stopes-Rowe and Cochrane (1990) show that these issues are similar to their own sample of Asians in Britain, and that the wish to emigrate is common, and often a 'defence' against racism.

One interesting perspective on the parent's dealing with identity is the process by which the children were named. In some cases naming was not an issue, for example Sally and Victor named Cassie just because they liked the name. Dick and Shirley and Linda and Ezekiel did not mention naming as an issue. However, naming was mentioned by all the couples with an Asian partner.

Seree was so named because, as Ruth said:

We wanted a name that was Indian, but that sounded OK in English. We didn't want people to find the name too strange.

Theresa and Sanjay, after much discussion gave their children both western and Indian names. Joan and Hari gave their children Indian names, but Joan and the children kept her surname, and this caused a lot of friction with Hari's family. Michelle and Salman gave their first child a Moslem name, Farida. The second child, Abel, was named after consultations with Salman's extended family in South Africa, who eventually approved it after agreeing that as a biblical name, it would be acceptable. The third child was simply given a name they liked, and they were no longer very concerned about the family's reactions. Harriet and Pargat named their children after Asian friends whom they admired. The names, however are Moslem, and this has caused friction in Pargat's family who refuse to call one of the girls by her real name, using a similar Punjabi name.

In these families naming was a difficult balancing act in which the parents had sought to value both cultures positively and to take the extended family's views into account. In each family naming the children was a carefully thought out strategy for the child's future identity.

All the parents who had children over three years old confirmed that they were very aware of identity issues such as race and culture. However, the children did not have a set view of their own identity. Many of the children were reported to refer to themselves as half-Indian or half-Malaysian and so forth. All the children aged under five seemed to be very aware of both colour and culture and represented this in various ways. Ravinder for example was able to do 'Indian' as well as 'non-Indian' drawing. The twins Ben and Peter said to their mother:

'Why can't you be brown like us?' (Note: Not 'Why can't we be white like you?')

They saw themselves as brown, the father as black and mother as pink. Similarly Nusrat had been ashamed on one occasion of her mother coming to the nursery school where her father was well-known. She didn't want them to see she had a white mother. At different times, Nusrat had drawn herself as white, pink, or brown and her parents felt that this was a process by which she was testing out different views of herself and through which she would eventually come to terms with her own identity. Chrisopher said to Theresa about his school friends:

They're just white, but I'm half Indian.

and Seree:

I'm half Indian, What are you half?

The parents saw the children as developing their identities in different ways and described varying degrees of confusion, contentment and happiness around the area of identity. Identity was an issue with which the children were coming to terms over time. Over time they were learning who they were, who was the same and who was different.

At a very young age the children were developing notions of culture, race, gender and nation. These were sometimes confused and conflictual, and the parents reacted with amusement, joy and concern.

One interesting observation about these families is that virtually all the parents themselves had some sort of 'mixed identity'. I have already noted that Ezekiel, for example had a 'Ghanaian self' and an 'English self', that Sanjay was mixed Punjabi and Hindi, and that many of the white parents came from mixed class backgrounds. For all the parents who had emigrated to the UK, both black and white, emigration had caused an enormous discontinuity in their identities, and many of the 'givens' of their lives were radically altered. For some, forming a relationship with a British person served to cement these changes and to accentuate the 'otherness' of their culture of origin. This shows that discontinuity and change in identity can occur both because of changes over time and because of contrasting cultural or racial forces. On this basis the notion that families can 'provide' a stable, core identity for their children must be challenged – identity depends on circumstances as much as on family relationships, and in the world today many people will have mixed identities without necessarily suffering catastrophic psychological consequences.

All the families studied, except for the A family, were middle class. Most of them were very familiar with anti-racist theories. In the interviews they were able to talk fluently about the abstract notions of race, culture, self-esteem and so on and to use these notions to reflect on their own lives. This illustrates another aspect of identity – the reflexive nature of social theory. Anti-racist theory provided many of the parents with the vocabulary to make sense of their own experiences. Others felt threatened by some aspects of anti-racist theory and practice. Virtually all had integrated elements of the theory into their parenting and their life choices.

The way the families made sense of themselves and their current situations – the family myths – grew out of complex relationships within the family and outside. The description of the children's development of identity shows that development of identity is not a simple progression from non-identity to some fixed identity. The development was often painful, discontinuous, context bound, and fractured by class and gender. Choices were being offered to the children in some areas of their lives but not others. Whereas the racial and cultural elements were one step removed and were seen as open to negotiation, class, gender, language, family structure and even political beliefs were seen as 'givens' within the family rather than issues which were negotiable between children and parents. Race, as opposed to culture was seen as an issue which related to conflict either within the family or outside. So race was seen in terms of power while culture was seen in terms of desire.

The Interview Process

The accounts given by the couples of their histories and current situations were provided in a particular context; the research interview with a white, male South African stranger. In the first part of the book I commented on how this may have affected their responses and my interpretation of them. I would like to make some further points. Because most of these interviews were conducted with both partners, the 'audience' for the life stories was different in the second set of interviews. Interestingly, several of the women commented that they had never heard their partners talk about themselves for so long. There were also several comments that it was very positive to take a break from child care and spend time discussing adult topics.

I was also surprised at how similar some of my own experiences of emigration had been to many of the respondents, both black and white, and how my own feelings about Britishness and the difficulties of maintaining peripheral culture in Britain were reflected by their accounts. However, accounts of racism were outside my own experience. An interesting example of this was provided by Pargat. In talking of racism he experienced, he mentioned that canvassers and officials would often ask him where he came from. He interpreted this as them questioning his right to be in the country, and his response is that it is none of their business. Pargat had asked me where I came from at the beginning of the interview, guessing that I was a South African. I had not even remembered this until this discussion. I did not point it out to Pargat. This incident illustrates how white people may experience situations as non-threatening or even positive, but the same situation can be experienced by black people as insensitive or attacking.

Discussion

The advantage of seeing the families' views of themselves, their histories, their current situation and their future as 'myths' or as narratives should now be apparent. In the first part of this study the parents' account of development was taken at face value and task of the researcher was to look for commonalities which would show how racial identity in mixed-raced children develops. In this phase of the research I turned the question on its head. Instead of asking 'How does the mother's past history affect her current beliefs and actions and in turn the development of her child?' I have asked 'Why is it, given the current circumstances, that parents provide this particular account of their own history, their present and their child's future?'. I have therefore moved away from the question of providing a truer or more accurate framework of identity development than for example that of Goodman or Katz and instead have began to develop a way of looking at a family which shows how they construct reality rather than how their reality can fit into a framework constructed by a theorist.

CHAPTER TEN

Conclusions

Introduction

This chapter will bring together the main findings of all three phases of the study, and will relate them to the nature of early racial identity development and its connections with the infant–mother relationship. In some ways the second set of observations represent a radical break from the first two parts of the study. They challenged some of the assumptions on which the study was originally based, especially in the expanded notion of 'identity' and the narrative rather than cause–effect nature of development. In other ways they were a continuation of the conclusions arrived at after the observations and the first interviews.

Summary of Findings

Observations

The observations confirmed how important the early relationship between the mothers and infants were in the early development of identity. They showed how mothers brought into the relationships beliefs and feelings from their pasts, and that these affected the way they related to their children. These fantasies and beliefs seemed to change soon after the children were born, when the mothers were faced with a real person. They changed further as the infants became individuals who developed their own personalities and initiated part of the relationship. In the A family the mother was also changing in response too her partner and her older daughter. Mothers' past experiences were therefore only one element which influenced the way they thought about their infants and their identity.

In both these families 'racial' issues were a central part of the family dynamic, and became part of the context in which the children grew up. For these two families, race was largely based on physical colour, although in both families there were some cultural elements. In the B family Rose made a conscious effort to bring 'black culture' into the home, but the African Caribbean presence in the A family was more immediate because of the father's presence. In the A family conflict was often racialised, and the children received some negative messages about black people from their mother. In contrast, Rose seemed to idealise 'black culture' and black people, who represented spontaneity and freedom.

Both these families were in the process of developing methods of dealing with difference, and negotiating boundaries, not only in the racial and cultural domains, but also gender, generational and interpersonal ones. Each child's development was characterised by a 'theme' or meta-narrative which developed and changed over time. In the case of Cathy the theme was her response to the chaos of the family and her mother's initial hostility towards her. For Dave the theme was his struggle to individuate and separate from his mother. Both infants developed 'selves' which were distinct ways of being in the world. The different 'selves' manifested in different situations, and it was hypothesised that they may become associated with different 'racial' selves. However, it was noted that the course of development was dependent on external events (such as father leaving the home) and children and parents' feelings, so that predictions could not be made.

Semi-Structured Interviews

These interviews found that meeting a black partner was often part of a wider 'meta-narrative' in the mothers' lives. Most of the mothers had described their background as sheltered or restricted, and they had broken away from this in their teens or early adulthood. Meeting a partner who was 'different' was part of this process. All of them saw this as a positive aspect of the relationship, but all faced challenges integrating the difference into their relationship. The difference was not universal, and the partners were invariably matched in personality, class and educational terms. The black partners had also mostly moved away from their own backgrounds, and several mothers commented that their partners related better to their family than to their own.

Children had a paradoxical effect on mothers. On the one hand it made them more aware of differences and the need to bring minority cultures into their day-to-day lives. On the other hand having grandchildren in the family brought together the extended family and allowed them to overcome some of the emotional distance.

Race and culture were dealt with very differently in the different families. In some families conflict was racialised, but culture played little part. In other families culture was more important than 'race' or colour, and some mothers felt that neither of these issues was important. It seemed that class rather than race had played a central role in the family 'culture', and for the parents it was the reproduction of class values that were most important. These values were often unspoken and accepted, rather than the subject of negotiation within the family. The children were aware of cultural and racial issues from an early age, and most felt positively about them rather than confused or upset.

No general connection could be found between mothers' early life and either their partner choice or parenting style, although each mother was able to make some connections. These things were too individual to develop any 'theory' of identity development or its relationship with mothers' past experiences.

'Life History' Interviews

The second set of interviews revealed an enormous variation in the meaning of 'race', 'culture' and 'identity' in different families. The interviews confirmed that these issues were negotiated in all the families from before the childrens' birth. The interviews confirmed the importance of parents' past experiences in allowing them to make sense of their current family situations. However, these connections were not generalisable or predictable, and made sense in narrative rather than causal terms. An example of this was that every parent felt that they were giving their children something they had lacked in their own parenting, but were also continuing some of the positive features of their original families. There were both conscious and unconscious narrative connections. Parenting style did not only relate to past experience, however, but also to current concerns within the family and their social context.

All the parents wanted their children to have a positive 'mixed' identity, but the content of this 'identity' was seen as variable and open for the child to choose. The families self-consciously exposed the children to the 'culture' of the black parent, but the exposure differed – in some the black parent was already rather distant from the culture, while in others the extended family offered easy access to it. The culture itself, however, was not a unified set of sounds, tastes, practices or beliefs; its nature was being constructed and negotiated continuously within the families. This negotiation of 'sameness' and 'difference' was seen as the fundamental process by which identity was constructed. Thus the future identity of the children was not predictable, and the families saw identity as being contingent on what choices the children make, where the family lives and what particular experiences the children will have.

In summary the three phases of the research confirmed some of the original hypotheses:

- the early age at which 'racial' identity begins

- the importance of the mother–infant relationship

- the importance of past experience

- the importance of current social context

- the location of racial identity within the broader identity.

However, these hypotheses were confirmed only by adopting an expanded view of 'identity' and 'development' and by seeing the connections as narrative rather than causal. Fathers and the 'marital' relationship were found to be almost as important as mothers in this process, not simply as 'role models' but as an integral part of the negotiations around difference. 'Culture' was seen as constructed in families rather than transmitted through generations. The 'self' was seen as a construction rather than a set of characteristics and beliefs. The relationship between 'race' culture, gender and class was seen as interactive and fluid rather than as primary and secondary identities or as coexisting 'selves'.

Sameness and Difference

The most striking similarity between all the parents was that they all were in a constant process of negotiating difference. In virtually every case (except perhaps that of Salman, where this process had occurred a generation before) the parents had begun to deal with differences between themselves and their families or between themselves and their own societies before they had met a partner from a different ethnic group. They tended to see their childhoods as pleasant but confined, and their adolescence or early adulthood as a time of separation and exploration. This meant that forming a relationship with a 'different' person was confirmation of already established themes in their live and not a complete break from their past. This was despite resistence by some parents to these relationships which ruptured their sense of continuity.

Hostility was experienced from some of both the black and white extended families, but the couples themselves tended to experience the white hostility as more threatening. In all these families the birth of the children heralded some form of reconciliation, and re-established a sense of continuity.

Other than this there were no identifiable characteristics or experiences which all the adults shared. Even those who experienced similar events such as emigration attributed different meanings and importance to them.

The common theme of these stories – a happy but confining childhood, a rupture with that childhood, a relationship with a 'different' person which confirmed the rupture and then a return to the 'roots' after the birth of children – should not be seen in causal terms. It may have been that the parents reconstructed their narratives in similar ways because of the nature of the interview situation. It may also be that these themes apply to many adults in London, where large numbers of people have left their 'roots' for all sorts of reasons, but few form inter-racial families. The interviews with black parents confirmed that this pattern was not restricted to white women. Black and white parents who had emigrated had experienced particular issues in dealing with their separation and difference from their parents and their cultural 'roots'.

The parents had all originated from, or had moved into, similar educational or class situations. This meant that they were with, in many ways, the kind of people whom they may have been expected to be partners, differing only in that they were from a different 'race'. There were as many similarities in the couples' respective backgrounds and they often perceived symmetries between themselves.

Interestingly, many of the parents, both white and black, saw positive opportunities as well as challenges in being part of the margins of conventional ethnicity.

Although some parents pointed out their lack of role models and media coverage of inter-racial families, others pointed out that the lack of stereotypes meant that they were able to negotiate culture and ethnicity within the family in a way that they could not have done with a member of their own group.

Another important factor in most of these families was that the family contacts invariably transcended national boundaries. All the families had close relatives in other countries. This meant that they did not feel bound by all the categories and assumptions of nation and race which pertain in contemporary Britain and saw these categorisations as contingent rather than essential. This enabled them to provide their children with choices which transcened conventional notions of ethnicity.

Some couples had experienced enormous hostility from both black and white families. The arrival of children often brought families closer together, often helping to overcome the differences with their own families. This meant that although in some families the children did come to symbolise racial difference, in others they represented conciliation and coming together of families. This finding contradicts the psychoanalytic assumption that black children will inevitably represent the split off 'bad' elements of white mother's personality and will be subject to unconscious racism.

Issues of 'race', 'culture' and 'ethnicity' were part of every family's lifestyle, and although there were a very wide range of issues that the families dealt with, all of them had involved their children in these matters from a very young age. In all the families these issues were part of the larger process of negotiating the questions around 'sameness' and 'difference', and were combined with other differences such as age, gender and class. They were also part of the negotiation of family values which was ongoing in all the families. The narrow question of 'racial identity' within the context of black/white identification was not dealt with by all the families, some of whom denied that this was an issue for them at all. In families where race was dealt with directly, this tended to be connected with conflict and power, whereas culture was more associated with desire, memory and a feeling of belonging.

Class was a fundamental factor in all these families, especially in the way the parents perceived their task and were able to talk about it. Class affected the family lifestyle more than race and culture, partly because class norms pervaded the parent's thinking in a much more unconscious (and therefore less challengeable) way than culture or race. Parents never asked themselves 'What aspects of middle class culture should we introduce in the home?' This was part of the fabric of their lives. In many cases there was a blurring of culture and class. For example, virtually every parent emphasised the value of education (and how their own parents had pushed them educationally). In the case of the black parents this was often attributed to the cultural expectations of Asian, African or African Caribbean parents. But white parents reported similar pressures and did not relate them to culture or ethnicity. Class seemed also to influence the kind of choices which the parents consciously provided for their children. In every middle class family the children were brought up so that they could be free to choose their identifications. In the A family, who were the only working-class (or rather under-class) family the children were not given those choices. It may be that the 'post-modern' identities which these children were being offered are only really available to middle-class children. This finding would be in line with those of Walkerdine (1985) who found differences in the language used by middle-class and working class mothers to discipline their children. Walkerdine found that middle-class mothers were much more likely to provide 'choices' to their children. Tizard and Phoenix (1993), however, found no strong relationship between class and racial identification in mixed-race adolescents, although Wilson (1987) found that middle-class children tended to misidentify more than working-class children in the doll tests.

There is a risk attached to the strategy which the middle-class families adopted. Anti racist and marginal theory predicts that mixed-race children will grow up thinking themselves white, and will have an 'identity crisis' when they discover that society treats them as black. By extension, children who see themselves as 'mixed' or who believe they have choice, may similarly suffer from identity problems when confronted with the polar dichotomy by society into black and white. The theories differ in their predictions about what age this crisis will occur. Maximé (1993) predicts problems in childhood, Small (1986) in adolescence and Stonequist (1937) in early adulthood. Research by Wilson (1987) and Tizard and Phoenix (1993), however, has shown little psychological disturbance or identity problems in mixed-race children and adolescents, who are able to develop 'situational ethnicity'. So it seems that this strategy can work, and the parents are not only providing the illusion of choice. Perhaps it is the parents' decision to introduce these issues consciously into the family when the children were young that may prevent the 'identity crisis' predicted by so may theories.

Almost all the black parents in the study had suffered some form of racism, although the degree differed. For many racism and the struggle against it was a major issue in their lives. Some white partners had also suffered because of their relationship with a black person, and some couples had suffered discrimination from black people as well. The white partners, however, were rarely aware of how much their partner had suffered from the threat of racism, and some were quite surprised by this.

Nevertheless, the direct causal link between institutional and individual racism, both within the family and from the outside, and identity development was not confirmed. This link was based on anti-racist theories who saw white mothers as the unwitting purveyors of socialised racist beliefs. The link between racism and identity sounds logical enough – if a black child is led to believe that all black people are inferior and she is black, she must therefore be inferior. However, this is only true if her primary reference group is black people as a whole. In reality children may identify with their family, friends, the local youth club, their school or many other groups or individuals, which may mitigate the effects of racism on personal identity. In this group of families racism was interpreted in many different ways, and it was the *interpretation* of racism that was important. Incidents that in some families would have caused a major crisis were seen as unimportant in other families. For the children it seems to be important that parents are able to deal with the issues of race and culture in a relaxed though vigilant way and that children should be encouraged to explore these issues for themselves with parental support.

The families differed in how they positioned themselves in terms of racism. Some families perceived themselves as a safe haven of tolerance within a hostile sea of racism, while others saw the family itself as a forum for working through racial differences. The parents were all aware of the likelihood of racism being an important factor in the children's future lives, and all had developed strategies to enable the children to deal with racism. These strategies varied according to class. Despite the extra challenge for the children of being mixed-race, the mothers all felt optimistic about their children's chances of developing a positive mixed-race identity.

Most of the children who were verbal described themselves as 'mixed' in some way. This does not mean that they were 'mixed up', although some of their understandings were at times confused. The parents saw this confusion as part of a process whereby they were exploring their own identity. Only one child (Roberta) had associated black with 'bad'. Most of the children saw their mixed identity in terms of culture rather than race for example, 'half Indian' rather than 'half white'. Interestingly, the exceptions to this were Roberta in the A family, and the twins, who called themselves 'brown'. In both these families the black partner was African Caribbean. This confirms the finding that for African Caribbeans the term black is used spontaneously to describe themselves, but this is not shared with other black groups such as Asians or even Africans, who tend to use cultural, religious or national descriptions (see Modood, 1992 for a discussion of this point). The families all chose to live in multi-racial areas, and all the children had contact with children from a wide range of backgrounds, although the degree of contact varied.

Parents related their own parenting style to their early experiences of being parented, but there was no direct causal relationship. The second set of interviews, by focusing on themes in the parent's stories, were able to point to more subtle ways in which the parents repeated elements of their own parenting unconsciously. However, the way their own parents had treated them did not cause them to become particular kinds of parents, nor did their early parenting determine their children's specific identities. These were seen to be dependent on a number of different factors, including their relationship with the partner, the child's own personality and dispositions, and the milieu in which they were living at the time. One example is that parents often responded to each other's parenting styles, so that they adapted to form complementary styles of parenting for their children.

Another important influence was that of contemporary theories (or accepted social ideologies) about parenting, not least anti-racist theories which encouraged some parents to choose multi-racial areas and to introduce children's 'roots' into the home consciously. Only one parent saw her children as essentially 'English' in identity, and none saw their major task as integrating their children into mainstream culture. Rather they saw their task as providing 'choices'. This stance was informed by contemporary beliefs, and may be restricted to middle-class parents in the early 1990s rather than being an a-historical characteristic of inter-racial families.

The finding that there was a narrative rather than a causal relationship between being parented and being a parent raises the question of the relationship between early parenting and later identity development in the children. Some of these issues have been addressed, but I believe that the findings were somewhat paradoxical. Parenting is fundamentally important in the early development of identity. The observations showed how children organise their personalities into configurations or 'selves' which are formed in the process of interactions with the parents. The interviews confirmed that very subtle interventions by the parents may have profound effects on the children, that 'selves' can persist into later life, and that they can be 'racialised' or 'ethnicised'. Some of the parents felt and behaved differently in different 'racial' situations. But it was not necessarily true that those aspects of the self which developed chronologically prior were those which were experienced as being more authentic or 'true'. These 'selves' will not neccesarily have any direct causal relationship to later identity or even identifications. The relationship is likely to be a narrative link rather than a causal one. The children's later identifications will depend not only on continuity of parenting, but also on the social context in which they find themselves. For example, they might depend on whether, by the time they are teenagers, the black community in Britain has developed the totalised or synthesised black identity which Gilroy believes it is doing, or whether it develops 'hyphenated identities' such as 'Muslim-British' and 'African-British', which Modood (1992) advocates.

These findings were common to all three phases of the research. However the third phase questioned some of the basic assumptions about 'race', 'identity' and 'development' each of which were based on a narrow and conventional set of assumptions held by both psychoanalytic and anti-racist theories, and which informed the way the questions and hypotheses in the first phases had been formulated.

Race

In the initial part of the study, 'race' was used to mean exclusively black or white. The cultural, class and gender influences within the families were not dealt with as central issues. Prevailing social theories treated race as a separate dynamic which was either subsumed under class or transcended class barriers. Culture was seen as a sub-category of race (Gilroy, 1987). Both families I observed saw race in these terms. In the A family, for example, the sign on the amplifier was '*Black* (Not 'Jamaican') man music'. Similarly when Norman argued with Tracy about child rearing, he said 'I bring my children up like a *black* parent...' The racialisation in this family was expressed in terms of colour. Because of this I anticipated that Cathy's identifications and her sense of self (or selves) would be experienced in terms of race rather than culture. This pattern was repeated in Family B, where Rose's struggle with dependence and independence was expressed in terms of race. It may be because in both these families the black element was African Caribbean that they associated racial identity in terms of black and white. The women in the first set of interviews widened the definition of race, and confirmed the intricate relationship between race, class, culture and gender in the identifications of their children, and in the way they saw themselves and their families.

The interviews therefore confirmed that racial identity could not be seen merely as a set of identifications with set 'racial' aspects of the self or of society. It also became apparent that the children did not have a set of racial or cultural 'roots' which were being transmitted by the parents. Each family was negotiating the issues of race and culture in different ways, both within the family and with the extended family and society as a whole. Thus it was clear that the issue of 'racial' identity was much wider than the issue of racism. The concept of a 'positive identity' was seen as a value judgement rather than a description.

Nevertheless, the semi-structured nature of these interviews, the fact that they were conducted with mothers alone, and the hypotheses they were testing (i.e. the causal relationships between mother's pasts and children's identities) limited the extent to which family dynamics and the way the family made sense of identity were uncovered. A good example of this was my own interpretation of Lucy's assertion that race played no significant part in the family's life. I treated this as an example of a denial of racism, and as almost racist in itself. I failed to see that this may well have been my own construction of the situation. Racism is endemic in British society but it does not necessarily affect every person in the same way, and it may well be that for particular families race plays little part.

Although the first interviews confirmed the heterogeneity of identities, they were still based on the notion that there was a 'core' identity which was a fundamental and stable characteristic of the individual, and that the 'core' identity chronologically preceded the other secondary selves which may develop. In the second part this was challenged – the history of the black parents in particular showed that the notion of 'primary' and 'secondary' identity was too narrow, and that these are relative to the current situation and how it is dealt with. Cathy and Dave's 'selves' were therefore not necessarily permanent structures, but were their ways of making sense and coping with painful, contradictory reality.

In the observations it had already become clear that despite what psychoanalytic theory postulated, the father had played a central role in Cathy's identity development. The mothers' accounts confirmed the importance of fathers, but were not able to provide the fathers' own perspectives. The interviews in the third stage with black parents and white fathers provided further evidence that my original assumption, that white mothers' task would be fundamentally different from that of black mothers, was erroneous. The interviews with Kathy and Shirley showed that even these two women dealt with their children's identity differently from each other, but both were similar to some of the white mothers. Shirley had been in a white environment most of her life, and for her there were few problems about cultural or racial issues other than her daughters' need to feel positive about themselves and to be protected from racism. Kathy had emigrated to the UK as an adult, and was more concerned about the cultural balance within the family. Both women shared with the white mothers the task of negotiating difference within the family. A similar point can be made about the fathers. All the fathers (except Paul who had no contact with Rose) felt that there were issues around culture, race or gender that were being resolved in the family. They all shared some responsibility for providing their children with cultural input. None of them saw this as the exclusive role of the mother. Having said this, there were variations, and mothers did tend to shoulder most of the burden in some families.

In the second interviews the focus was more on how families perceived and managed difference, and this wider focus provided much richer information, and much clearer links than the narrow focus on race and racism. The second interviews widened the definitions of identity even further than the first, adding religion and nation to the range of issues which interacted with race, gender, class, colour and culture in the process of 'racial' identity formation.

Some of the families showed a degree of racialisation, and the observations in particular showed how racialisation can affect family dynamics. Nevertheless, it would be wrong to conclude that these tensions always dominated the relationships in the families, and it would be especially wrong to see them as problem families who mirrored the wider problems of racial politics in society. Although researchers and social workers like to seek out pathology, viewing these families only as 'problems' adds to the discrimination against them, not to understanding them more fully. The view of these families as a microcosm is based on a notion of racism which is individualised to the study of 'racists', and also the view that racism is endemic in society and therefore every white is a racist. Post-modern anti-racists have challenged this unidimensional, personalised view of race relations. The pathologisation of these families is unfair, untrue and theoretically invalid.

Identity Development

This study was initially based on the accepted views of psychoanalysts, developmental psychologists and racial preference researchers that racial identity development is a linear, cumulative process in which cognitive and emotional structures are provided with content by the processes of identification with, and internalisation of mother's beliefs and attitudes. The 'self' which was developed was seen as a collection of dispositions, characteristics, behaviours and beliefs which needed to be more or less in tune with 'society's' perceptions of the individual. Identity was originally seen as mediated through parents, who were seen as transmitting accepted social values. This view has now been substantially altered, because it is seen as prescriptive and static, and does not reflect the dynamic and fluid nature of development which has elements of discontinuity, disjuncture and conflict as well as continuity and stability. Now identity development is seen as negotiated within the family, between individuals and the outside world, and between the family and the outside world, which itself is changing and contradictory.

The findings were in some ways paradoxical – they confirmed that early parenting plays a crucial role in children's early identity formation, and that this role is subtle and powerful. The children in the observations were shown to develop a sense of self largely as a response to this parenting. On the other hand, parents do not determine future identity. This means that the analogy used by psychoanalysis and racial identity theory is inaccurate. The family's role is not analogous to a gun shooting a bullet in a predetermined direction. They are more like authors who write the first chapter of a book, leaving the children to write the rest of the story. They set the scene for later development which may constantly refer back to them, but they do not determine the story. If this analogy is accepted, it is in principle impossible to predict future development, and the assumption made when this project began was misplaced. The findings do not, however, confirm the full-blown post-modernist assertion that identity is a fabrication by the individual which is used to paper over the cracks of discontinuous and contradictory experience, with no reference to 'real life'. Later identity was not simply created by the individuals, but was based on earlier experiences. However, these experiences were often reinterpreted by the parents. A good example of this was their accounts of their own early parenting. Many parents said that after they had children, they had reassessed their own parenting in a much more sympathetic way, while others were determined to give their children a better deal than they had.

Identity

Identity is seen by anti-racism and psychoanalysis as essentially a set of stable beliefs, characteristics and behaviours, and an individual's perception of themselves in relation to a unified, established 'society'. At first identity was seen as a set of roles combined into 'selves'. Now identity is seen as a set of experiences, memories, selves, which are ever-changing unconnected and conflicting, retold as a story so that the person has a sense of a coherent self, but each telling is different. The 'selves' which were described in the observations can be seen as strategies developed by the infants to deal with 'difference' in their lives by retaining both 'sameness' and 'difference' in their responses to the world. They can be seen as two 'themes' which were emerging in the narrative of the children's identity development.

Methodology

In this section I will discuss some of the major methodological points which have arisen from the present study. In Chapter 4 I have outlined the methods used in the study and the adaptation of the observational method from training to research. Chapters 4 and 7 commented on the validity and reliability of the data. I will confine myself here to issues which may have significance for other studies.

Observations

The Tavistock model of infant observation stresses the need for the observer to be receptive to the raw experience of the family and his own responses to them – to *know* the family rather than *knowing about* them (Bion, 1984b), and to enter into the field with as few theoretical assumptions as possible. By examining his/her 'pre-verbal' experiences the observer gains a better understanding of the baby's experience.

Using this model made my task as an observer analogous to the infants' own task in identity development. This was the case especially in analysing the data which arose from those observations. Like the infants I entered into an unfamiliar environment and began to receive an overwhelming amount of information which seemed to have little coherence. The task was to identify meaningful patterns and then develop an explanation for the patterns by categorising them.

The transcripts turned out to be a rich source of data, providing an excellent basis for the narrative of the children's identity development to be told. Interviews with parents, videos of short interactions and behaviour check lists had seemed to offer a more cost effective way of learning about the infants' development, but no other method would have demonstrated the interactions and their influence on development. The method was extended in this study by the use of interviews. I believe that the Tavistock method of infant observation can be further adapted without losing its essential character. Some researchers have already extended the method, for example Piontelli (1987), who has pioneered the use of ultrasound to observe foetuses. Further adaptations could include the use of video to look at particular interactions in more depth, interviewing other family members and observations outside the home.

The observation method may be further strengthened by introducing the 'narrative' nature of development into the analysis of the material, with a greater recognition of the social and cultural context in which the observation is taking place, and the fluid nature of the higher-order structures being developed. In the observation seminars there was a tendency to see a rigid relationship between the 'signifier' and the 'signified'. For example, babies who turned toward the light were invariably seen as 'looking to the nipple for reassurance'. Post-modernism should warn us against over confidence in interpreting subjective meanings. Both the 'observed infant' and the 'clinical infant' should be seen as adult reconstructions, not necessarily as real entities.

Semi-Structured Interviews

Analysis of the material from these interviews was far more straightforward than the observations. This was because the interviews were designed to elicit responses to pre-set questions which were derived from theory and from experiences in the observations. The method of data analysis was influenced by Miles and Huberman's (1984) model, which involves tabulating the raw data and then noticing patterns which emerge. The idea is eventually to develop higher order classifications to explain patterns of information so that theoretical explanations of the phenomena can be developed.

Not all the original hypotheses were confirmed by these interviews. Some of the patterns elicited in the interviews contradicted the theoretical hypotheses on which the questionnaires were based. An example of this was the expected link between mothers' early experiences and their parenting and attitudes towards race. The responses showed little evidence of my (perhaps naive) expectation of a clear link. It was partly because of these findings that the method was changed for the second set of interviews.

The mothers provided a great deal of information, but the restriction to mothers limited the amount of useful information about the families.

Biographical Method

Because of the gaps which emerged in the first set of interviews, the second set were conducted using a different methodology based on the biographical method. This method has the advantage of being almost completely unstructured, allowing the parents to develop their own stories rather than responding to my pre-set questions. The emphasis on narrative rather than delving for causes allowed them to give accounts of their lives which showed more clearly the continuity and the differences between past and present. Jointly interviewing both partners gave me a flavour of the family which I could not get from individual interviews. The interview in this phase with only the mother of a two parent family (the K family) was disappointing in the amount of material it produced.

The biographical method asserts that different life stories may be told in different situations, These interviews with a white, middle class ex-South African must surely have influenced the way the stories were told. My version of their stories was also affected by these factors. Nevertheless this approach denies that there is a 'true' story.

By laying open my own position and train of thought as clearly as possible I have tried to make the process of theorising as 'transparent' as possible. Readers can draw their own conclusions about the accuracy of the inferences I have drawn from the material. Researchers from different backgrounds would amplify, challenge or add to some of my conclusions. The account given here is intended to be part of a discourse rather than a statement of 'truth'. This is not to say that the findings of this study are any less significant than those which used quantitative methodology. The huge raft of quantitative studies which have been conducted on racial identification have produced no 'truth' even about the relationship between racial choices and racial identity, let alone the process of identity formation. After 50 years of study there are still calls for more research (Jackson *et al.* 1988; Tizard and Phoenix, 1989).

Qualitative methodology is always open to the accusation that it is merely an account of the researchers' opinion and not a legitimate part of social science. The systematic nature of the data collection and interpretation, and its openness to scrutiny means that this study is not simply another anecdotal contribution to the debate. Rustin (1987) argues that that the Tavistock model of infant observation: '...lends itself more easily than clinical work to public scrutiny and replication.' (p.119)

It is particularly suitable for studies such as this in which individual aspects of development need to be studied in the context of developing relationships. It requires entering the turbulent world of infant–mother relationships with a deliberately theory-free mind, and therefore little guidance as to what to look for, and no guarantee that anything observed will have any bearing on the subject one wishes to study. But there are no short cuts to the rich data available from this method.

There is no 'holy grail' for either qualitative or quantitative methods in this field. I believe that the biographical method provides a much more fruitful way forward than the endless attempt to isolate the variables which will determine the form of children's racial identity. Research based on the notion that identity is like a physical object which can be studied is bound to lose its fluid, changing and contextual nature. Perhaps it is the search itself that is important rather than the elusive 'truth' which it hopes to uncover (Semin and Gergen, 1990). The scientific 'truth claims' of psychoanalysis in this search must be limited, as Wolfenstein (1991) so graphically states:

'...we commit epistemic suicide when we attempt to make ourselves into Galileos of the mind.' (p.544)

Ethics

In a study such as this one where intimate details of peoples' lives are being studied, there are bound to be difficult ethical dilemmas. I will only address the main ones here.

Researcher's Background

The fundamental ethical question is: 'What right has a white, middle-class South African Jew to study this topic?' The ethical point is that by studying race and motherhood, white males perpetuate current power relationships; the researcher has a voice, and the objects of study are merely there to further his theory.

To this I can only answer 'What right have I to avoid studying the topic?'. The issues of race and culture have been crucial to my political and personal life, and it would be hypocritical to ignore them and avoid difficult issues.

Confidentiality and Consent

To what extent is it justified to enter into a family's private life, observe and ask questions, and then write about those observations? When the observations were conducted I used the accepted informal methods of consent which were used at the Tavistock Centre. Issues around partnership and consent are now much more prevalent (Broom and Steiglitz, 1992) and the shortcomings of this approach are apparent. The Statement on Professional and Ethical Responsibilities of The Society for Applied Anthropology says:

> 'To the people we study we owe disclosure of our research goals, methods and sponsorship. The participation of people in our research activities shall only be on a voluntary and informed basis...' (1983, in Bernard, 1988, p.458)

Withholding information about the purpose of the study is not in the spirit of this statement. I believe that if it is to be extended to research, infant observation will need to formalise the method of consent used.

CHAPTER ELEVEN

Revisiting the Theory

This chapter will revisit some of the theoretical assumptions which were made in the first part of the study about identity and racial identity development and will focus on current social work and psychological anti-racist literature which addresses the question of identity development in black and mixed-race children. These theories will be examined in the light of post-modernist new anti-racist theorising and recent research in the area. The concept of 'Narrative Identity' will be expanded and it will be argued that this is a much more appropriate framework for addressing racial identity than the 'structural-developmental' theories on which this study was originally based. Some conclusions will be drawn about social services policy and practice in relation to inter-racial families.

Narrative Identity

Chapter 3 ended with an account of the main tenets of post-modern philosophy as they relate to the issue of identity development. I will very briefly repeat the main thrust of this argument.

Post-modernism denies the basis on which the structural-developmental view of identity posited by Berger and Luckmann, Erikson, Piaget and Winnicott rests. It contends that personal identity is not a fixed set of beliefs or dispositions that develops into a stable structure over time. It denies fixed causal links between past and future, rather focusing on the different constructions of reality which individuals or groups formulate in different circumstances to maintain the fantasy of coherence. Thus it sees the 'self' and personal identity as an unstable and conflicting set of meanings and emotions held together by narratives which cover the cracks of contradiction and discontinuity. It concentrates particularly on the construction of 'difference' and 'otherness', and abandons the bi-polar notions in favour of multiplicity. Post-modernism abandons the attempt to create teleological meta-theories of development, preferring to focus on the particular and the local.

If the 'structural-developmental' model is abandoned, what alternative can post-modernism offer? One possible alternative is the notion of 'Narrative Identity' offered by Ricoeur (1991, 1992). Ricoeur's concept of narrative identity is based on many post-structuralist assumptions, but he does not go as far as Derrida in seeing identity as being totally contingent or constructed (Bernstein, 1991).

However, narrative identity does provide a way of conceptualising how humans construct their own identity. Ricoeur (1991) summarises as follows:

> It is thus plausible to endorse the following chains of assertions: self knowledge is an interpretation; self interpretation, in its turn finds in narrative, among other signs and symbols, a privileged mediation; this mediation draws on history as much as it does on fiction, turning a story of a life into a fictional story or historical fiction, comparable to those biographies of great men in which history and fiction are intertwined. (p.188)

Identity is constructed and reconstructed on a continuous basis. The narrative can change and evolve over time and in different contexts. Although the narrative is used to maintain a sense of unity, this unity is used to cover up an underlying discontinuity and conflict (Jameson, 1984).

Narratives are told by someone (the sender) about something (the referent) to someone (the addressee). The 'self' can be both the sender, the referent or the addressee of a narrative of identity, but it is different 'selves' who take up these different positions. In some ways, therefore, when I talk about myself I am actually talking about someone else. The narrative may also change depending on the addressee so that the construction of the self can be different with different people and in different situations.

The narrative is accompanied by a meta-narrative which 'legitimates' it. The legitimation of the narrative can be in terms of a theory or a reference to the cultural or societal norm. So the question 'Why am I like I am?' is accompanied by a (usually unspoken) question of 'Why are there people like me or like us?' The discussion of family myths (which are a kind of meta-narrative) in the preceding chapters shows how pervasive meta-narratives can be.

Although narratives are changeable they exist within a framework and only certain types of narratives are legitimised for particular individuals. When narratives challenge the 'rules of the game' powerful forces may intervene to force the narrative back to an acceptable story. These forces can be internal, for example guilt or fear of fragmentation, or external, for example threat or the withdrawal of information. The meta-narrative especially is affected by the legitimating forces which society operates on the individual's narrative.

Narratives answer the questions 'How did I get here?', 'What am I doing here?' and 'Where am I going?' Narrative identity does not only operate on the individual level. Families, ethnic groups, cultures and nations can all be seen as having narrative identities, all of which are accompanied by meta-narratives which legitimise them, and all of which contain diachronic and synchronic elements.

In this view of identity, the mature individual would be someone who is willing to face the contradictions and discontinuities in their own lives, to live with the uncertainty and disjuncture of a changing world and who attempts to understand and confront the forces which are involved in 'writing their story' (Dreyfus and Rabinow, 1986).

Maturity here is not seen as a stage in identity development but rather as a stance or position which individuals, and also families, cultures and societies can take towards themselves, their origins, their current position and their future aspirations.

The notion of narrative identity extends the psychoanalytic and child development frameworks. It frees the researcher from having to find the 'essential' nature of inter-racial relationships or mixed-race identity or from having to find some new way of redefining the stages of identity development.

Biography is often used by 'Critical' social science, with the intention of providing a voice for voiceless members of society (see Hammersley, 1993). Some recent social work writings for example Rees (1991) use biography as the starting point of empowerment in social work practice, and this way of thinking can go beyond research and into practice itself.

Race and Racial Identity

Thus far I have confined my argument to a general discussion of identity development and critiques of modernist theories of identity. I would now like to turn to how recent post-modernist theory has influenced the thinking on race, racism and racial identity. Modernist theories of race are set out above in Chapters 1 and 2, but I will recapitulate briefly the development of modernist anti-racism in order to set the scene for the post-modernist critique.

Modern anti-racism started in the 1960s with the 'colour blind' approach. This approach saw the task of black people as integrating into British society, and the role of social work and other professionals was to help this integration take place. The next phase during the 1970s was multi-culturalism. Multi-culturalism acknowledged that individuals do have different cultures and practices. Instead of creating a melting pot of individuals who would all become English, multi-culturalism envisaged a melting pot of cultures, whose ideal was a society in which people of different cultures would live together and tolerate each other. Thus the task of teachers and social workers was seen as helping individuals to understand and live with each other's cultures.

Anti-racism, in a reaction to this, claims that both these stances left out the oppressive forces which prevail on all black people in British society. Anti-racists see the division of black people into ethnic or cultural groups as a denial of their common historical subjection to colonialism and racism and of the institutional nature of racism in society (Dominelli, 1988; Husband, 1991). Anti-racism challenges professionals to rout out racist beliefs and practices in both individuals and institutions. More recent anti-discriminatory theory sees racism as one of a number of oppressive forces, for example sexism, disabilism, ageism. (Thompson,

1993). Thus the notion of 'multiple oppressions' or hierarchies of oppression was developed, in which black women were seen as more oppressed than black men, black disabled women were more oppressed than black women and so forth.

At first glance anti-racism itself seems like a post-modernist attack on modernist British liberal ideals. Anti-racism attacks the totality of 'Britishness' and shows how notions of 'Britishness' are racist (Husband, 1991). The attempt to integrate black people into British society holds an underlying assumption that British culture is better than their own cultures, and that any rational person living in this country would want to become fully, that is, nationally and culturally 'British'. Similarly, anti-racism attacks the teleology and essentialism of these notions of Britishness. The anti-racists show how British society and culture has always treated black people as the 'other' and even liberal and radical white activists have excluded them and colluded in their oppression (Dominelli, 1988; Harris, 1991). The notion of 'institutional racism' can be seen as an example of 'decentering of the (British) subject'; in other words, racism is not seen as individual pathology, but is rather part of a web of cultural, political and institutional practices (Ballard, 1989; Husband, 1991). (But contrast Husband's rather unidimensional decon-struction of new right views about race with the much more complex picture provided by Saggar (1993).) The notions of 'black identity' and the 'black family' embraced by anti-racists are close to the 'incommensurability' (i.e. non-translata-bility) of discourses posited by post-modernists.

Post-modernist anti-racists such as Rattansi, Cohen, and Gilroy point out, however, that instead of deconstructing racist ideologies and practices, modern anti-racists have simply inverted them. Instead of there being only one way of being British, there are now two ways: black and white. Modernist anti-racism views 'culture' and 'race' in essentialist terms and imposes its own teleology. So for modernist anti-racists, black children have a right to their 'roots' and 'culture' which are given to them by 'the black family'. 'The black family' itself is seen as having strengths which have allowed it to survive through the tests of racism. According to the post-modernist anti-racists, these essentialist notions are a simplification. They note that the relationship between, race, culture, class and gender are complex and fractured, rather than hierarchial (Brah, 1992). Racism, too, is seen as a much more complex phenomenon than multi-culturists or modernist anti-racists acknowledge. Rather than seeing a totalised, unitary insti-tutional racism they see different racisms which are local, context bound, and time limited. Anti-racism, they claim, must therefore address racism on a local and appropriate level (Cohen, 1992). Discussing anti-racism Rattansi (1992) says:

Race can produce simplified interpretations of complex social, economic and cultural relations for anti-racists as well as racists. (p.29)

Gilroy (1987) points out that anti-racism and racism share the same discourse of totality and exclusion, he shows that the definition of black used in modern anti-racism means that other groups such as Jews, Irish and so on are excluded from the anti-racist analysis (see also Alderman, 1993). In addition, individual black people are included only in regard to being black; other aspects of their identity are disregarded. Gilroy maintains that rather than having a black identity imposed by anti-racist theorists, black people in Britain should, and are, developing their own common identity through 'street culture' and forms of local political action. Gilroy believes that different black peoples in Britain are in the process of developing a 'national' identity but are still far from achieving it. Ironically, Modood (1988) criticises Gilroy for marginalising Asian Britons, who are seen as possessing 'Black British' identity only in so far as they participate in African Caribbean inspired 'street culture'.

Gilroy's critique shows some of the difficulties in notions of positive' black identity. The 'modern' view, is still part of social work orthodoxy, both here and in the United States, and has been confirmed by such recent authors as Ahmad (1991), BAAF (1987), Banks (1992a and b), Dominelli (1988), Macdonald (1991), McMahon and Allen-Meares (1992) and Maximé (1993). These modernist accounts continue to see black identity as something which is essential to all black people, including mixed-race children. A positive black identity is seen by these authors as consisting of positive identification, self-esteem and pride. Many of these authors point out that whites are able to, and indeed encouraged to, question, doubt and challenge their own identity. Thus white identity is seen as fragmented, contradictory and contested whereas black identity is proud, unified, and essential. Maximé (1993) says: 'Racial identity represents the ethnic/biological dimension of the person' (p.177).

She sees black identity as an essential, fundamental, and genetic property of black people. A 'positive identity' rather than being descriptive of well adjusted black people becomes prescriptive, and deviations are seen as pathological. Her slogan 'Love is not enough', which is intended to show that black children's identity needs nurturing, betrays her belief that all black parents offer something extra, no matter who they are or what their background. This extra dimension of black parenting remains undefined and therefore unchallengeable. Ironically, Maximé's and Small's (1986) conception of racial identity echo the biologically based racist views of the early twentieth century which Park and Stonequist set out to challenge in their marginality studies. Black people are seen as having a (modern) identity in which meta-narratives are not challenged, where a black 'essence' underlies superficial cultural differences. Whites, in contrast, are privileged with a post-modernist identity which incorporates difference and challenges meta-narratives.

Maximé does not differentiate between the black identity of a child living in a close knit community whose first language is not English and a black British child who lives in a multi-ethnic environment. All black children are seen to have a need for the same kind of black identity irrespective of gender, class, culture and family type. Rattansi and Gilroy especially believe that the black community in Britain has reached a point where post-modernist or 'mature' identities are not only possible but essential for black people in this country to understand their own position and confront racism.

'Mixed-Race' Identity

How does the modernist/post-modernist anti-racist debate impinge on the analysis of mixed-race children and their identity? Within modernist anti-racist texts, mixed-race children are either ignored, totalised, that is seen as black with the same problems and issues to confront as every black child (BAAF, 1987), or pathologised. The concern for positive black identity pathologises mixed-race identity. Examples of this pathologisation are provided by the articles by Maximé and Banks.

Banks's two articles (1992a,1992b) are similar and both illustrate his technique of cognitive ebonisation. In the first, however, this is described as a technique of working with 'mixed ethnicity' children and their mothers. In the second it is described as a technique for direct identity work with black children. So although he makes a distinction between 'mixed ethnicity' and black children in his first article, he does not in fact see a difference at all. He sees his technique as applying universally to black children with 'identity confusion'. Similarly Banks takes an ambivalent stance towards the concept of race. Citing De Montague (1965), he vigorously denies that race has any 'real' meaning saying:

> ...the social and biological idea of race represents a collection of pseudo-logical rationalisations based on a confusion of emotions, prejudiced judgements and disordered values. It is for this reason that I prefer the term 'mixed ethnicity' rather than mixed-race to describe children of mixed background. (Banks, 1992b, p.37)

Even excepting the fact that 'mixed-ethnicity' must surely include Jewish/Irish, English/French, and Sikh/Jamaican combinations amongst many others, it is difficult to understand why Banks rejects the term 'race' altogether on the one hand, but on the other hand has developed a therapeutic technique for making children proud of the very entity of which he denies the existence. Significantly Banks has later changed the terminology to 'Black mixed parentage' Banks (1995).

Virtually every anti-racist text seems to start off making the point that race is socially constructed and therefore not a biologically valid term. But this is a spurious point for three reasons:

- It is rooted in a biologistic (Anglo-Saxon) assumption that the biological is primary, and that biological differences are more real than social differences.

- It implies that there are other categorisations which are a 'valid' basis for discrimination. But feminists (Walkerdine, 1985; Nice 1992) and disability theorists (Oliver 1990) show that 'biological' differences such as gender and disability are socially constructed.

- ° All theorists agree that it is legitimate to use political beliefs such as Nazism, which are obviously not biologically determined, as bases for judging people. The claim that 'race' does not exist in reality is thus a rhetorical point rather than part of a coherent anti-racist argument.

Banks further asserts that all black people are 'mixed-race' because all have white ancestors, and therefore the group we are discussing are 'directly mixed'. But he here confuses the *biological* with the *social* meaning of race, resulting in an echoing of eugenicist arguments.

Banks bases his view of identity development on that of Erikson whom he calls the 'pioneer of the concept of identity'. He goes on to challenge Tizard and Phoenix's (1989) view that mixed-race children can have a range of identities. He says:

> The Eurocentric foundation on which (such) psychological perspectives are based need a significant perceptual shift to even begin to be relevant to considering the identity needs of black children and adolescents. (1992c, p.21)

Accusations of 'Eurocentrism' against psychological theories are common in modern anti-racist writings (Dominelli, 1988; Ahmad, 1990). However, it is difficult to know what is Eurocentric and what not. Why is it that Tizard and Phoenix's view is considered to be Eurocentric, whereas Erikson's theory is not? There is a double irony here. Erikson's theory is based on Ego Psychology, which has been attacked by European theorists such as Lacan (see Sarup, 1990) and Løvlie 1993) as being a product of western, and particularly Anglo-Saxon, conceptions of the self and identity. Thus Banks is using an 'Anglo-Saxon' theory to challenge the 'Eurocentric' theories of those whom he opposes. 'Eurocentrism' for Banks has become a term with little meaning other than that he disagrees with the theory.

Further difficulties become apparent when Banks's (1992b) technique of Cognitive Ebonisation is considered in detail. Part of this technique involves:

> imaginative stories...which attempt a subliminal reversal of the negative connotations of blackness and hence black people. A brief example would be: 'Basil was a beautiful shiny black beetle. All the other animals wanted to look like him'. 'We love your glossy black coat' said the white pelican. 'I wish I had one as nice as you'. Basil was very proud indeed, no other animal looked as smart as him and he was very happy to be so handsome'. In this example the traditional portrayal of the term 'blackness' as often depicted in children's literature is modified from negative to positive. (p.22).

Quite how subliminal this story is, is open to question, but it is a good example of a modern anti-racist strategy. Although on the surface the story is meant to counteract negative connotations of blackness the narrative contains a 'hidden agenda':

- ° The most important attribute of people is the colour of their skin.

- People should be judged according to a hierarchy in which skin colour is the main determinant of their position in the hierarchy.

- Skin colour should be associated with pride and envy.

Cohen (1989, 1992), Rattansi (1992) and Troyna and Hatcher (1992) have all shown that simple reversals of racism in stories and didactic techniques are largely ineffective in anti-racist teaching. Rattansi (1992) says:

> Both multi-cultural and anti-racist critiques ignore the actual literary and pedagogic devices involved in the construction of subject position for the child/reader in school texts. They neglect *how* texts construct meanings, as opposed to *what* they supposedly mean...too often all the protagonists make some simplistic assumptions about the ease with which subjectivities are produced by racist or anti-racist texts. (p.35)

Other aspects of Cognitive Ebonisation involve the use of books with black heros, positive labelling of black features and so forth. Citing Piaget, Banks (1992a) advises parents to:

> ...guard against imposing the term black on a child who rejects the word, until the child has reached an appropriate development for understanding of its abstract political meaning...some parents are unaware that rejection of the term black may be due to a child's literal or concrete understanding of colour labels rather than a rejection of group identity or denial of political affinity. (p.22)

Banks (1992c) advocates:

> Blackness as a positive aspirational goal to be achieved can also be useful with statements such as 'when you understand more about the world you will like being black' or 'when you find out the good things black people have done you will be so happy to be black.' (p.23)

Setting aside the fact that it is rather patronising towards children, there are major difficulties with this statement. First, Banks' use of Piagetian theory to explain the child's misidentification is rather disingenuous. Unless he is talking about children under the age of four he is simply mistaken. All theories of racial development acknowledge that children have some sense of racial identity by the age of four, and this age could easily be pushed back even further. Second, by Banks's own account, some of his teenage subjects talked of themselves as 'brown' rather than black. Brown does not have the same abstract political connotation as black, so is Banks saying that these teenagers had not yet developed an abstract understanding of the term?

By Banks's definition the children who described themselves as 'half-Indian' or 'half-Ghanaian' must be suffering from confusion or some other psychopathology because these half identities are untenable and a sign of racial confusion.

All this points to a simple view of black identity which is possessed by all black children, no matter what their background, which needs to be nurtured by an identity worker. Any definitions by the children of themselves which contradict the identity worker's view are seen as a result either of identity confusion or of immaturity. How cultural, gender and class identities interface with this essential black identity is not described by Banks, or Maximé. Presumably these other identities are seen as non-problematic and not in need of an identity worker.

Would Banks extend his technique to 'Cognitive Feminisation' for girls who wanted to be fire fighters or judges? They could also be told stories about housewife heroines, or told that when they are older they will want to be a secretary and will be shown pictures of beautiful, slim and well-made up animals being envied by scruffy, obese and trousered companions.

Banks presents a view of black identity which is the mirror image of a stereotypically positive white identity complete with heroes, villains and so on. It represents exactly the kind of anti-racist essentialism which Gilroy, Cohen, Rattansi, Modood and Brah wish to transcend.

Owusu-Bempah (1994) criticises all 'identity work'. He claims that the proponents of such intervention are themselves racist, because the basis of this work is the assumption that all black children have a basic wish to be white. He points out the severe consequences which these assumptions can have for social work intervention and decision making, and calls to task not only the social work theorists who advocate these methods, but also the whole tradition of research, including the doll studies, which give scientific credence to the notion of the inevitability of low self-esteem for black children.

My purpose in providing this critique of Banks's and Maximé's theories is not because I think they are wholly inadequate. Pride and positive feelings are surely important for all mature identities. I do believe, however, that prescriptions for healthy identity should not be decreed by 'experts'. I have tried to show the consequences of the modernist view of racial identity and its potential impact on mixed-race children and inter-racial families. From Park and Stonequist onwards, marginality and hybridity have been seen as either pathological states with dire psychological consequences for all those involved or alternatively as a celebration of difference and a sign of breaking down barriers. I believe that neither is the case. This study has shown that inter-racial families do have to deal with specific issues and choices. Different families deal with these issues differently and there is no one 'inter-racial' family in the same way as there is no one black family. Inter-racial families may be harmonious, conflictual or both. When conflict does arise it may be around race, culture, values or it may be a personality clash. It is likely to involve a complex combination of all these factors. When children do show signs of distress this distress is likely to have multiple inter-relating causes, as does most psychological damage to children. It also shows that all the theorists, including Benson and Tizard and Phoenix, who see the inter-racial family as a microcosm of race relations are only seeing one aspect of a multi facetted phenomenon. Race and ethnicity are not monolithic features of society which are reproduced in families, and racism is not reducible to the interactions within families – it is built into the institutions of society as much as being manifested in the psyches of individual racists.

Gilroy (1987) believes that black people in Britain are moving away from defining themselves purely as victims, and are involving themselves in political and cultural activity which is positive and affirming to black people rather than reactive to white culture. Victims are prevented from achieving 'maturity' in the definition which Dreyfus and Rabinow provided. For a victim self-doubt is an indulgence which merely strengthens the hand of oppressive forces, allowing them to divide and rule. The kind of identity presented by Maximé and Banks is appropriate under certain conditions, but need not be universal. I believe that this study has confirmed that black and interracial families do not view themselves merely as victims of either black or white hostility, although that hostility is all too present in their lives. They are actively engaged in the process of developing new conceptions of identity which transcend the old totalising categories of race, class and nation.

These families have shown that this is not an easy task. Marginality or 'hybridity' is not simply a celebration of difference. Difficult and painful choices confront these families. The children and parents may go through traumatic phases in which external and internal forces will combine to undermine their stability. As Bhaba (1990a) says:

> Cultural difference must not be understood as the free play of polarities and pluralities in the homogeneous empty time of the national community. It addresses the jarring of meanings and values generated in between the variety and diversity associated with cultural plentitude; it represents the process of cultural interpretation formed in the perplexity of living, in the disjunctive, liminal space of national society... In erasing the harmonious totalities of culture, cultural difference articulates the difference between representations of social life without surmounting the space of incommensurable meanings and judgements that are produced within the process of transcultural negotiation. (p.316)

and similarly

> The marginal or minority is not the space of a celebratory or utopian self marginalisation. It is a much more substantial intervention into those justifications of modernity – progress, homogeneity, cultural organicism, the deep nation, the long past – that rationalise the authoritarian 'normalising' tendencies within cultures in the name of the national interest or the ethnic prerogative...the culture boundaries of the nation...may be acknowledged as containing thresholds of meaning that must be crossed, erased, and translated in the process of cultural production (p.4).

Bhaba here points to perhaps the biggest problem for modernist anti-racism. This is the assumption that what is good for their defined black collectivity must also be good for each black individual. This assumption explains why all modernist accounts of racial identity slip into a totalising and prescriptive discourse which imposes their own essentialist view of identity.

Mothers

Having shown how modern anti-racism deals with mixed-race children, I would like to turn to the portrayal of their mothers. Two views emerge from the literature. On the one hand is the view that these mothers are racist, with the implication that they are the cause of the psychopathology in their children (Banks, 1992a; Maximé, 1993). Some theorists, using a psychoanalytic framework go further to explain their racism in terms of their early relationships with their fathers and their association of 'blackness' with 'badness' (Henriques, 1974; Holland and Holland, 1984). In this view, the mothers' low self-esteem is caused by poor bonding with their fathers. They feel unworthy of white men like their idealised father, and the relationship with the black man symbolises their anger with both their fathers and themselves. Children are a concrete symbol of this anger and ambivalence, and so the anger towards the black partner is projected onto the children.

On the other hand, some theorists see the mothers as being 'mature', civilised or rational in their ability to overcome difference. Rustin (1992) says:

'Rationality and the capacity to enjoy differences depend on a continuing developmental struggle within each individual and social group,...' (p.60)

This dichotomy reproduces the modern anti-racist debate and its totalising celebration of either homogeneity or heterogeneity.

Neither of these positions acknowledge that both love and fear of difference may have motivated the mothers. Holland and Holland see their patients as depressed women who are rejected by their parents, spouses and children. All white mothers are seen as having similar motivations and pathologies, with similar consequences for themselves and their families. These articles do not show how a successful interracial relationship might be achieved. They assume that the 'blackness' of their partner is the only significant factor about him, and this is either treated in an idealised or denigrated way. They also deny that a partner or child might symbolise many things other than blackness and badness. This point is highlighted by the television series *The Bhudda of Suburbia* by Hanif Kureshi which shows an Asian/English family. This is one of the very few portrayals of inter-racial families in the media, and shows how complex race, racism and sexuality can become. However, the mother is still seen as a passive foil to the father and son, so even this programme does not escape stereotyping.

These accounts have an even more disturbing message than mere pathologisation of the inter-racial situation. They imply that the children's problems are solely the mother's responsibility. Fathers are absent except occasionally as 'role models'.

The implication is that black fathers, as long as they are present, are by definition positive role models for their children. Mothers, on the other hand are subjected to intense scrutiny to discover the 'roots' of their racism. White fathers are not considered important because all the theories, in particular object relations theory, see the mother as the primary carer, and the father is therefore given little responsibility for his children's identity development. Black mothers are assumed to provide adequate parenting – they are are seen as nurturing mothers and positive role models.

Walkerdine (1985) shows how damaging these assumptions are for women, whose role is seen as producing and nurturing children to facilitate their 'natural' ability to become productive, autonomous, rational and happy adults. Mothers are thereby seen as 'irrational' and their own feelings and desires are suppressed and discounted. This applies especially to working class mothers, whose disciplining style is seen as harmful and pathogenic. This view of motherhood is extended by the modern anti-racists to seeing the mother's role as providing nurturance for the natural 'black identity' of her children (see especially Maximé on this point). Since the mothers' choice of black partners is already a sign of their pathology, by definition they cannot be 'efficient producers' of children with a positive black identity. Nice (1992) shows how black mothers are similarly pathologised by modern social theories, either by being seen as overbearing or as having unlimited capacity to parent with no support.

The accounts provided here and in Alihbai-Brown and Montague (1992) show that modern anti-racist views of parents in inter-racial families are limited. It is obviously true that some mothers are racist, and most will have some racist beliefs or feelings, but their motivations are complex, conflicting, and variable. Conflict can produce racialisation, but even this connection is not ubiquitous. Over time motivations change and individuals may develop different, perhaps conflicting, motivations and feelings. All the women in this study, and most in Alihbai-Brown and Montague's book, chose partners of similar educational and class background. But why should this choice of 'sameness' be any more natural or rational than the choice of 'difference' in cultural or racial background. Rationality is equated by these authors to their (dare I say it... Eurocentric) version of 'normality' which is seen as equivalent to 'conformity'. Those who challenge the natural order are seen as pathological. Bhabha counters this view, asserting that hybridity challenges orthodox notions of culture. Those who see it as their task to uphold cultural values (i.e. maintain sameness opposed to difference) seek to pathologise and further marginalise those who cross boundaries. But Bhabha is not merely celebrating difference. This is not a naive 'melting pot', assimilationist or multiculturalist discourse. Difference is a form of disjuncture, interruption and fracture, as well as of celebration.

Interestingly, Holland and Holland, as well as Banks refer specifically to working class women. The sample in this study was overwhelmingly middle class, and it may be that social situations and choices are more limited for working class mixed-race children, although Maximé (1993) specifically denies this, saying that all black children have the same identity issues to face. Nevertheless I doubt that all white working class women in this situation are racist, or that their racism has a single, common psychological cause. Psychoanalytic accounts of racism tend to see it as a manifestation of psychotic defenses of splitting and projective identification, so that black people are given the negative 'split off' attributes of the racist (see Young, 1990) But if racism is multi-faceted, local and context specific, why should it be associated with one particular psychological process?

Another problem with modernist accounts, especially psychoanalytic ones, is that the analytic discourse is aimed at providing an objective picture of the sequence of significant events and interpretations which predate the pathology, and in which cause and effect are determined. Thus Adorno *et al.*, Holland and Holland and Rustin all see the roots of racism in early life, just as Stonequist, Park and Maximé all see the causes of pathology for people of mixed parentage as being in early parenting. What they seldom consider is that later events such as becoming a fascist or having a mixed-race child might affect how early family life has been reconstructed, and that the context in which the narrative is given also plays a part.

Narrative analysis sees causation in a more circular way than does psychoanalysis, so that effects and causes are more difficult to uncouple from each other. If narrative reality takes precedence over 'truth', then psychoanalysis, along with virtually all social science, loses its claim for 'scientific' validity. Psychoanalytic accounts, together with other modernist psychologies can legitimately claim to be meaningful but cannot claim to provide ultimate truth (Kvale, 1992; Sass, 1992). What is interesting about all the anti-racist accounts, even some post-modernist ones, is that their discussions of race and racism contain the metaphors of disease. Like the eugenicist racists and the cultural racists who saw black immigration as a 'disease' affecting the body politic, modernist anti-racists treat racism as if it is a disease of thought (Dominelli, 1988; Ahmad, 1990) or a form of psychosis (Frosh, 1989; Holland and Holland, 1984; Rustin, 1991; Wolfenstein, 1991). It is this metaphor which leads to the pathologisation of inter-racial families, and leads most authors to take the stance of social 'doctors' whose job it is to cure society of the infection. But Cohen, Gilroy, Troyna and Hatcher and van Dijk show the inadequacy of this metaphor, and how misguided it is as a basis for anti-racist action. Foucault and Lyotard also show that 'power' and 'difference' can be seen as much more complicated and multi-faceted phenomena than 'social diseases'.

Trans-Racial Fostering and Adoption

This research does not directly address trans-racial adoption and fostering. However, as mentioned in Chapter 2, trans-racial adoption and interracial families have been treated by anti-racists similarly because in both cases black children are being brought up by white parents who are believed to lack the skills to protect their children from racism (Bagley, 1993a; Banks, 1992a, 1992b; Small, 1986, 1992; Tizard and Phoenix, 1993). Some anti-racists go further than this, claiming that black and white children live in such different worlds that even the concepts of care and bonding used by western thought are not appropriate for black children. This takes the claim of incommensurability to its extreme, denying even the possibility of meaningful parent-child relationships between black and white people. Harris (1991) says:

> ...the Black child can only experience bonding in a Black family. The phenomenon experienced by Black children in a White family is merely 'sham bonding' which soon dissipates once the issue of colour and race becomes a factor for the child. (p.143)

Rhodes' (1993) recent study of the introduction of same-race placements in an Inner London authority shows the process by which this policy became accepted practice. Barn (1993) studied all black children in care in a similar local authority, and focused on their admission, patterns of placement and outcomes. Neither of these authors questions her modernist anti-racist assumptions. Rose points out the facility with which same-race policies were adopted. She sees this as a result of the political skills of the workers who originated the policy. She does not acknowledge that one reason for the ease of implementation may have been the resonance of same race policies with right-wing elements who were similarly trying to break down the hegemony of local government professionals, nor that these policies may have succeeded because they resonate with the long-standing resistance to miscegenation by racists. She uncritically accepts modernist anti-racist definitions of 'blackness' and marginalises children of mixed parentage, citing Small (1986), BAAF (1987).

Barn similarly deals almost exclusively with African Caribbeans, commenting only briefly about the situations of 'mixed-origin' and Asian children. While acknowledging the over-representation of 'mixed-origin' children in care, and pointing out that her sample were almost exclusively from white mothers and black fathers, she offers no explanations as to why this may be. There were no children from Asian-white unions at all. Barn found that trans-racial placements were invariably traumatic and caused identity problems for the children. Rowe, Hundleby and Garnett (1989) found in a study of six local authorities that children of mixed parentage were far more likely to be in care than either white or black children (Asian children were grossly under represented), and that the patterns of their care differed considerably from both black and white children. Like Barn, they offer no explanation for these findings.

Gilroy (1992) is less enthusiastic about 'same-race' policies, claiming that they were developed to protect black workers, who are in an untenable position in local authority employment. He strongly challenges the orthodoxy:

Same race adoption and fostering for minority ethnics is presented as an unchallenged and seemingly unchallengeable benefit for all concerned. What is most alarming about this is not its inappropriate survivalist tone, the crudity with which racial identity is conceived nor even the sad inability to see beyond the conservation of racial identities to the possibility of their transcendence. It is the extraordinary way in which the pathological imagery has simply been inverted, so that it forms the basis of a pastoral view which asserts the strength and durability of black family life, and in present circumstances retreats from confronting the difficult issues which result in black children arriving in care in the first place. The contents of the racists' pathology and the material circumstances to which it can be made to correspond are thus left untouched. The tentacles of racism are everywhere, except in the safe haven which a nurturing black family provides for delicate, fledgling racial identities. (p.58)

Bagley (1993a and b) conducted a long-term follow up of adopted children in Britain and Canada. The sample contained same-race, inter-country and trans-racially placed children with a control group of natural children. Bagley found no differences in the mental health of adoptive children except for Innuit children adopted by Canadians. With regard to identity problems Bagley found that about 20 per cent of adoptive children develop identity problems, but trans-racial adoption is no more likely to result in identity difficulties by any measurement than in-racially adopted teenagers. Hayes (1993) points out that none of the literature shows any connection between adoptive parent's behaviour or attitudes and identity problems, a point confirmed by Bagley, who says that difficulties occur randomly.

An interesting phenomenon in the studies of identity problems in trans-racial adoption is the range of ages at which these problems are expected to materialise. Banks and Maximé see the problems as occurring in early childhood. BAAF, Barn and Rose see them as manifesting in adolescence, whereas Small sees them occurring (like Stonequist's 'marginal man') in early adulthood.

Bagley points out that although the evidence is that trans-racial and inter-country adoption is successful personally for those concerned, it does threaten minority communities, who see it as an attack on their integrity. Although Bagley and Gilroy disagree with Barn and Rose's conclusions about trans-racial placement, there is consensus that African Caribbean children are over-represented in the care system, children of mixed parentage are even more over-represented and Asian children are under-represented. Similarly, they all note the one-way nature of trans-racial placement. They point out, as does Ahmad (1990), that it is social workers' inadequacy in assessing and working with natural families that causes this over-representation, and that practice must change.

Despite recent attempts (e.g. by Lau, 1993; Adcock, 1993; Smith and Berridge, 1994) to formulate a consensus about trans-racial adoption, the two sides of the debate are still far apart (Harris, 1991; Hayes, 1993), and the rhetoric on both sides is still very strong. Virginia Bottomley introduced an adoption white paper saying:

We shall reinforce the general preference of authorities and agencies for recommending married couples as adoptive parents...there should be no place for ideology in adoption. We want common sense judgements, not stereotyping. There are, for example, no good grounds for refusing on principle transracial adoptions... (Department of Health Press Release, 3/11/93)

Barnardos criticised the white paper for:

failing to recognise the right of black children to a black adoptive family. (Dyer, 1993)

'Common sense' is ranged against 'children's rights', neither acknowledging their own ideological roots.

This is a classic post-modern dilemma: trans-racial adoption is successful for most individuals, but the institution itself has resonances of racism and colonialism which make it reproduce unequal power relationships between communities.

The real policy question is not the outcomes for the children concerned but the extent to which institutions should be focused on individual rather than community need when these are in conflict. By focusing on social processes individual children may suffer, but by focusing on individuals, inequitable social relations are not challenged. I believe that the biographical approach, which contextualises individual and group histories, may be a starting point for a new phase of anti-racist social work practice in this area.

Three further conceptual problems cloud the trans-racial adoption debate. First, it is assumed by both sides that the interests of all groups of black children are identical. However, all the research shows that the patterns of care for different groups of black children are at least as variable as the differences between aggregations of black and white children. (White children are never disaggregated, so it is impossible to tell what the patterns are for different groups of white children.) Second, the nature of 'race' and ethnicity are seldom examined, and the modenist assumption that a child's ethnicity is transmitted from one generation to another is used. Ethnicity is not seen as a changing set of meanings and beliefs which each child constructs. This means that the definitions of 'same race' or 'same ethnicity' are either ignored or are seen as a practical rather than conceptual issue. Both sides confuse the causes and effects of racism with the notions of culture and ethnicity, resulting in convoluted and confusing justifications. The third conceptual problem is that the debate does not acknowledge the changes in society. Children adopted in the 1960s may have a very different experience from those adopted in the 1990s, because the institution of adoption itself has changed considerably over the years. This means that no research project can claim to decide ultimately whether trans-racial adoption is 'successful', no matter how comprehensive the research design.

In relation to children of mixed parentage the trans-racial adoption debate is even more complex because of the added difficulty of defining their ethnicity. It does seem clear that these children are disproportionately represented in the care system, especially if their mothers are white (Banks, 1995) and that this is likely to be due to social workers' moral judgements about white women's ability to look after black children.

Children

Tizard and Phoenix (1993) studied 56 teenagers who had one African Caribbean and one white parent. The subjects were 15-year-olds from inner and outer London. They also interviewed 16 parents. The interviews with parents and children were confidential, so they were not able to relate individual parents' attitudes to those of their children.

Tizard and Phoenix found that less than 50 per cent of their subjects considered themselves to be black; most saw themselves as 'mixed-race' or 'brown'. Most had suffered from racism, and had developed strategies to cope with this. Most of the children had high self-esteem and positive identities, although there were a small number who showed marked identity problems. There was no evidence that having a black identity correlated with it being 'positive' or with high self-esteem. Parents had helped with the strategies, but there was no evidence that black parents were more influential that white ones in developing identity or strategies, and the strategies of black and white parents were similar. Interestingly, their sample of parents were much less politicised than those in the present study. Many considered race not to be an issue, and only two couples saw race in political terms.

Despite its different theoretical basis, methodology and sample, Tizard and Phoenix's findings are remarkably similar to those of this study, and those of Wilson (1987). This is particularly interesting because the three studies cover the three age ranges in which identity confusion is deemed to occur, and none has found evidence that this phenomenon is widespread. There is little evidence that these families show marked pathology or marginality. The three studies show that inter-racial families sometimes face particular problems, especially hostility from both communities and a lack of role models in the media with which to identify. Nevertheless there is no inter-racial family 'type' and the families are more diverse than similar. Class background and nationhood are the main forces which seem to determine how the families see themselves and cope with their lives.

Other recent research such as that by Back (1993), Bennet, Dewberry and Yeels (1992) and Troyna and Hatcher (1992) confirm that patterns of racism and identity in children and adolescents are not straightforward. They neither conform to modernist anti-racist categories nor are amenable to simple didactic solutions. Like this study they all found that racism is a constant threat to many of their subjects. The painful effects of racism on children of mixed parentage are dramatically highlighted in the video *Coffee Coloured Children* (1988) confirming that scrubbing, self-mutilation and self-hate can occur to mixed-race children in their natural families.

Implications for Social Work

I am not advocating that modern theories of development, racism and racial identity should be jettisoned in favour of post modern theory. I believe that there are times when totalisation is absolutely necessary. It would be self-indulgent and morally unacceptable not to support the anti-racist forces which are attempting to unite black people, and a white person has no right to tell black people how to organise their resistance. However, I believe that solidarity with anti-racism should not be equated with an uncritical and 'knee-jerk' acceptance of social work's anti-discriminatory orthodoxy. I hope that by introducing new concepts from the educational anti-racist debate into the social work discussion that anti-racism will be strengthened rather than weakened. Racisms and racist discourses have an unnerving capacity to evolve, adapt and disseminate to meet the challenges of a changing world. I believe that if anti-racism does not do the same then the anti-racist gains made in social work, already under threat, will be completely reversed (Rooney, 1993). Interestingly, there are a few signs that CCETSW's supposed rigid adherence to classic anti-racism is responding to other anti-racisms (see discussion of 'same race' placements' Gambe *et al.*, 1991, pp.62–73).

I recognise that this could be taken as being part of a *racist* rather than an anti-racist discourse. Indeed, post-modernism has been accused by its less sophisticated critics of celebrating the *status quo*. Some of these conclusions could indeed be used by racists. I think this is a risk worth taking. It is a risk shared by all anti-racist discourses, many of whose arguments are very similar to those who they supposedly oppose. Gilroy's point about this similarity of discourses, quoted above, is graphically highlighted by recent debates about single parenthood, education and crime, in which the traditional 'British family' and 'British culture' are being portrayed as the panacea for all social ills, which is being threatened by alien forces. British family and culture is described by the new right in virtually identical, almost mystical, terms to social work anti-racist's black families and culture (Jones and Novak, 1993; Saggar, 1993) leaving little room for variation, and confusing description with prescription. The danger of emphasising 'sameness' which is rightly criticised by all anti-racists is counterbalanced by the danger of emphasising 'difference' or incommensurability, because it invites the racist's argument that 'different' peoples are 'exotic' and too unlike British people to fit into this society. Thus every deconstruction of racist thinking holds a danger of being deconstructed itself, and there is no right answer. As Hari said, we have to live with the undecidability.

Post-modern discourses can add a depth and richness to many debates in social work, not only anti-racism. Some of these concepts are already being used by a few authors (e.g. Rojek *et al.* 1988; Parton, 1991; Sands and Nuccio, 1992; Harris and Timms, 1993). Social work, however, is developing a culture in which professional judgement is being increasingly devalued. This is a culture where policy makers and academics do the thinking and social workers use checklists, where theories are constantly being simplified into diagrams with concentric circles, ladders, steps, and flow charts, and where good practice is equated with efficiency and economy. Post-modernism provides a potent rebuttal of this approach, as well as to traditional Marxist and Feminist approaches (Rojek *et al.* 1988; Sands and Nuccio, 1992). It shows that any construction of social situations and problems is contextual, temporary and ideologically framed, that every inclusion is also an exclusion and that opposites can be the same. The potential for informing the debate is staggering. The use of narrative and biography as a tool for empowering practice has already been suggested by Rees (1991) and similarly holds tremendous potential for future exploration, as a counter to the normalising systems approaches which are so prevalent in the profession.

Bibliography

Aboud, F.E. and Skerry, S.A. (1984) 'The development of ethnic attitudes.' *Journal of Cross-Cultural Psychology 15*, 1, 3–34.

Adcock, M. (1993) 'Perspectives on transracial placement.' *ACPP Review and Newsletter 15*, 4, 170–172.

Adorno, T.W., Frenkel-Brunswik, E., Levinson, D. and Sanford, R.N. (1950) *The Authoritarian Personality*. New York: Harper.

Ahmad, B. (1990) *Black Perspectives in Social Work*. Birmingham: Venture Press.

Alderman, G. (1993) 'The Jewish dimension in British politics since 1945.' *New Community 20*, 1, 9–26.

Alibhai-Brown, Y. and Montague, A. (1992) *The Colour of Love: Mixed Race Relationships*. London: Virago.

Allport, G.W. (1979) *The Nature of Prejudice*. Reading, MA: Addison-Wesley.

Ammons, R.B. (1950) 'Reactions in a projective doll-play interview of white males two to six years of age to differences in skin colour and facial features.' *Journal of Genetic Psychology 76*, 323–341.

Back, L. (1993) Race, identity and nation within an adolescent community in South London. *New Community 19*, 2, 217–233.

Bagley, C. (1993a) 'Transracial adoption in Britain: a follow up study with policy considerations.' *Child Welfare 22*, 3, 285–299.

Bagley, C. (1993b) *International and Transracial Adoptions A Mental Health Perspective*. Aldershot: Avebury.

Bagley, C., Verma, K.V., Mallick, K. and Young, L. (1979) *Personality, Self-esteem and Prejudice*. Farnborough: Saxon House.

Ballard, R. (1989) 'Social work with black people: what's the difference?' In C. Rojek, G. Peackock and S. Collins (eds) *The Haunt of Misery. Critical Essays in Social Work and Helping*. London: Routledge.

Banks, N. (1992a) 'Mixed-up kid.' *Social Work Today 24*, 3, 12–13.

Banks, N. (1992b) 'Techniques for direct identity work with black children.' *Adoption and Fostering 16*, 3, 19–25.

Banks, N. (1992c) 'Some considerations of "Racial" identification and self esteem when working with mixed ethnicity children and their mothers as social services clients.' *Social Services Research 3*, 32–41.

Banks, N. (1995) 'Children of black mixed parentage and their placement needs.' *Adoption and Fostering 19*, 2, 19–24.

Banks, W.C. (1976) 'White preference in blacks: A paradigm in search of a phenomenon.' *Psychological Bulletin 83*, 6, 1179–1186.

Barker, M.W. (1982) 'Through experience towards theory: psychodynamic contribution to social work education.' *Issues in Social Work Education 2*, 1, 3–25.

Barn, R. (1993) *Black Children in the Public Care System*. London: Batsford.

Barthes, R. (1973) *Mythologies*. St Albans: Granada.

Bennet, M., Dewberry, C. and Yeels, C. (1991) 'A reassessment of the role of ethnicity in children's social perception.' *Journal of Child Psychology and Psychiatry 32*, 6, 969–982.

Benson, S. (1981) *Ambiguous Ethnicity. Interracial Families in London.* Cambridge: Cambridge University Press.

Bentovim, A. (1979) 'Child development research findings and psychoanalytic theory: an integrative technique.' In D. Shaffer and J. Dunn (eds) *The First Year of Life... Psychological and Medical Implications of early Experience.* Chichester: John Wiley.

Berger, P.L. and Luckmann, T. (1966) 'The social construction of reality.' Doubleday Anchor, New York.

Bernard, H.R. (1988) 'Research methods in cultural anthropology.' Newbury Park, CA: Sage.

Bernstein, J.M. (1991) 'Grand narratives.' In D. Wood (ed) *On Paul Ricoeur.* Warwick Studies in Philosophy and Literature. London: Routledge.

Bernstein, R.J. (1991) *The New Constellation.* Cambridge: Polity Press.

Bertaux, D. (ed) (1981) *Biography and Society The Life History Approach in the Social Sciences.* Beverly Hills CA: Sage.

Bhabha, H.K. (1990a) 'DissemiNation: time, narrative and the margins of the modern nation.' In H.K. Bhabha (ed) *Nation and Narration.* London: Routledge.

Bhabha, H.K. (1990b) 'Narrating the nation.' In H.K. Bhabha (ed) *Nation and Narration.* London: Routledge.

Bick, E. (1964) 'Infant observation in psycho-analytical training.' *International Journal of Psycho-Analysis 45*, 558–566.

Bick, E. (1968) 'The experience of skin in early object relations.' *International Journal of Psycho-Analysis 49*, 484–486.

Bion, W.R. (1984a) *Learning From Experience.* London: H. Karnac.

Bion, W.R. (1984b) *Elements of Psychoanalysis.* London: H. Karnac.

Boden, M.A. (1979) *Piaget.* London: Fontana Modern Classics.

Bourne, S. and Lewis, E. (1984) 'Delayed psychological effects of perinatal deaths: The next pregnancy and the next generation.' *British Medical Journal 289*, 6438, 147–148.

Boyd, C.G. (1989) 'Mothers and daughters: a discussion of theory and research.' *Journal of Marriage and the Family 50*, 291–301.

Brah, A. (1992) 'Difference, diversity and differentiation.' In A. Rattansi and J. Donald (eds) *'Race' Culture and Difference.* London: Open University and Sage.

Brand, E.S., Ruiz, R.A. and Padilla, A.M. (1974) 'Ethnic identification and preference: A review.' *Psychological Bulletin 81*, 11, 860–890.

Brazelton, T.B. and Cramer, B.G. (1991) *The Earliest Relationship. Parents, Infants and the Drama of Early Attachment.* London: Karnac Books.

British Agencies for Adoption and Fostering (1987) *The Placement Needs of Black Children.* Practice Note 13.

Broom, M.E. and Steiglitz, K.A. (1992) 'The consent process and children.' *Research in Nursing and Health 15*, 147–152.

Butterworth, G. (1982) 'A brief account of the conflict between individual and the social in models of cognitive growth.' In G. Butterworth and P. Light (eds) *Social Cognition. Studies of the Development of Understanding.* Brighton: The Harvester Press.

Call, J.D. (1964) 'Newborn approach behaviour and early ego development.' *International Journal of Psyco-Analysis 45*, 286–294.

Charles, M., Thoburn, S. and Rashid, S. (1992) 'The placement of black children with permanent new families.' *Adoption and Fostering 16*, 3, 12–19.

Cheetham, J., James, W., Loney, M., Mayor, B. and Prescott, W. (eds) (1981) *Social and Community Work in a Multi- Racial Society.* London: Harper and Row.

Chestang, L. (1972) 'The dilemma of biracial adoption.' *Social Work 17*, 2, 100–105.

Chodorow, N. (1978) *The Reproduction of Mothering.* Berkley, CA: University of California Press.

Clancier, A. and Kalmanovitch, J. (1987) *Winnicott and Paradox*. London, Tavistock.

Clark, K. (1955) *Prejudice and Your Child*. Boston, Beacon Press.

Clark, K. (1965) *Dark Ghetto*. London, Gollancz.

Clark, K. and Clark, M. (1939) 'The development of consciousness of self and the emergence of racial identification in Negro pre-school children.' *Journal of Social Psychology* SSPSI Bulletin 10, 591–599.

Clark, K. and Clark, M. (1947) 'Racial identification and preference in Negro children.' In T.M. Newcomb and E.L. Hartley (eds) *Readings in Social Psychology*. New York: Holt.

Cohen, P. (1989) 'Reason, racism and the popular monster.' In B. Richards (ed) *Crises of The Self Further Essays on Psychoanalysis and Politics*. London: Free Association Books.

Cohen, P. (1992) '"Its Racism what dunnit": Hidden narrative in theories of racism.' In A. Rattansi and J. Donald (eds) *'Race' Culture and Difference*. London: Open University and Sage.

Community Care (1993) Who's Racially Naive? editorial 9 September 1993.

de Man, P. (1984) 'Autobiography as defacement.' In P. de Man (ed) *The Rhetoric of Romanticism*. Ithaca, NY: Cornell University Press.

Denzin, N.K. (1983) 'Interpretive Interactionism.' In G. Morgan (ed) *Beyond Method Strategies for Social Research*. Newbury Park, CA: Sage.

Denzin, N.K. (1989) *Interpretive Biography*. Newbury Park, CA: Sage.

Department of Health (1993) *Adoption White Paper: Statement by Secretary of State for Health*. Press Release 3/11/1993.

Devereux, G. (1978) *Ethnopsychoanalysis. Psychoanalysis and Anthropology as Complementary Frames of Reference*. Berkeley, CA: University of California Press.

Dollard, J., Miller, N.E., Doob, L.W., Mowrer, O.H. and Sears, R.R. (1939) *Frustration and Aggression*. New Haven, MA: Yale University Press.

Dominelli, L. (1988) *Anti-Racist Social Work*. London: Macmillan.

Donaldson, M. (1978) *Children's Minds*. London: Fontana Press.

Dreger, R.M. and Miller, K.S. (1968) 'Comparative psychological studies of Negroes and whites in the US.' *Psychological Bulletin 57*, 361–402.

Dreyfus, H.L. and Rabinow, P. (1986) 'What Is Maturity? Habermas and Foucault on "What is Enlightenment?"' In D.C. Hoy (ed) *Foucault A Critical Reader*. Oxford: Blackwell.

Dunn, J. (1979) 'The first year of life: continuities in individual differences.' In D. Shaffer and J. Dunn (eds) *The First Year of Life... Psychological and Medical Implications of Early Experience*. Chichester: John Wiley.

Dyer, C. (1993) 'Bottomley adoption code outlaws ideology.' *The Guardian* 4/11/1993 8.

Eichenbaum, L. and Orbach, S. (1983) *Understanding Women*. New York: Basic Books.

Erikson, E.H. (1963) 'Youth: fidelity and diversity.' In E. Erikson (ed) *Youth: Change and Challenge*. New York: Basic Books.

Erikson, E.H. (1977) *Childhood and Society*. London: Paladin Grafton Books.

Erikson, E.H. (1980) *Identity and the Life Cycle*. New York: Norton.

Escalona S.K. (1968) *The Roots of Individuality*. Chicago: Aldine.

Eysenck, H.J. (1986) *Decline and Fall of the Freudian Empire*. Harmonsworth: Penguin.

Fanon, F. (1968) *Black Skin, White Masks*. London: MacGibbon and Kee.

Foucault, M. (1987) 'What is Enlightenment?' In P. Rabinow and W.M. Sullivan (eds) *Interpretive Social Science A Second Look*. Berkeley, CA: University of California Press.

Fox, D.J. and Jordan, V.B. (1973) 'Racial preference and identification of black, American Chinese and white children.' *Genetic Psychology Monographs 88*, 229–286.

Freud, S. (1910) *The Future Prospects of Psycho-Analytic Therapy*. Standard Edition, 11. London: Hogarth Press.

Freud, S. (1913) *Totem and Taboo: Some Points of Agreement between the Mental Lives of Savages and Neurotics* Standard Edition 13, 1. London: Hogarth Press..

Freud, S. (1930) *Civilisation and its Discontents.* Standard Edition 21, 59. London: Hogarth Press..

Frosh, S. (1989) 'Psychoanalysis and racism.' In B. Richards (ed) *Crises of The Self Further Essays on Psychoanalysis and Politics.* London: Free Association Books.

Gambe, D., Gomes, J., Kapur, V., Rangel, M. and Stubbs, P. (1992) *Improving Practice with Children and Families: A Training Manual.* Antiracist Social Work Education Two. Central Council for Education and Training in Social Work Northern Curriculum Development Project CCETSW, Leeds.

Gergen, K.J. (1967) 'The significance of skin colour in human relations.' *Daedalus* Spring, 390–406.

Gergen, K. J., Gloger-Tippelt, G. and Berkowitz, P. (1990) 'The cultural construction of the developing child.' In G.R. Semin and K.J. Gergen (eds) *Everyday Understanding. Social and Scientific Implications.* London: Sage.

Gill, O. and Jackson, B. (1983) *Adoption and Race.* London: Batsford Academic and Educational.

Gilroy, P. (1987) *There Ain't no Black in the Union Jack.* London: Routledge.

Gilroy, P. (1992) 'The end of Antiracism.' In A. Rattansi and J. Donald. *'Race' Culture and Difference.* London: Open University and Sage.

Ginsburg, H. and Opper, S. (1979) *Piaget's Theory of Intellectual Development,* Second Edition. Engelwood Cliffs, NJ: Prentice-Hall.

Gitter, D., Mostowski, P. and Satow, Y. (1972) 'The effect of skin colour and physiognomy on racial misidentification.' *Journal of Social Psychology 88,* 139–143.

Glaser, B. and Strauss, A. (1967) *The Discovery of Grounded Theory.* Chicago IL: Aldine.

Glover, D. and Strawbridge, S. (1985) *The Sociology of Knowledge.* Ormskirk: Causeway.

Goodman, M.E. (1946) 'Evidence concerning the genesis of interracial attitudes.' *American Anthropologist 48,* 624–30.

Goodman, M.E. (1952) *Race Awareness in Young Children.* Cambridge, MA: Addison-Wesley

Gordon, M.M. (1978) *Human Nature, Class and Ethnicity.* New York: Oxford University Press.

Greenwald, H.J. and Oppenheim, D.B. (1968) 'Reported magnitude of self-misidentification among Negro Children: artifact?' *Journal of Personality and Social Psychology 8,* 49–52.

Hammersley, M. (ed) (1993) *Social Research: Philosophy, Politics and Practice.* London: Sage.

Hammersley, M. and Atkinson, P. (1983) *Ethnography. Principles in Practice.* London: Tavistock.

Harbin, S.P. and Williams, J.E. (1966) 'Conditioning of color connotations.' *Perception and Motor Skills 22,* 217–218.

Harland, H. (1987) *Superstructuralism The Philosophy of Structuralism and Post-Structuralism.* London: Methuen.

Harris, R. and Timms, N. (1993) *Secure Accommodation in Child Care: Between Hospital and Prison or Thereabouts.* London: Routledge.

Harris, V. (1991) 'Values of Social Work in the Context of British Society in Conflict with Anti-Racism. in Curriculum Development Project Steering Group.' (ed) *Setting the Context for Change. Anti-Racist Social Work Education 1.* Leeds: CCETSW.

Hayes, M.M. (1990) *Placing Black Children.* London: ABSWAB.

Hayes, P. (1993) 'Transracial Adoption: Politics and Ideology.' *Child Welfare 22,* 3, 301–309

Heimann, P. (1950) 'On Counter-transference.' *International Journal of Psycho-Analysis 31,* 81–84.

Henriques, F. (1974) *Children of Caliban.* London: Secker and Warburg.

Holland, R. and Holland, K. (1984) 'Depressed women: Outposts of empire and castles of skin.' In B. Richards (ed) *Capitalism and Infancy Essays on Psychoanalysis and Politics.* London: Free Association Books..

Hook, R.H. (ed) (1979) *Fantasy and Symbol. Studies in Anthropological Interpretation.* London: Academic Press.

Horowitz, E.L. (1936) 'Development of attitudes towards Negroes.' *Archives of Psychology 194.*

Horowitz, E.L. and Horowitz, R.E. (1939) 'Development of social attitudes in children.' *Sociometry 1,* 307–338.

Hraba, J. and Grant, G. (1970) 'Black is beautiful: A re-examination of racial identification and preference.' *Journal of Personality and Social Psychology 16,* 398–402.

Hunt, J.C. (1989) *Psychoanalytic Aspects of Fieldwork.* Newbury Park, CA: Sage.

Husband, C. (1991) '"Race", Conflictual Politics and Anti-Racist Social Work: Lessons from the past for action in the 90s.' In Curriculum Development Project Steering Group (ed) *Setting the Context for Change. Anti-Racist Social Work Education 1.* Leeds: CCETSW. 46–73.

Isaacs, S. (1952) 'The Nature and Function of Phantasy.' In J. Reviere (ed) *Developments in Psycho-analysis.* The International Psycho-analytical Library,; 43. London: Hogarth Press..

Jackson, J.S., McCulloch, W.R. and Gurin, G. (1988) 'Family, socialisation environment, and identity development in Black Americans.' In H.P. McAdoo (ed) *Black Families,* Second Edition. Newbury Park, CA: Sage.

Jameson, F. (1984) Foreward to Lyotard, J-F. *The Postmodern Condition: A Report on Knowledge.* Manchester: Manchester University Press.

Johnson, R.C. and Nagoshi, C.T. (1986) 'The adjustment of offspring of within-group and interracial/intercultural marriages: a comparison of CT factor scores.' *Journal of Marriage and the Family 48,* 279–284.

Johnson, P., Shireman, J.F. and Watson, K.W. (1987) 'Transracial adoption and the development of black identity at age eight.' *Child Welfare 66,* 1, 45–55.

Jones, C. and Novak, T. (1993) 'Social work today.' *British Journal of Social Work 23,* 3, 195–212.

Katz, P.A. (1976) *Towards the Elimination of Racism.* New York: Pergammon.

Kean, J. (1992) 'The modern democratic revolution: reflection on Lyotard's the post modern condition.' In A. Benjamin (ed) *Judging Lyotard.* London: Routledge.

Kearney, R. (1986) *Modern Movements in European Philosophy.* Manchester: Manchester University Press.

Kirk, J. and Miller, M. (1986) *Reliability and Validity in Qualitative Research.* Beverley Hills, CA: Sage.

Klein, M. (1955) 'On identification.' In M. Klein, P. Heimann and R. Money-Kyrle (eds) *New Directions in Psycho-Analysis.* London: Maresfield.

Klein, M., Heimann, P. and Money-Kyrle, R. (1955) New Direction in Psycho-Analysis. London: Maresfield.

Kuhn, T.S. (1962) *The Structure of Scientific Revolutions.* Chicago, IL: University of Chicago Press.

Kvale, S. (1992) 'Postmodern psychology: a contradiction in terms?' In S. Kvale (ed) *Psychology and Postmodernism.* London: Sage.

Lacan, J. (1977) *Ecrits: A Selection.* London: Tavistock.

Laplanche, J. and Pontalis, J.B. (1983) *The Language of Psycho-Analysis.* London: Hogarth Press and The Institute of Psycho-Analysis.

Lather, P. (1992) 'Postmodernism and the human sciences.' In S. Kvale (ed) *Psychology and Postmodernism.* London: Sage.

Lau, A. (1993) 'Report of NETCAP Working party on Transracial Adoption.' *ACPP Review and Newsletter 15,* 4, 165–169.

Leach, P. (1979) *Baby and Child. From Birth to Age Five.* Harmondsworth: Penguin.

Lichtenberg, J.D. (1983) *Psychoanalysis and Infant Research.* Hillsdale, NJ: Analytic Press.

Loney, M. (1981) 'Immigration and social welfare.' Preface to J. Cheetham, W. James, M. Loney, B. Mayor and W. Prescott (eds) (1981) *Social and Community Work in a Multi-racial Society.* London: Harper and Row.

Løvlie, L. (1992) 'Postmodernism and subjectivity.' In S. Kvale (ed) *Psychology and Postmodernism.* London: Sage.

Luster, T. (1989) 'The relation between parental values and parenting behaviour: A test of the Kohn hypopthesis.' *Journal of Marriage and the Family 51*, 139–147.

Lyotard, J-F. (1984) *The Postmodern Condition: A Report on Knowledge*. Manchester: Manchester University Press.

Lyotard, J-F. (1992) *The Postmodern Explained to Children Correspondence 1982–1985*. London: Turnaround.

Macdonald, S. (1991) *All Equal Under the Act?* London: REU, NISW.

Mahler, M., Pine, F. and Bergman, A. (1975) *The Psychological Birth Of The Human Infant*. London: Hutchinson.

Maier, H.W. (1969) *Three Theories of Child Development Contributions of Erik H. Erikson, Jean Piaget and Robert R. Sears, and their Applications*, Revised Edition. New York: Harper and Row.

Mann, J. (1973) 'Status: The marginal man reaction – mixed- nloods and Jews.' In P. Watson (ed) *Psychology and Race*. Harmonsworth: Penguin.

Mattinson, J. (1975) *The Reflection Process in Casework Supervision*. London: Institute of Marital Studies.

Maximé, J.M. (1993) 'The importance of racial identity for the psychological well-being of Black children.' *ACPP Review and Newsletter 15*, 4, 173–179.

McAdoo, H.P. (1985) 'Racial attitude and self concept of young black people over time.' In H.P. McAdoo and J.J. McAdoo (eds) *Black Children Social, Educational and Parental Environments*. Newbury Park, CA: Sage.

McAdoo, H.P. (ed) (1988) *Black Families*, Second Edition. Newbury Park, CA: Sage.

McMahon, A. and Allen-Mears, P (1992) 'Is social work racist? A content analysis of recent literature.' *Social Work 37*, 6, 533–539.

Mead, M. (1979) 'The influence of methods of observation on theory, with particular reference to the work of George Devereax and Margaret Lowenfeld.' In R.H. Hook (ed) *Fantasy and Symbol. Studies in Anthropological Interpretation*. London: Academic Press.

Meltzoff, A.N. and Moore, M.K. (1983) 'The origins of imitation in infancy: Paradigm, phenomena and theories.' In L.P. Lipsett (ed) *Advances in Infancy Research*. Norwood, NJ: Ablex.

Miles, M. and Hubermann, A. (1984) *Qualitative Data Analysis: A Sourcebook of New Methods*. Newbury Park, CA: Sage.

Miller, L., Rustin, M., Rustin, M. and Shuttleworth, J. (eds) (1989) *Closely Observed Infants*. London: Duckworth.

Milner, D. (1983) *Children and Race. Ten Years On*. London: Ward Lock Educational.

Mishler, E.G. (1986) *Research Interviewing: Context and Narrative*. Cambridge, MA: Harvard University Press.

Mitchell, D. (1988) 'Alton accuses Liverpool over race adoption policy.' *Community Care 1/9/1988* 727, 2.

Modood, T. (1988) '"Black" racial equality and Asian identity.' *New Community 14*, 3, 397–404.

Modood, T. (1992) *Not Easy Being British: Colour, Culture and Citizenship*. Stoke-on-Trent: Trentham Books.

Morland, J.K. (1962) 'Racial acceptance and preference of nursery school children in a Southern City.' *Merrill-Palmer Quarterly 8*, 271–80.

Morland, J.K. (1963) 'Racial self-identification: A study of nursery school children.' *American Catholic Sociological Review 24*, 231–42.

Mullender, A. and Miller, D. (1985) 'The Ebony group: black children in white foster homes.' *Adoption and Fostering 9*, 1, 33–40.

Nanton, P. (1989) 'The new orthodoxy: racial categories and equal opportunities policy.' *New Community 15*, 4, 549–64.

Nice, V.E. (1992) *Mothers and Daughters The distortion of a Relationship*. Basingstoke: Macmillan.

Non-Aligned Productions (1988) *Coffee Coloured Children* (Video). London: Albany Video Distribution.

Oakley, A. (1981) *Subject Women.* Oxford: Martin Robertson.

Oliver, M. (1990) *The Politics of Disablement: Critical Texts in Social Work and the Welfare State.* Basingstoke: Macmillan.

Owusu-Bempah, C. (1994) 'Race, self-identity and social work.' *British Journal of Social Work 24,* 128–136.

Park, R.E. (1964) *Race and Culture.* New York: Free Press.

Parton, N. (1991) *Governing the Family: Child Care, Child Protection and the State.* London: Macmillan.

Patton, M.Q. (1990) *Qualitative Evaluation and Research Methods,* Second Edition. Newbury Park, CA: Sage.

Penny, P. and Best, F. (1990) *How the Black family is Pathologised by the Social Services Systems.* London: ABSWAB.

Peters, M.F. (1988) 'Parenting in black families with young children: a historical perspective.' In H.P. McAdoo (ed) *Black Families,* Second Edition. Newbury Park, CA: Sage.

Phillips, A. (1988) *Winnicott.* London: Fontana Modern Masters.

Phoenix, A. (1987) 'Theories of gender and black families.' In G. Weiner and M. Arnot (eds) *Gender Under Scrutiny.* Milton Keynes: Open University Press.

Piaget, J. (1953) *The Origin of Intelligence in the Child.* London: Routledge and Kegan Paul.

Piaget, J. (1951) *Play, Dreams and Imitation in Childhood.* London: Routledge and Kegan Paul.

Piaget, J. (1972) *Psychology and Epistemology. Towards a Theory of Knowledge.* Harmondsworth: Penguin.

Piaget, J. and Inhelder, B. (1973) *Memory and Intelligence.* London: Routledge and Kegan Paul.

Piaget, J. and Weil, A. (1951) 'The development in children of the idea of the homeland and of relations with other countries.' *International Social Sciences Bulletin 3,* 531–537.

Pinker, R. (1993) 'A lethal kind of looniness.' *Times Higher Education Supplement,* 10th September, 1993.

Piontelli, A. (1985) *Backwards in Time. A Study in Infant Observation by the Method of Esther Bick.* London: Clunie Press.

Piontelli, A. (1987) 'Infant observation from before birth.' *International Journal of Psycho-Analysis 68,* 453–463.

Plummer, K. (1983) *Documents of Life: An Introduction to the Problems and Literature of a Humanistic Method.* London: Allen and Unwin.

Popper, K.R. (1972) *Conjectures and Refutations: The Growth of Scientific Knowledge.* London: Routledge and Kegan Paul.

Pulaski, M.A.S. (1980) *Understanding Piaget. An Introduction to Children's Cognitive Development.* New York: Harper and Row.

Racker, H. (1968) *Transference and Countertransference.* London: Maresfield.

Rattansi, A. (1992) 'Changing the subject? Racism, culture and education.' In A. Rattansi and J. Donald (eds) *'Race' Culture and Difference.* London: Open University and Sage.

Rees, S. (1991) *Achieving Power Practice and Policy in Social Welfare.* Sydney: Allen and Unwin.

Rex, J. (1986) *Race and Ethnicity.* Milton Keynes: Open University Press..

Rhodes, P.J. (1992) 'The emergence of a new policy: "Racial matching" in fostering and adoption.' *New Community 18,* 2, 191–208.

Rhodes, P.J. (1993) *'Racial Matching' in Fostering.* Aldershot: Avebury.

Ricoeur, P. (1991) 'Narrative Identity.' In D. Wood (ed) *On Paul Ricoeur.* Warwick Studies in Philosophy and Literature. London: Routledge.

Ricoeur, P. (1992) *Oneself as Another.* Chicago: University of Chicago.

Ritchie, J. (1973) 'Culture, personality and prejudice.' In P. Watson (ed) *Psychology and Race.* Harmondsworth: Penguin Education.

Rojek, C., Peackock, G. and Collins, S. (1988) *Social Work and Received Ideas.* London: Routledge.

Rooney, B. (1993) 'Questioning anti-racist quality.' *Community Care* 7 October 1993 12.

Rowe, J., Hundleby, M. and Garnett, L. (1989) *Child Care Now: A Survey of Placement Patterns*. British Agencies for Adoption and Fostering Research Series 6. London.

Rustin, M. (1987) 'Psychoanalysis, philosophical realism and the new sociology of science.' *Free Associations 9*, 102–136.

Rustin, M. (1991) *The Good Society and the Inner World. Psychoanalysis, Politics and Culture.* London: Verso.

Rutherford, J. (1990) 'The third space: interview with Homi Bhabha.' In J. Rutherford (ed) *Identity: Community, Culture, Difference.* London: Lawrence and Wishart.

Rutter, M. (1982) *Maternal Deprivation Reassessed,* Second Edition. Harmondsworth: Penguin.

Saggar, S. (1993) 'Black participation and the transformation of the "race" issue in British Politics.' *New Community 20*, 1, 27–42.

Samuels, A. (1979) 'Trans-racial adoption – adoption of the black child.' *Family Law 9*, 8, 237–239.

Sands, R. and Nuccio, K. (1992) 'Postmodern feminist theory and social work.' *Social Work 37*, 6, 489–494.

Sarup, M. (1992) *Jaques Lacan.* Hemel Hempstead: Harvester Wheatsheaf.

Sass, L.A. (1992) 'The epic of disbelief: the postmodernist turn in contemporary psychoanalysis.' In S. Kvale (ed) *Psychology and Postmodernism.* London: Sage.

Sattler, J.M. (1973) 'Racial experimenter effects.' In K.S. Miller and R.S. Dreger (eds) *Comparative Studies of Blacks and Whites in the US.* New York: Seminar Press.

Schneider, E.L. (1991) 'Attachment theory and research: review of the literature.' *Clinical Social Work Journal 19*, 3, 251–266.

Segal, H. (1979) *Klein.* London: Fontana Modern Masters.

Semin, G.R. and Gergen, K.J. (eds) (1990) *Everyday Understanding. Social and Scientific Implications.* London: Sage.

Sherif, M. (1966) *Group Conflict and Co-operation: Their Social Psychology.* London: Routledge and Kegan Paul.

The Shorter Oxford Dictionary. (1973) Oxford: Oxford University Press.

Simpson, G.E. and Yinger, J.M. (1985) *Racial and Cultural Minorities. An Analysis of Prejudice and Discrimination,* Fifth Edition. New York: Plenum Press.

Small, J.M. (1986) 'Transracial placements: conflicts and contradictions.' In S. Ahmed, J. Cheetham and J. Small (eds) *Social Work with Black Children and their Families.* London: Batsford.

Small, J.M. (1992) 'Ethnic and racial identity in adoption within the United Kingdom.' *Adoption and Fostering 16*, 4, 61–69.

Smith, P.M. and Berridge, D. (1994) *Ethnicity and Childcare Placements.* London: National Children's Bureau.

Spencer, M.B. (1984) 'Black children's race awareness, racial attitudes and self concept: a reinterpretation.' *Journal of Child Psychology and Psychiatry 25*, 3, 433–441.

Stern, D.N. (1977) *The First Relationship: Infant and Mother.* Cambridge, MA: Harvard University Press.

Stern, D.N. (1985) *The Interpersonal World of the Infant. A View from Psychoanalysis and Developmental Psychology.* New York: Basic Books.

Steuerman, E. (1992) 'Habermas vs Lyotard: modernity vs postmodernity.' In A. Benjamin (ed) *Judging Lyotard.* London: Routledge.

Stonequist, E.V. (1937) *The Marginal Man. A Study in Personality and Culture Conflict.* New York: Russel and Russel.

Stopes-Roe, M. and Cochrane, R. (1990) *Citizens of This Country: The Asian-British.* Clevedon: Multilingual Matters.

Sudman, S. and Bradburn, N.M. (1982) *Asking Questions.* San Francisco, CA: Jossey-Bass.

Talberg, G., Couto-Rosa J.A.A. and O'Donnell, M. (1988) 'Early affect development: empirical research.' *International Journal of Psycho-Analysis 69*, 239–259.

Thompson, N. (1993) *Anti-Discriminatory Practice*. London: Macmillan.

Tizard, B. (1990) 'Ex-institutional children: a follow-up study to age 16.' *Adoption and Fostering 14*, 1, 17–20.

Tizard, B. (1979) 'Early experience and later social behaviour.' In D. Shaffer and J. Dunn (eds) *The First Year of Life... Psychological and Medical Implications of Early Experience*. New York: John Wiley.

Tizard, B. and Phoenix, A. (1989) 'Black identity and trans-racial adoption.' *New Community 15*, 3, 427–38.

Tizard, B. and Phoenix, A. (1993) *Black, White or Mixed-Race? Race and Racism in the Lives of Young People of Mixed Parentage*. London: Routledge.

Troyna, B. and Hatcher, R. (1992) *Racism in Children's Lives A study of Mainly-White Schools*. London: Routledge.

van Dijk, T.A. (1987) *Communicating Racism Ethnic Prejudice in Thought and Talk*. Newbury Park, CA: Sage.

Walkerdine, V. (1985) 'On the regulation of speaking and silence: subjectivity, class and gender in contemporary schooling.' In C. Steedman, C. Urwin and V. Walkerdine (eds) *Language, Gender and Childhood*. London: Routledge and Kegan Paul.

Ward, S.H. and Braun, J. (1972) 'Self esteem and racial preference in black children.' *American Journal of Authopsychiatry 42*, 4, 644–647.

Wilson, A. (1987) *Mixed Race Children*. London: Allen and Unwin.

Winnicott, D.W. (1941) 'The observation of infants in a set situation.' In D.W. Winnicott (1965) *The Maturational Process and the Facilitating environment. Studies in the Theory of Emotional Development*. London: Hogarth Press and the Institute of Psycho-analysis.

Winnicott, D.W. (1951) 'Transitional objects and transitional phenomena.' In D.W. Winnicott (1965) *The Maturational Process and the Facilitating Environment. Studies in the Theory of Emotional Development*. London: The Hogarth Press and the Institute of Psycho-analysis.

Winnicott, D.W. (1957) 'On the contribution of direct child observation to psycho-analysis.' In D.W. Winnicott (1975) *Through Paediatrics to Psychoanalysis*. London: The Hogarth Press and the Institute of Psycho-analysis.

Winnicott, D.W. (1965) *The Maturational Process and the Facilitating environment. Studies in the Theory of Emotional Development*. London: The Hogarth Press and the Institute of Psycho-analysis.

Winnicott, D.W. (1974) *Playing and Reality*. London: Penguin Books.

Winnicott, D.W. (1975) *Through Paediatrics to Psychoanalysis*. London: The Hogarth Press and the Institute of Psycho-analysis.

Winnicott, D.W. (1980) *The Piggle. An Account of the Psychoanalytic Treatment of a Little Girl*. London: Penguin Books.

Winnicott, D.W. (1988) *Human Nature*. London: Free Association Books..

Wolfenstein, E.V. (1991) 'On the uses and abuses of psychoanalysis in cultural research.' *Free Associations 2*, 24, 515–547.

Young, L. (1990) 'A nasty piece of work: a psychoanalytic study of sexual and racial difference in "Mona Lisa".' In J. Rutherford (ed) *Identity: Community, Culture, Difference*. London: Lawrence and Wishart.

Young, R. (1992) 'Colonialism and humanism.' In A. Rattansi and J. Donald (eds) *'Race' Culture and Difference*. London: Open University and Sage.

Subject Index

Author Index

Lightning Source UK Ltd.
Milton Keynes UK
UKOW04f2321290816

281769UK00001B/18/P